Oxford German Series

GENERAL EDITOR: JULIUS GOEBEL, PH.D.

PROFESSOR OF GERMANIC LANGUAGES IN THE UNIVERSITY OF ILLINOIS

A PRACTICAL GUIDE

TO A SCIENTIFIC STUDY OF

THE GERMAN VOCABULARY

BY

AUGUST PREHN, PH.D. (MÜNSTER)

NEW YORK UNIVERSITY, NEW YORK

NEW YORK

OXFORD UNIVERSITY PRESS

AMERICAN BRANCH: 35 WEST 32ND STREET

LONDON, TORONTO, MELBOURNE, AND BOMBAY
HUMPHREY MILFORD

1913

TO
F. W. C. LIEDER

PREFACE

In the present manner of teaching the vocabulary of the German language much time and energy are wasted. This waste is due chiefly to a general lack of system in the traditional method of teaching a vocabulary.

The several hundred words presented in grammatical text-books are extremely difficult to memorize, and after they have been committed to memory, it is equally difficult to identify them in a printed text or in conversation. After pupils have received instruction for two or three years, they are unable to read at sight an easy German book, and neither they nor their teachers have cause to remember with pleasure these years of toil.

Many years ago the author, realizing this condition, attempted in his own classes to remove as many obstacles as possible. Primitive experiments justified the labor involved. Continued work along those lines has resulted, after many years, in the present text.

The general appearance of school-books creates impressions upon the minds of pupils which, as a rule, become permanent. Bulky grammars with small vocabularies are largely responsible for the mistaken idea that lists of declensions and conjugations represent the soul and body of a language.

In preparing this book the author has been guided by the following beliefs: (1) That the vocabulary of the German language may easily be grasped by ordinary minds; (2) That acquiring

a vocabulary is the most important feature in learning the language; (3) That grammar is a subordinate part of the work;
(4) That the vocabulary and the grammar of a language should
be acquired simultaneously; (5) That the grammar ought to be
used as an aid in securing correctness.

As most teachers of German are accustomed to follow the
lead of a text-book containing a limited vocabulary and an
extensive grammar, the author offers to users of this book the
following

SUGGESTIONS

Before assigning a definite lesson, read with the class in
different parts of the first division a few pages for the specific
purpose of displaying the great possibilities for rapid advance-
ment. The identification by inspection of hundreds of words
arouses in the pupils' minds a liking for the new study which
cannot possibly be attained by the sight of disconnected words
of strange appearance.

Point out in the second division the more important inter-
relations of consonants. While theoretical explanations gen-
erally fail to produce the expected results, the tabulations of
words as presented in this book strongly appeal to the fancy
of the pupils.

Base the first lesson on Chapter I, C (Self-explanatory Verbs),
assign by way of an experiment from twenty to thirty words
for the first recitation, and increase or decrease the volume of
the daily lesson according to the capacity of the class.

At the same time teach as rapidly as possible, from the
grammar selected for the purpose, an outline of conjugation,
beginning with the synopsis of the auxiliary verbs. Add the
synopsis of both regular and irregular verbs with haben and
sein.

Take the principal parts of the most important irregular verbs, distinctly grouped according to vowel gradations, and form from the very outset sentences for the purpose of showing the characteristic features of German construction. Have every sentence recited orally and from memory. This exercise, which develops the faculty of connected speech, is of the utmost importance.

Select next in order Chapter I, B (Self-explanatory Adjectives and Adverbs), and proceed to the declension of the definite article and of the pronouns which imitate its declension, to pave the way to an intelligent study of the most desirable nouns contained in Chapter I, A.

This part of the work ought to be followed by selections from Chapter III (Derivatives).

Numerous primary words having become the mental property of the pupils, the process of acquiring a knowledge of secondary and further formations does not offer any difficulty. The faculty of word composition and word analysis is almost imperceptibly developed, and after about six weeks' study the first attempt at reading a complete book can be safely made. If the teacher feels that the class is ready to translate a book, he ought to write on the blackboard, by way of experiment, a paragraph from some easy German story and, according to the result, proceed immediately or wait a few more weeks.

The discovery by the pupils that they can identify most of the words occurring in the text without consulting a dictionary is one of their most gratifying experiences, and the enthusiasm of the pupils will be heartily shared by the teacher who realizes that he does not depend any longer on the dreaded introductory reader.

The presentation to the class, at this early period, of reading-matter that appeals to the pupils and shows the German people in the light of an intelligent and progressive nation creates an interest which is a safeguard against the old-time spirit of ridicule which, in many instances, leads to an aversion to the study of German and to greater difficulties in discipline than any other line of instruction has to countenance.

At this juncture the study of word-groups ought to be taken up. It would, of course, not be wise to follow the alphabetical order of events, and teachers ought to make their own selections (for instance, alt, jung, groß, neu, Freund, Land, Waſſer, etc.).

The introduction of these groups has been in all classes under the author's charge and observation a source of delight to students of all grades in the schoolroom and, in colloquial courses, in evening schools, to the educated and the illiterate. The opportunity of learning, without any special effort, from six to twelve or even more words just as easily as one word fascinates any pupil. It does not, however, impress every teacher as the proper thing to do. There are many members of the profession who earnestly believe that the sledge hammer is a more efficient tool than reasoning, and that saving of time for the pupil is an educational felony.

While reducing the labor of word study to a considerable extent, the fundamental idea on which this book is based leaves a very great margin for study for pupils of every description. Constructional difficulties of German texts and the intricacies of German grammar will remain the same that they were before. But besides eliminating the most obnoxious feature of word study, this method will enable the advocates of enormous assignments for home work to attain results which it has been impossible to accomplish by means of memorizing.

Teachers who prefer courses in reading can, by strictly adhering to the preceding outline, cover in sight translation during the first year with beginners from 400 to 600 pages of the texts which are used in all schools for second and third reading.

Advocates of oral courses will be particularly benefited by taking up the study of word-groups at the earliest possible moment. The author's experiments in this field have led him to adopt a method which, after a few months of word study, can be easily applied in any grade. Tell, in the beginning, stories in German adapted to the character of the pupils, and have these translated into English by members of the class. After several months add stories in English and have these translated orally into German, or use a composition book.

It has been claimed by teachers who have tried on the basis of Grimm's law to accustom their pupils to the identification of German words that such translations as Graf, giraffe, Gesell, gazelle, have led to a discontinuation of their attempts of developing the system any further. Similar mistakes are, doubtless, inevitable, but the sum total is as insignificant as the number of accidents resulting from the use of machinery by which millions of people are benefited.

Pupils of German descent, who bring in a vocabulary which, in most cases, is far more limited than they imagine, can be associated with beginners without any disadvantage to them.

The above outline of application has also been successfully applied to pupils who had had several years of previous experience in memorizing words. The immediate relief and the clear prospect of faster progress are quickly perceived and appreciated by this class of students.

For those who wish to trace the association of words that could not be alphabetically arranged a special index has been added in which will be found the number of the group to which the word belongs. As, however, this book is not intended to be a cyclopedia but a guide for teachers and students through school and college, its volume has been limited in proportion to the purpose which it is expected to serve, and the seeker for information is likely to miss, at times, what he is looking for and to find what he did not expect to see, and it is hoped that such discoveries may prove a compensation for omissions.

It has been the experience of many teachers that too many rules rather confuse than enlighten the students. While, in mathematics, hundreds of examples are offered to illustrate certain conditions, books dealing with the study of a language present too many generalizations instead of examples.

For this reason, the lists of prefixes and suffixes and the theory of Grimm's law, which can be found in almost every grammar, have been omitted, and their places have been taken by the lists of words which clearly show what those generalizations mean.

Moreover, nouns of like gender have been characterized as such; instead of repeating the definite article or the customary abbreviations, *m.*, *f.*, *n.*, for instance, nouns ending in ḥeit, feit, ſchaft, ung, etc. have been marked, "All feminine," and as they represent, in most cases, great numbers of words, the impression will be produced that the majority of German nouns can be easily classified as to gender, and that it is the minority that fail to indicate their gender.

It is obvious that Kluge's *Etymologisches Wörterbuch der deutschen Sprache* has been consulted in many instances; digressions from Kluge's interpretations will be quickly detected

and, it is hoped, appreciated by those who are thoroughly
familiar with Kluge's book. The general plan and the inter-
pretation of numerous derivations which naturally lie beyond
the scope of Kluge's dictionary are original.

The author owes a debt of gratitude for encouragement and
advice to Dr. F. W. C. Lieder, Instructor in German in Har-
vard University, Mr. Paul R. Lieder, Professor Frank Vogel
of the Massachusetts Institute of Technology, Mr. D. B.
Duncan, teacher of English in the Columbia Grammar School,
New York, and for many valuable suggestions regarding the
general arrangement of the subject-matter, to the General
Editor of the Oxford University Press, Professor Julius Goebel
of the University of Illinois.

It is the author's sincere wish that the users of this book
will derive from its pages as much gratification as he himself
and his pupils have done during the preparation of this volume,
when even the limited material that could be offered to the
class in default of the complete book has been productive of
results which have made the study of the German language
what every teacher expects it to be.

CONTENTS

A PRACTICAL GUIDE TO A SCIENTIFIC STUDY
OF THE GERMAN VOCABULARY

A PRACTICAL GUIDE TO A SCIENTIFIC STUDY OF THE GERMAN VOCABULARY

I. SELF–EXPLANATORY GERMAN WORDS AND THEIR DERIVATIONS

A. NOUNS

1. Geography and Astronomy

Masculine

Äquator, equator
Astronom, astronomer
Atlas, atlas
Berg, (iceberg) mountain
Grund, ground
Hafen, haven, port
Horizont, horizon
Kanal, canal
Kanton, canton
Komet, comet
Krater, crater
Norden, north
Osten, east
Plan, plan
Planet, planet
Pol, pole
See, (sea) lake
Strom, (stream) river
Süden, south
Sund, sound
Tunnel, tunnel
Vulkan, volcano
Westen, west
Zenith, zenith

Feminine

Bai, bay
Karte, chart, map
Lagune, lagoon
Meile, mile
Oase, oasis
Platte, plateau
Provinz, province
Pyramide, pyramid
See, sea, ocean
Sphäre, sphere
Terrasse, terrace
Zone, zone

Neuter

Kap, cape
Klima, climate
Moor, moor (heath)
Riff, reef
Territorium, territory

Plural only

Tropen, tropics

DERIVATIVE NOUNS

Masculine

Abgrund, abyss
Gründer, founder

Feminine

Astronomie, astronomy
Begründung, founding

Gründlichkeit, thoroughness
Gründung, foundation
Strömung, current

Neuter

Gebirge, range of mountains

DERIVATIVE ADJECTIVES

astronomisch, astronomical
bergig, mountainous
gebirgig, mountainous
gründlich, fundamental
horizontal, horizontal
klimatisch, climatic

nördlich, northern
östlich, eastern
südlich, southern
vulkanisch, volcanic
westlich, western

DERIVATIVE VERBS

abkarten, concert, plot
begründen, found, prove
entströmen, stream from

gründen, ground, found
strömen, stream

2. Town, House, and Household

Masculine

Architekt, architect
Balkon, balcony
Damm, dam, carriage road
Distrikt, district
Flur, floor (hall)
Giebel, gable
Palast, palace
Plunder, plunder
Sparren, spar
Stall, stall, stable
Stuhl, stool, chair

Feminine

Burg, borough, castle
Gabel, (gable?) fork
Garderobe, wardrobe
Gaze, gauze
Halle, hall
Hütte, hut
Lampe, lamp
Matratze, mattress
Matte, mat
Nische, niche
Residenz, residence
Ruine, ruined castle
Schindel, shingle
Villa, villa, cottage

Neuter

Haus, house
Hotel, hotel

Kabinett, cabinet, room
Magazin, magazine, storehouse

DERIVATIVE NOUNS

Masculine

Bürger, citizen

Feminine

Architektur, architecture
Behausung, lodging
Bürgerschaft, commonalty

Häuslichkeit, household
Plünderung, pillage
Stallung, stall, stable

Neuter

Gehäuse, casing

DERIVATIVE ADJECTIVES

bürgerlich, civic

häuslich, domestic

DERIVATIVE VERBS

eindämmen, dam in
plündern, plunder

ruinieren, ruin

3. Nature

Masculine

Äther, ether
Brand, brand, fire
Magnet, magnet
Sand, sand
Strand, strand, beach
Sturm, storm
Wind, wind

Lava, lava
Natur, nature
Temperatur, temperature

Neuter

Echo, echo
Eiland, island
Eis, ice
Feuer, fire
Firmament, firmament
Fossil, fossil
Graphit, graphite
Phänomen, phenomenon
Phantom, phantom
Wetter, weather

Feminine

Asche, ashes
Atmosphäre, atmosphere
Düne, down
Ebbe, ebb, tide
Flamme, flame
Grotte, grotto

Derivative Nouns

Feminine

Beftürmung, storming
Einäſcherung, incineration
Feuerung, fuel
Natürlichkeit, naturalness

Strandung, running aground

Neuter

Gewitter, thunderstorm
Unwetter, stormy weather

Derivative Adjectives

ätheriſch, ethereal
atmoſphäriſch, atmospheric
eiſig, icy
feurig, fiery
magnetiſch, magnetic

natürlich, natural
phänomenal, phenomenal
ſtürmiſch, stormy
windig, windy

Derivative Verbs

abfeuern, fire off, discharge
anfeuern, inflame
beſtürmen, storm, assail
einäſchern, incinerate
entflammen, inflame
feuern, fire

magnetiſieren, magnetize
ſtranden, strand, be beached
ſtürmen, storm
verſanden, get covered with sand
wittern, scent

4. Mammals

Masculine

Bock, buck
Büffel, buffalo
Bulle, bull
Dachs, (dachshound) badger
Drache, drake (*poetical*), dragon
Elefant, elephant
Eſel, ass, donkey
Froſch, frog
Fuchs, fox
Hund, hound, dog
Kater, (tom)cat
Luchs, lynx
Marder, marten

Ochs, ox
Panter, panther
Pudel, poodle
Schimpanſe, chimpanzee
Stier, steer
Tiger, tiger
Vampyr, vampyre
Wolf, wolf
Zobel, sable

Feminine

Dogge, (bull)dog
Gazelle, gazelle
Giraffe, giraffe

Hyäne, hyena
Katze, cat
Kuh, cow
Maus, mouse
Ratte, rat
Sau, sow

Neuter
Füllen, filly
Kalb, calf

DERIVATIVE NOUNS

Masculine
Schäfer, shepherd

Feminine
Eselei, stupidity
Eselin, jenny-ass
Füchsin, she-fox, vixen

Kamel, camel
Lamm, lamb
Reh, roe
Renntier, reindeer
Schaf, sheep
Schwein, swine, hog
Wiesel, weasel
Zebra, zebra

Hündin, dog
Nachäffung, aping, imitation
Panterin, jaguar
Schäferin, shepherdess
Schweinerei, filth
Tigerin, tigress
Wölfin, she-wolf

DERIVATIVE ADJECTIVES

affig, apish
hündisch, doggish

kalberig, acting like a calf, silly
schweinig, dirty

DERIVATIVE VERBS

kälbern, act like a calf, silly
mausen, steal like a mouse

nachäffen, ape, imitate
verhunzen, (dog) spoil

5. Body of Mammals

Masculine
Huf, hoof

Feminine
Mähne, mane
Nüster, nostril

Neuter
Horn, horn
Vließ, fleece

DERIVATIVE NOUN

Neuter
Gehörn, horns

Derivative Adjective

hörnern, horny

6. Fishes and Reptiles

Masculine

Aal, eel
Fisch, fish
Flunder, flounder
Hering, herring
Karpfen, carp
Krebs, crab
Rogen, roe, spawn
Salm, salmon

Feminine

Finne, fin
Otter, adder
Sardine, sardine

Neuter

Krokodil, crocodile
Netz, net

Derivative Nouns

Masculine

Fischer, fisherman

Feminine

Fischerin, fisher-woman
Fischerei, fishery

Derivative Verbs

fischen, fish

krebsen, crab

7. Birds

Masculine

Falk(e), falcon
Fasan, pheasant
Fink, finch
Habicht, hawk
Kapaun, capon
Kranich, crane
Kuckuck, cuckoo
Pelikan, pelican
Rabe, raven
Storch, stork

Feminine

Brut, brood
Daune, down
Henne, hen
Krähe, crow
Lerche, lark
Schnepfe, snipe
Schwalbe, swallow
Turteltaube, turtledove

Neuter

Nest, nest

Derivative Nouns

Masculine

Falkner, falconer
Gänserich, gander
Hahn, rooster
Täuberich, cock-pigeon

Neuter

Gefieder, feathers, plumage
Huhn, chicken

Derivative Verbs

brüten, brood, hatch

nisten, nest

8. Insects and Worms

Masculine

Floh, flea

Feminine

Biene, bee
Fliege, fly
Hornisse, hornet

Larve, larva
Motte, moth
Trichine, trichina
Wespe, wasp

Neuter

Insekt, insect

Derivative Noun

Neuter

Gewürm, worms, vermin

Derivative Verb

wurmen, fret, vex

9. Plants, Shrubs, and Trees

Masculine

Apfel, apple
Baum, (beam) tree
Block, block, log
Buchweizen, buckwheat
Busch, bush
Dünger, dung
Epheu, ivy
Flachs, flax

Forst, forest
Garten, garden
Hanf, hemp
Hopfen, hop
Jasmin, jessamine
Kakao, cocoa
Kaktus, cactus
Knollen, knoll
Lattich, lettuce

Moder, mud
Park, park
Reis, rice
Rhabarber, rhubarb
Stamm, stem
Stumpf, stump
Tabak, tobacco
Trog, trough
Wald, woods
Zweig, twig

Feminine

Ähre, ear
Aprikose, apricot
Beere, berry
Birke, birch
Blume, (bloom) flower
Bohne, bean
Botanik, botany
Buche, beech
Dattel, date
Eiche, oak
Esche, ash
Espe, aspen
Flora, flora
Föhre, fir
Haselnuß, hazelnut
Hürde, hurdle
Kastanie, chestnut
Kerbe, carve, notch
Kresse, cress
Lilie, lily
Linde, linden

Melone, melon
Myrte, myrtle
Nessel, nettle
Nuß, nut
Olive, olive
Palme, palm
Pappel, poplar
Rinde, rind, bark
Rose, rose
Rosine, raisin
Sellerie, celery
Stoppel, stubble
Tulpe, tulip
Ulme, elm
Vanille, vanilla
Walnuß, walnut
Zeder, cedar

Neuter

Beet, bed
Bouquet, bouquet
Farnkraut, fern
Feld, field
Gras, grass
Heu, hay
Korn, corn, grain
Laub, (leaf) foliage
Mais, maize, corn
Malz, malt
Radieschen, radish
Stroh, straw
Veilchen, violet

DERIVATIVE NOUNS

Masculine

Förster, forester

Gärtner, gardener
Müller, miller

Feminine

Abſtammung, descent
Abzweigung, branching off
Laube, bower
Stämmigkeit, sturdiness
Verzweigung, ramification

Waldung, woodland

Neuter

Gebüſch, bushes, thicket
Gefilde, fields
Gezweig, branches

DERIVATIVE ADJECTIVES

belaubt, leafy
bewaldet, wooded
buchen, beechen
buſchig, bushy
flachſen, flaxen

roſig, rosy
ſtämmig, sturdy
ſtrohig, strawy
verzweigt, ramified
waldig, wooded

DERIVATIVE VERBS

abrinden, bark
abſtammen, rise from the stem, descend
abzweigen, branch off
bäumen, rise like a tree, prance
baumeln, dangle (as from a tree)
belauben, cover with leaves
botaniſieren, botanize

düngen, dung, fertilize
entlauben, shed the leaves
entſtammen, descend
graſen, graze, cut grass
heuen, make hay
kerben, carve, notch
modern, rot, decay
verblümen, express figuratively

10. Stones and Metals

Masculine

Diamant, diamond
Jaspis, jasper
Marmor, marble
Nickel, nickel
Quarz, quartz
Rubin, ruby
Stahl, steel
Stein, stone

Feminine

Bronze, bronze
Gemme, gem
Kohle, coal
Koralle, coral
Perle, pearl

Neuter

Gold, gold
Kryſtall, crystal

Metall, metal
Mineral, mineral
Platin, platinum

Silber, silver
Zink, zinc
Zinn, tin

DERIVATIVE NOUN
Feminine

Versteinerung, petrifaction

DERIVATIVE ADJECTIVES

golden, golden
marmorn, made of marble
metallisch, metallic
mineralisch, mineral
silbern, made of silver

stählern, made of steel
steinern, stony
steinig, stony
zinnern, made of tin

DERIVATIVE VERBS

krystallisieren, crystallize
perlen, rise in pearls
stählen, steel, harden
vergolden, gild
verkohlen, carbonize

vernickeln, plate with nickel
versilbern, silver, plate
versteinern, petrify
verzinnen, tin

11. Time

Masculine

Freitag, Friday
Herbst, (harvest) autumn
Kalender, calendar
Mittag, (midday) noon
Mittwoch, (mid-week) Wednesday
Monat, month
Montag, Monday
Sommer, summer
Sonntag, Sunday
Winter, winter
Januar, January
Februar, February
März, March

April, April
Mai, May
Juni, June
Juli, July
August, August
September, September
Oktober, October
November, November
Dezember, December

Feminine

Minute, minute
Periode, period
Sekunde, second

Weile, while
Woche, week

Neuter

Datum, date
Jahr, year

DERIVATIVE NOUNS

Masculine

Nachmittag, afternoon
Vormittag, forenoon

Verjährung, superannuation
Vertagung, adjournment

Neuter

Feminine

Tagung, convention

Jahrhundert, century
Jahrtausend, millenary
Jahrzehnt, decade

DERIVATIVE ADJECTIVES

abendlich, evening
bejahrt, aged
betagt, elderly
herbstlich, autumnal
jährlich, yearly
monatlich, monthly

periodisch, periodical
sommerlich, summer-like
sonntäglich, Sunday-like
täglich, daily
winterlich, winterly
wöchentlich, weekly

DERIVATIVE VERBS

datieren, date
tagen, dawn, hold a meeting
verjähren, superannuate

vertagen, adjourn
verweilen, while, linger
weilen, while, linger

12. Chemistry

Masculine

Alkohol, alcohol
Asphalt, asphalt
Balsam, balsam
Gips, gypsum
Kalf, (chalk) lime
Kampfer, camphor
Leim, lime, glue
Phosphor, phosphorus

Salmiak, sal-ammoniac
Schmeer, (smear) grease
Spiritus, spirits, alcohol
Talg, tallow
Teer, tar
Terpentin, turpentine
Tropfen, drop
Wismut, bismuth
Zinnober, cinnabar

Feminine

Apotheke, apothecary's shop
Chemie, chemistry
Pottasche, potash
Rakete, (sky)rocket
Retorte, retort
Salbe, salve
Schlacke, slag
Zelle, cell

Neuter

Cement, cement

Chinin, quinine
Chlor, chlorine
Gas, gas
Glyzerin, glycerine
Hydrat, hydrate
Jod, iodine
Pulver, powder (pulverize)
Quecksilber, quicksilver
Salpeter, saltpeter
Strychnin, strychnine
Sublimat, sublimate
Vitriol, vitriol

DERIVATIVE NOUNS

Masculine

Apotheker, druggist
Chemiker, chemist
Glaser, glazier
Tropfer, dropper
Vergaser, carbureter

Feminine

Einbalsamierung, embalming
Glasur, potter's glazing
Verkalkung, calcination

DERIVATIVE ADJECTIVES

alkoholisch, alcoholic
balsamisch, balmy

chemisch, chemical
kalkig, limy

DERIVATIVE VERBS

asphaltieren, asphalt
einbalsamieren, embalm
einkampfern, cover with camphor
glasieren, glaze
leimen, glue
salben, anoint

teeren, tar
tröpfeln, drop, trickle
tropfen, drop
verglasen, glaze, vitrify
verkalken, calcinate

13. Measures and Weights

Masculine

Sack, sack, bag

Feminine

Kanne, can
Kapsel, capsule

Maſſe, mass
Mitte, middle
Mulde, mold
Rute, rod
Unze, ounce

Neuter

Ende, end
Format, form, size
Gran, grain
Karat, carat
Paar, pair, couple
Pfund, pound

DERIVATIVE NOUNS

Masculine

Vermittler, middleman

Endloſigkeit, endlessness
Unendlichkeit, endlessness
Vermittelung, mediation
Vollendung, completion

Feminine

Beendigung, termination

DERIVATIVE ADJECTIVES

endlich, final

endlos, endless

DERIVATIVE VERBS

beenden, finish
beendigen, finish
einſäckeln, put into a sack
enden, end

formieren, form
vermitteln, act as a middleman
vollenden, complete

14. Instruments and Utensils

Masculine

Apparat, apparatus
Ballon, balloon
Bolzen, bolt
Cylinder, cylinder
Drillbohrer, drill (bore)
Haken, hook
Hammer, hammer
Kamm, comb
Keſſel, kettle
Krahn, crane

Schaft, shaft
Spaten, spade
Stock, stick
Stöpſel, stopper
Strang, string
Zirkel, (circle) compass

Feminine

Bahre, bier
Büchſe, box
Feile, file

Kurbel, (curve) crank
Laterne, lantern
Linſe, lens
Maſchine, machine
Mechanik, mechanics
Pumpe, pump
Ramme, ram
Raſpel, rasp
Rolle, roll
Schaufel, shovel
Schraube, screw
Sichel, sickle

Spindel, spindle
Spule, spool
Uhr, (hour) clock, watch
Vaſe, vase

Neuter

Inſtrument, instrument
Joch, yoke
Kabel, cable
Lineal, (line) ruler
Pendel, pendulum
Teleſkop, telescope

DERIVATIVE NOUNS

Masculine

Maſchiniſt, machinist
Mechaniker, mechanic

Feminine

Unterjochung, subjugation

DERIVATIVE ADJECTIVES

cylindriſch, cylindrical
hakig, hooky

mechaniſch, mechanical

DERIVATIVE VERBS

bohren, bore
feilen, file
haken, hook
hämmern, hammer
kabeln, cable
kämmen, comb
liniieren, line, rule

pumpen, pump
rammen, ram
rollen, roll
ſchaufeln, shovel
ſchrauben, screw
unterjochen, subdue
zirkeln, move in a circle

15. The Human Body

Masculine

Bart, beard
Buſen, bosom
Ellbogen, elbow

Finger, finger
Fuß, foot
Gaumen, gum
Hunger, hunger

Knöchel, knuckle, ankle
Muskel, muscle
Nabel, navel
Nacken, neck
Nerv, nerve
Puls, pulse

Mumie, mummy
Nase, nose
Rippe, rib
Schulter, shoulder
Sehne, sinew
Zunge, tongue

Feminine

Braue, brow
Brust, breast
Faust, fist
Fiber, fiber
Figur, figure
Galle, gall
Hand, hand
Hüfte, hip
Hygiene, hygiene
Leber, liver
Lende, loin
Locke, lock, curl
Lunge, lung

Neuter

Bein, bone, leg
Blut, blood
Fleisch, flesh
Haar, hair
Kinn, chin
Knie, knee
Mark, marrow
Ohr, ear
Organ, organ
Schienbein, shinbone
Schulterblatt, shoulderblade
Skelett, skeleton

DERIVATIVE NOUNS

Masculine

Fleischer, butcher
Handel, handling of goods, commerce
Organismus, organism
Vierfüßler, quadruped
Vierhänder, quadrumane

Brüstung, parapet
Fleischerei, butcher's store
Handhabung, handling
Handlichkeit, handiness
Handlung, action, store
Muskulatur, muscling
Neckerei, nagging, teasing

Feminine

Behandlung, treatment
Behendigkeit, agility
Blutung, bleeding

Neuter

Geblüt, race, lineage
Genick, neck
Gerippe, skeleton

Derivative Adjectives

bartlos, beardless
bebartet, bearded
behaart, hairy
blutig, bloody
figürlich, figurative
fleischig, fleshy
fleischlich, carnal
haarig, hairy
haarlos, hairless

handlich, handy
hungrig, hungry
knöchern, bony
lockig, curly
muskulös, muscular
nervös, nervous
organisch, organic
sehnig, sinewy
vierfüßig, quadruped

Derivative Verbs

behaaren, cover with hair
behandeln, handle, treat
bluten, bleed
brüsten sich, boast
fußen, foot, rely upon
handeln, handle goods, trade
handhaben, handle
hungern, be hungry
knieen, kneel
locken, curl

näseln, speak through the nose
necken, nag, tease
nicken, bend the neck, nod
pulsieren, pulsate
schultern, shoulder
verbluten, bleed to death
verhungern, die of hunger
zerfleischen, tear up the flesh
züngeln, shoot out in tongues

16. Family and Persons in General

Masculine

Assistent, assistant
Bräutigam, bridegroom (elect)
Bruder, brother
Gast, guest
Ingenieur, engineer (civil)
Kannibale, cannibal
Kumpan, companion
Lakei, lackey
Mann, man, male person
Mensch, man, human being
Nachbar, neighbor

Name, name
Neffe, nephew
Neger, negro
Onkel, uncle
Pöbel, people, mob
Sklave, slave
Sohn, son
Stiefbruder, step-brother
Strolch, (stroller) tramp
Vagabund, vagabond
Vater, father

Feminine

Bande, band, gang
Braut, bride (elect)
Dame, dame, lady
Familie, family
Genealogie, genealogy
Generation, generation
Gilde, guild
Mutter, mother
Person, person

Rasse, race
Schwester, sister
Tochter, daughter
Witwe, widow

Neuter

Publikum, public
Volk, (folk) people
Weib, (wife) woman

DERIVATIVE NOUNS

Masculine

Gevatter, god-father
Vorname, Christian name
Witwer, widower
Zuname, family name

Feminine

Bemannung, crew
Bemutterung, motherly care
Bevölkerung, population
Gastlichkeit, hospitality
Gevatterin, god-mother
Gevatterschaft, god-fathership
Männlichkeit, manliness
Mannschaft, team, squad

Menschheit, mankind
Menschlichkeit, humanity
Nachbarschaft, neighborhood
Persönlichkeit, personality
Sklaverei, slavery
Sklavin, slave
Strolcherei, vagrancy
Verbrüderung, fraternization
Volkstümlichkeit, popularity
Weiblichkeit, womanhood

Plural only

Gebrüder, brothers (in a firm)
Geschwister, brothers and sisters

DERIVATIVE ADJECTIVES

beweibt, married
bräutlich, bridal
brüderlich, fraternal
familiär, familiar
gastlich, hospitable
kannibalisch, cannibal
lakeienhaft, officious
mannhaft, manly, valiant

männlich, manly, masculine
menschlich, human
mütterlich, maternal
nachbarlich, neighborly
namenlos, nameless
namentlich, by name, particularly
namhaft, renowned
nämlich, namely

perſönlich, personal
pöbelhaft, vulgar
ſchweſterlich, sisterly
väterlich, paternal

volkstümlich, popular
weibiſch, womanish
weiblich, female, feminine

DERIVATIVE VERBS

bemannen, man
bemuttern, treat like a mother
benamſen, give a name
bevölkern, populate
beweiben ſich, take a wife
ſtrolchen, stroll
vagabundieren, ramble

verbrüdern ſich, fraternize

Used in the Past Participle only

benachbart, neighboring
entmenſcht, brutalized
verwitwet, widowed

17. Clothing

Masculine

Flanell, flannel
Gürtel, girdle
Hut, hat
Kattun, (cotton) muslin
Kittel, (coat) frock
Knopf, (knob) button
Mantel, mantle, cloak
Muff, muff
Pelz, pelt, fur
Plüſch, plush
Ring, ring
Schal, shawl
Schlitz, slit
Schuh, shoe
Tüll, tulle

Feminine

Jacke, jacket

Kappe, cap
Kutte, (coat) frock
Livree, livery
Nadel, needle
Sandale, sandal
Schärpe, scarf
Socke, sock
Sohle, sole
Spange, spangle
Watte, wadding
Wolle, wool

Neuter

Garn, yarn
Hermelin, ermine
Juwel, jewel
Leinen, linen
Muſſelin, muslin

DERIVATIVE NOUNS

Masculine

Gürtler, girdler
Handſchuh, glove

Hüter, (heeder) keeper
Juwelier, jeweler
Schuſter, shoemaker

Feminine	**Befohlung**, repair of soles
Bemäntelung, excuse	

DERIVATIVE ADJECTIVE
wollig, woolly

DERIVATIVE VERBS

behüten, heed, keep	**nähen**, sew (needle)
bemänteln, excuse	**ringeln**, curl
beschuhen, supply with shoes	**schlitzen**, slit
besohlen, sole	**umgarnen**, ensnare
gürten, gird	**verkappen**, disguise
hüten, heed, keep	**verknüpfen**, connect
knöpfen, button	**wattieren**, wad
knüpfen, connect	

18. Food and Beverages

Masculine	*Feminine*
Appetit, appetite	**Butter**, butter
Honig, honey	**Cichorie**, chicory
Kaffee, coffee	**Lakritze**, licorice
Käse, cheese	**Limonade**, lemonade
Kaviar, caviar	**Mandel**, almond
Kuchen, cake	**Milch**, milk
Mostrich, mustard	**Nudel**, noodle
Pfeffer, pepper	**Portion**, portion, dish
Punsch, punch	**Restauration**, restaurant
Rum, rum	**Schokolade**, chocolate
Saft, sap, juice	**Spezerei**, spices
Salat, salad	**Suppe**, soup
Spinat, spinage	**Torte**, tart
Syrup, syrup	**Zigarre**, cigar
Tee, tea	
Vegetarier, vegetarian	*Neuter*
Wein, wine	**Bier**, beer
Zucker, sugar	**Brot**, bread
	Futter, fodder, food

Mahl, meal, repast

Mehl, meal, flour

Salz, salt

Soda, soda

DERIVATIVE NOUNS

Masculine	*Feminine*
Restaurateur, caterer	Fütterung, feeding
Winzer, vintner	Milcherei, creamery

DERIVATIVE ADJECTIVES

appetitlich, appetizing

käsig, caseous

mehlig, mealy

pfefferig, peppered

saftig, juicy

salzig, salted

DERIVATIVE VERBS

füttern, feed

pfeffern, pepper

salzen, salt

versalzen, oversalt

zuckern, sugar

19. Medicine

Masculine	*Feminine*
Doktor, doctor	Beule, boil
Idiot, idiot	Blattern, (bladder) smallpox
Karbunkel, carbuncle	Cholera, cholera
Katarrh, catarrh	Diagnose, diagnosis
Krampf, cramp, spasm	Diät, diet
Krüppel, cripple	Dosis, dose
Patient, patient	Epidemie, epidemic
Quacksalber, quack	Hysterie, hysteria
Rheumatismus, rheumatism	Krisis, crisis
Sarg, sarcophagus, coffin	Kur, cure
Scharbock, scurvy	Masern, measles
Scharlach, scarlet	Medizin, medicine
Skorbut, scurvy	Pein, pain
Stich, stitch, stab	Pest, pest
Typhus, typhoid	Pille, pill
Veitstanz, St. Vitus' dance	Plage, plague

Praxis, practice
Seuche, sickness
Strophel, scrofula
Sonde, sound, probe
Therapie, therapeutics
Warze, wart
Wunde, wound

Neuter

Fieber, fever
Hospital, hospital
Pflaster, plaster
Rezept, recipe, prescription
Symptom, symptom
Spital, hospital

DERIVATIVE NOUNS

Masculine

Peiniger, tormentor
Rezeptar, prescription clerk

Feminine

Einsargung, placing into a coffin

Peinlichkeit, painfulness
Quacksalberei, quackery
Sucht, disease
Verkrüppelung, stunt

DERIVATIVE ADJECTIVES

epidemisch, epidemic
fieberisch, feverish
hysterisch, hysterical
krampfhaft, spasmodic
kritisch, critical
medizinisch, medical

peinlich, painful
praktisch, practical
rheumatisch, rheumatic
skrophulös, scrofulous
typhös, typhoid
verkrüppelt, crippled

DERIVATIVE VERBS

bepflastern, cover with plasters
einsargen, place into a coffin
fiebern, be in a fever
kurieren, cure
peinigen, cause pains, torture
pflastern, plaster

plagen, plague, torture
praktizieren, practise
sondieren, sound
verkrüppeln, cripple
verseuchen, infect
verwunden, wound

20. Religion

Masculine

Abt, abbot
Apostel, apostle
Bischof, bishop

Christ, Christian
Geist, ghost, spirit
Gott, God
Jude, Jew

Kaplan, chaplain
Kardinal, cardinal
Katholik, Catholic
Klerus, clergy
Küster, custodian, sexton
Laie, layman
Märtyrer, martyr
Mönch, monk
Pastor, pastor
Pharisäer, Pharisee
Philister, philistine
Pilger, pilgrim
Pomp, pomp
Priester, priest
Psalm, psalm
Rabbiner, rabbi
Schrein, shrine
Superintendent, bishop of the
    Protestant Church
Tempel, temple
Teufel, devil
Vikar, vicar

Feminine

Bibel, Bible
Hölle, hell
Kanzel, chancel
Kapelle, chapel

Katakombe, catacomb
Kathedrale, cathedral
Kirche, church
Messe, mass
Moschee, mosque
Nonne, nun
Reformation, reformation
Religion, religion
Seele, soul
Sekte, sect
Sünde, sin
Synagoge, synagogue
Theologie, theology

Neuter

Almosen, alms
Grab, grave
Kloster, cloister, convent
Kreuz, cross
Münster, monastery, convent
Orakel, oracle
Ostern, Easter
Paradies, paradise
Sakrament, sacrament
Symbol, symbol
Testament, testament
Wunder, wonder, miracle

DERIVATIVE NOUNS

Masculine

Götz, idol
Graben, ditch
Kanzler, chancelor
Klausner, recluse
Sünder, sinner

Feminine

Abtei, abbey
Äbtissin, abbess
Begeisterung, inspiration
Bewunderung, admiration
Christenheit, Christianity
Christin, Christian

Geistlichkeit, clergy
Geistlosigkeit, dullness
Göttlichkeit, divine origin
Gottlosigkeit, impiety
Grube, pit
Jüdin, Jewess
Kanzlei, chancery
Katholikin, Catholic
Kreuzigung, crucifixion
Märtyrerin, martyr
Pilgerin, pilgrim
Priesterin, priestess
Seligkeit, bliss
Sühne, atonement

Sünderin, sinner
Teufelei, deviltry
Teufelin, devil
Vergötterung, apotheosis
Verwunderung, surprise
Wunderlichkeit, oddity

Neuter

Begräbnis, burial
Christentum, Christianity
Grübchen, (little pit) dimple
Judentum, Judaism
Pastorat, parsonage
Priestertum, priesthood

DERIVATIVE ADJECTIVES

apostolisch, apostolic
biblisch, biblical
bischöflich, episcopal
christlich, Christian
entseelt, inanimate
geistig, intellectual
geistlich, spiritual
geistvoll, ingenious
göttlich, divine
gottlos, godless
gottvoll, divine
höllisch, infernal
jüdisch, Jewish
katholisch, Catholic
kirchlich, ecclesiastical

klösterlich, monastic
orakelhaft, oracular
pharisäisch, pharisaic
philisterhaft, snobbish
priesterlich, priestly
religiös, religious
seelisch, psychic
selig, blissful
sündig, sinful
symbolisch, symbolical
testamentarisch, testamentary
theologisch, theological
wunderbar, wondrous
wunderlich, strange
wundervoll, wonderful

DERIVATIVE VERBS

abkanzeln, lecture a person
begeistern, inspire
begraben, bury
bekreuzen sich, cross oneself

beseelen, animate
beseligen, make happy
bewundern, admire
kreuzen, cross

kreuzigen, crucify
pilgern, wander
reformieren, reform
sühnen, atone for sins

sündigen, sin
vergeistigen, spiritualize
vergöttern, idolize
wundern sich, wonder

21. Political Terms

Masculine

Aristokrat, aristocrat
Demagog, demagogue
Demokrat, democrat
Despot, despot
Fürst, (first) prince, ruler
Insurgent, insurgent
Intrigant, intriguer
König, king
Kurier, courier
Magistrat, board of aldermen
Minister, member of the cabinet
Monarch, monarch
Polizist, policeman
Potentat, potentate
Präsident, president
Prinz, prince
Rang, rank
Rebell, rebel
Regent, regent
Sozialist, socialist
Staat, state
Sultan, sultan
Suverän, sovereign

Thron, throne
Usurpator, usurper
Vice, vice

Feminine

Debatte, debate
Dynastie, dynasty
Interpellation, interpellation
Katastrophe, catastrophe
Krone, crown
Nation, nation
Partei, party
Politik, politics
Polizei, police force
Reaktion, reaction
Republik, republic
Revolution, revolution
Tendenz, tendency

Neuter

Parlament, parliament
Ultimatum, ultimatum
Veto, veto
Votum, vote

DERIVATIVE NOUNS

Masculine

Despotismus, despotism
Parlamentär, truce-bearer
Parlamentarier, member of parliament

Politiker, politician
Reaktionär, reactionary
Revolutionär, revolutionist

Feminine

Aristokratie, aristocracy
Demokratie, democracy
Fürstin, princess
Königin, queen
Krönung, coronation
Monarchie, monarchy
Nationalität, nationality
Parteilichkeit, partiality

Präsidentschaft, presidency
Prinzessin, princess
Regentschaft, regency
Verstaatlichung, state ownership

Neuter

Fürstentum, principality
Königtum, royalty
Ministerium, ministry, cabinet

DERIVATIVE ADJECTIVES

aristokratisch, aristocratic
demokratisch, democratic
fürstlich, princely
königlich, royal
monarchisch, monarchical
national, national

parlamentarisch, parliamentary
parteiisch, partial
politisch, political
polizeilich, of the police
republikanisch, republican
staatlich, federal, national

DERIVATIVE VERBS

debattieren, debate
interpellieren, interplead
krönen, crown
politisieren, discuss politics
rangieren, rank
rebellieren, rebel

regieren, govern
revolutionieren, revolutionize
thronen, throne
usurpieren, usurp
verstaatlichen, turn over to the state
vetieren, veto

22. Army and Navy

Masculine

Ballast, ballast
Bord, board
Deich, dike
Deserteur, deserter
Drillmeister, drillmaster
Feind, (fiend) enemy
Grenadier, grenadier

Helm, helmet
Herold, herald
Husar, hussar
Invalide, invalid
Kadett, cadet
Kahn, canoe, boat
Kamerad, comrade
Kapitän, captain

Karabiner, carbine
Kavalier, cavalier
Kiel, keel
Koller, collar, cape
Kürassier, cuirassier
Major, major
Marsch, march
Mast, mast
Offizier, officer
Orden, order, decoration
Posten, post, sentinel
Proviant, provisions
Reiter, rider, horseman
Rekrut, recruit
Respekt, respect
Ritter, (rider) knight
Sattel, saddle
Schild, shield
Sekundant, second
Soldat, soldier
Speer, spear
Spion, spy
Sporn, spur
Tribut, tribute
Triumph, triumph
Trupp, troop
Tumult, tumult
Vasall, vassal
Veteran, veteran
Wall, wall, rampart
Zickzack, zigzag

Feminine

Artillerie, artillery
Barke, bark
Bastei, bastion
Batterie, battery

Boje, buoy
Bombe, bomb
Brigade, brigade
Flagge, flag
Flanke, flank
Flinte, (flint) gun
Flotte, fleet, navy
Galeere, galley
Garde, guard
Garnison, garrison
Gondel, gondola
Granate, grenade
Infanterie, infantry
Jacht, yacht
Kanone, cannon
Kavallerie, cavalry
Koppel, (coupler) belt
Krippe, crib
Majestät, majesty
Marine, (marine) navy
Meuterei, mutiny
Mine, mine
Miliz, militia
Pallisade, palisade
Parade, parade
Pike, pike
Pistole, pistol
Schaluppe, sloop
Schlacht, slaughter, battle
Schwadron, squadron
Truppe, troop
Waffe, weapon
Werft, wharf
Zitadelle, citadel

Neuter

Bataillon, battalion

Bollwerk, bulwark
Boot, boat
Duell, duel
Geschwader, squadron
Kaliber, caliber
Kastell, castle, stronghold
Leck, leak
Militär, military, army
Panier, banner
Quartier, quarters

Regiment, regiment
Ruder, rudder, oar
Scharmützel, skirmish
Schiff, ship
Schwert, sword
Steuer, steer(age)
Tau, tow, hawser
Turnier, tournament
Wrack, wreck
Zivil, civilians

DERIVATIVE NOUNS

Masculine

Artillerist, gunner
Beutel, (boodle) bag
Bombardier, gunner
Duellant, duellist
Fähn(d)rich, (flag) ensign
Gardist, guardsman
Infanterist, foot soldier
Kanonier, gunner
Meuterer, mutineer
Sattler, saddler
Schiffer, boatman
Schlächter, slaughterer, butcher
Söldner, hireling
Zivilist, civilian

Feminine

Ausbeutung, taking advantage of
Besoldung, salary
Bewaffnung, armament
Entwaffnung, disarmament
Feindin, enemy
Feindschaft, enmity
Kameradschaft, good-fellowship
Reiterei, cavalry
Ritterschaft, knighthood
Sattlerei, saddlery
Schlächterei, slaughter

DERIVATIVE ADJECTIVES

feindlich, hostile
flott, afloat
kameradschaftlich, companionable
leck, leaky
majestätisch, majestic

meuterisch, mutinous
militärisch, military
ritterlich, chivalrous
soldatisch, soldierly

Derivative Verbs

anspornen, spur, incite
befeinden, persecute
beflaggen, hang out flags
bemasten, supply with masts
bewaffnen, arm
bombardieren, shell
desertieren, desert
duellieren, fight a duel
eindeichen, dam up
einquartieren, quarter
entwaffnen, disarm
flaggen, flag
flankieren, flank
gondeln, ride in a gondola
kahnen, boat
koppeln, couple
lecken, leak
marschieren, march

meutern, mutiny
paradieren, parade
reiten, ride
rekrutieren, recruit
respektieren, respect
rudern, row
satteln, saddle
schiffen, navigate
sekundieren, second
spionieren, spy
steuern, steer
tauen, tow
triumphieren, triumph
unterminieren, undermine
verfeinden sich, fall out
verproviantieren, provision
verschiffen, ship

23. School, Art, and Literature

Masculine

Akt, act
Antiquar, dealer in old books
Artikel, article
Chor, chorus, choir
Dialekt, dialect
Dialog, dialogue
Diphthong, diphthong
Direktor, director, principal
Firnis, varnish
Foliant, folio
Gaukler, juggler
Humor, humor
Index, index
Kandidat, candidate

Karneval, carnival
Katalog, catalogue
Klassiker, classic
Kollege, colleague
Konsonant, consonant
Lack, lacquer
Pädagog, pedagogue
Philolog, philologist
Philosoph, philosopher
Photograph, photographer
Professor, professor
Prolog, prologue
Punkt, point, period
Reim, rhyme
Rhythmus, rhythm

Roman, romance, novel
Sockel, socle
Stil, style
Strich, stroke, line
Student, student
Text, text
Vers, verse
Vokal, vowel
Zirkus, circus

Feminine

Akademie, academy
Algebra, algebra
Arithmetik, arithmetic
Ballade, ballad
Büste, bust
Deklamation, declamation
Fabel, fable
Gallerie, gallery
Geographie, geography
Geometrie, geometry
Gestikulation, gesticulation
Grammatik, grammar
Grazie, grace
Grimasse, grimace
Gruppe, group
Hymne, hymn
Idee, idea
Idylle, idyl
Illusion, illusion
Illustration, illustration
Immatrikulation, matriculation
Interpunktion, punctuation
Karikatur, caricature
Klasse, class
Komödie, comedy
Konversation, conversation

Kopie, copy
Korrektur, correction
Kreide, crayon, chalk
Linie, line
Liste, list
Literatur, literature
Logik, logic
Lyrik, lyric poetry
Magie, magic
Maske, mask
Methode, method
Moral, morals
Muse, muse
Mythe, myth
Novelle, novel
Oper, opera
Pantomime, pantomime
Phantasie, fancy
Positur, posture
Prosa, prose
Satyre, satire
Scene, scene
Schule, school
Silbe, syllable
Skizze, sketch
Symmetrie, symmetry
Syntax, syntax
Theorie, theory
These, thesis
Tragödie, tragedy
Trilogie, trilogy
Vision, vision

Neuter

Ballet, ballet
Billet, billet, ticket
Buch, book

Diplom, diploma
Drama, drama
Fresko, fresco
Gymnasium, high school
Ideal, ideal
Idiom, idiom
Institut, institute
Modell, model
Museum, museum

Pastell, pastel
Pergament, parchment
Portrait, portrait
Programm, program
Synonym, synonym
Theater, theater
Thema, theme
Werk, work
Wort, word

DERIVATIVE NOUNS

Masculine

Akademiker, academician
Choral, hymn
Chorist, member of the chorus
Diplomat, diplomat
Dramatiker, dramatist
Grammatiker, grammarian
Gymnasiast, high-school boy
Humorist, humorist
Idealist, idealist
Komödiant, comedian
Korrektor, proofreader
Literat, man of letters
Lyriker, lyric poet
Modellierer, modeler
Phantast, visionary
Prosaiker, prose writer
Schüler, scholar, pupil
Theoretiker, theorist
Urtext, original text

Feminine

Antwort, answer
Beantwortung, reply
Befürwortung, support
Bücherei. library

Diplomatie, diplomacy
Gaukelei, jugglery
Kandidatur, candidacy
Maskerade, masquerade
Nachsilbe, suffix
Pädagogik, pedagogy
Philologie, philology
Philosophie, philosophy
Photographie, photography
Professur, professorship
Pünktlichkeit, punctuality
Schülerin, scholar, pupil
Schulung, training
Sophisterei, sophistry
Studentenschaft, student body
Vorsilbe, prefix
Wirklichkeit, reality
Wirksamkeit, efficiency
Wirkung, effect

Neuter

Antiquariat, second-hand book store
Direktorium, board of directors
Kollegium, faculty, lecture
Vorwort, preface

Derivative Adjectives

akademisch, academic
antiquarisch, second hand
diplomatisch, diplomatic
dramatisch, dramatic
fabelhaft, fabulous
geographisch, geographical
grammatisch, grammatical
graziös, graceful
humoristisch, humorous
ideal, ideal
idyllisch, idyllic
karnevalistisch, relating to carnival
literarisch, literary
logisch, logical
lyrisch, lyric
methodisch, methodical
moralisch, moral
mythisch, mythical

pädagogisch, pedagogical
phantastisch, fanciful
philologisch, philological
philosophisch, philosophical
prosaisch, prosaic
pünktlich, punctual
rhythmisch, rhythmical
romanhaft, romantic
romantisch, romantic
stilistisch, stylistic
symmetrisch, symmetrical
syntaktisch, syntactical
textlich, textual
theatralisch, theatrical
theoretisch, theoretical
wirksam, efficient
wörtlich, literal

Derivative Verbs

ankreiden, chalk down
beantworten, answer
befürworten, advocate
bewirken, work, effect
buchen, book
deklamieren, recite
dirigieren, direct
fabulieren, fabulize
firnissen, varnish
gaukeln, juggle
gestikulieren, gesticulate
gruppieren, group
idealisieren, idealize
illustrieren, illustrate
immatrikulieren, enroll
interpunktieren, punctuate

karikieren, caricature
kopieren, copy
korrigieren, correct
lackieren, lacquer
liniieren, line, rule
maskieren, mask
modellieren, model
moralisieren, moralize
phantasieren, wander (mind)
philosophieren, philosophize
photographieren, photograph
portraitieren, portray
punktieren, punctuate
reimen, rhyme
schulen, train
skizzieren, sketch

studieren, study
verwirklichen, realize

wirken, work, take effect

24. Music

Masculine

Baß, bass
Sopran, soprano
Tenor, tenor
Ton, tone
Triangel, triangle
Triller, trill, quaver
Virtuose, virtuoso
Walzer, waltz

Feminine

Akustik, acoustics
Arie, aria
Fiedel, fiddle
Flöte, flute
Guitarre, guitar
Harfe, harp
Harmonie, harmony
Kantate, cantata

Laute, lute
Leier, lyre
Melodie, melody
Musik, music
Oboe, oboe, hautboy
Orgel, organ
Posaune, bassoon
Symphonie, symphony
Trommel, drum
Trompete, trumpet
Zither, zither

Neuter

Duett, duet, duo
Pedal, pedal
Quartett, quartet
Quintett, quintet
Trio, trio
Violoncell, violoncello

Derivative Nouns

Bassist, bass-singer
Fiedler, fiddler
Flötist, flutist
Harfner, harpist
Musikant, musician
Musiker, musician
Oboist, oboe player

Organist, organist
Posaunist, performer on the trombone
Trommler, drummer
Trompeter, trumpeter
Violinist, violinist
Violoncellist, violoncellist

Derivative Adjectives

harmonisch, harmonious
musikalisch, musical

symphonisch, symphonious

Derivative Verbs

ableiern, drawl out
fiedeln, fiddle
flöten, blow the flute
musizieren, make music
nachleiern, imitate

tönen, sound
trillern, trill, quaver
trommeln, drum
trompeten, trumpet
walzen, waltz

25. Science

Feminine

Elektrizität, electricity
Formel, formula
Materie, matter
Nummer, number
Optik, optics
Perspektive, perspective
Phase, phase
Probe, probe, test
Technik, engineering
Vibration, vibration

Volte, volt
Ziffer, cipher, figure

Neuter

Barometer, barometer
Element, element
Experiment, experiment
Mikroskop, microscope
Quadrat, square
Thermometer, thermometer

Derivative Nouns

Masculine

Elektriker, electrician
Materialist, materialist
Optiker, optician

Techniker, technologist

Neuter

Material, material

Derivative Adjectives

elektrisch, electric
elementar, elementary
experimentell, experimental
formell, formal
materiell, material

mikroskopisch, microscopic
optisch, optical
quadratisch, quadratic
technisch, technical

Derivative Verbs

elektrisieren, electrify
entziffern, decipher
experimentieren, experiment
formulieren, formulate

numerieren, number
probieren, probe, test
quadrieren, square
vibrieren, vibrate

26. Law

Masculine
Advocat, lawyer
Arrest, arrest
Bann, ban
Galgen, gallows
Jurist, jurist
Notar, notary
Protest, protest
Prozeß, process, trial
Referent, referee

Feminine
Injurie, injury, insult

Instanz, instance
Jurisprudenz, jurisprudence
Justiz, justice
Klausel, clause
Marter, (martyr) torment

Neuter
Privileg, privilege
Register, register, record
Schafott, scaffold
Statut, statute
Tribunal, tribunal
Urteil, ordeal, sentence

DERIVATIVE NOUNS

Masculine
Arrestant, prisoner

Feminine
Advokatur, lawyer's office
Beurteilung, criticism

Registratur, registrar's office
Verbannung, exile
Verurteilung, condemnation

Neuter
Notariat, notary's office

DERIVATIVE ADJECTIVES
juristisch, juridic
notariell, certified by a notary

urteilslos, lacking in judgment

DERIVATIVE VERBS
arretieren, arrest
beurteilen, criticize
martern, torture
protestieren, protest
prozessieren, bring suit
referieren, report

registrieren, record
urteilen, judge
verbannen, exile
verklausulieren, guard by clauses
verurteilen, sentence

27. Transportation

Masculine

Paſſagier, passenger
Tender, tender
Transport, transportation
Viadukt, viaduct
Wagen, wagon, car

Feminine

Achſe, axle

Depeſche, despatch, telegram
Karre, cart
Kutſche, coach
Lokomotive, locomotive
Poſt, post, mail

Neuter

Automobil, automobile
Paket, package

DERIVATIVE NOUN
Masculine

Kutſcher, coachman, driver

DERIVATIVE ADJECTIVE

poſtaliſch, postal

DERIVATIVE VERBS

depeſchieren, telegraph
karren, cart

kutſchieren, drive a coach
transportieren, transport

28. Trades and Commerce

Masculine

Bäcker, baker
Ballen, bale
Brief, (brief) letter
Dukaten, ducat
Export, export
Import, import
Kautſchuk, caoutchouc
Koch, cook
Kork, cork
Kredit, credit
Markt, market

Paß, passport
Preis, price
Prinzipal, employer
Profit, profit
Rabatt, rebate
Reſt, rest, balance
Ruin, ruin
Schmied, (black)smith
Schmuggel, smuggle
Stapel, staple
Stempel, stamp
Subſkribent, subscriber

Tarif, tariff
Telegraph, telegraph

Taxe, tax
Tonne, ton
Ware, ware

Feminine

Adresse, address
Bank, bank
Finanzen (*plur.*), finance
Firma, firm
Flasche, flask, bottle
Industrie, industry
Kasse, cash, cashier's desk
Marke, mark
Masche, mesh
Notiz, notice, memorandum
Pappe, (pap) cardboard
Prämie, premium
Profession, profession
Qualität, quality
Quantität, quantity
Rente, rent
Sorte, sort
Summe, sum
Tabelle, tabulation

Neuter

Gummi, gum, rubber
Honorar, honorarium, fee
Inventar, inventory
Kapital, capital
Monopol, monopoly
Muster, muster, sample
Öl, oil
Pack, package
Papier, paper
Patent, patent
Pech, pitch
Salär, salary
Sortiment, assortment
Syndikat, syndicate
System, system
Telegramm, telegram
Telephon, telephone
Wachs, wax

DERIVATIVE NOUNS

Masculine

Adressat, addressee
Bankier, banker
Finanzier, financier
Importeur, importer
Kapitalist, capitalist
Kassier(er), cashier
Rentier, retired business man
Schmuggler, smuggler
Telegraphist, telegraph operator

Feminine

Bäckerei, bakery
Bäckerin, baker's wife
Briefschaften, mail
Köchin, cook
Notierung, quotation
Schmiede, smithy
Schmuggelei, smuggling
Telegraphie, telegraphy
Verpackung, packing

Neuter

Gebäck, pastry
Gepäck, baggage

Geschmeide, (gold)smith's work, jewelry

DERIVATIVE ADJECTIVES

brieflich, by letter
finanziell, financial
industriell, industrial
kapitalistisch, capitalistic
musterhaft, exemplary
ölig, oily
papieren, made of paper

qualitativ, qualitative
quantitativ, quantitative
systematisch, systematic
tabellarisch, tabular
telegraphisch, telegraphic
telephonisch, by telephone
wächsern, waxen

DERIVATIVE VERBS

adressieren, address
backen, bake
einkassieren, collect
honorieren, honor (draft)
importieren, import
kochen, cook
markieren, mark
notieren, quote
ölen, oil
packen, pack
profitieren, profit
salarieren, salary
schmieden, forge, frame

sortieren, assort
stapeln, staple
stempeln, stamp, cancel
summieren, sum up
taxieren, appraise
telegraphieren, telegraph
telephonieren, telephone
verbriefen, promise in writing
verkorken, cork up
verpacken, pack up

Used in the Past Participle only

erpicht, sticky, eager

29. Amusement and Games

Masculine

Ball, ball
Jubel, jubilee, exultation
Jux, joke
Tanz, dance
Trumpf, trump

Neuter

Billard, billiards
Domino, domino
Fest, feast, celebration,
Schach, chess

Derivative Adjective
festlich, festive

Derivative Verbs

ballen, form into a ball
jubeln, rejoice

tanzen, dance
trumpfen, trump

30. Abstracts

Masculine

Charakter, character
Egoismus, egotism
Grimm, grim, anger
Harm, harm
Instinkt, instinct
Schauder, shudder
Takt, tact
Titel, title
Witz, wit

Feminine

Initiative, initiative
Ironie, irony

Lust, lust, desire
Manier, manner
Miene, mien, air
Reue, rue, repentance
Scham, shame
Sorge, sorrow
Weise, wise, manner

Neuter

Phlegma, phlegm
Talent, talent
Temperament, temperament

Derivative Adjectives

besorgt, anxious
charakteristisch, characteristic
charakterlos, shifty
egoistisch, selfish
ergrimmt, enraged
grimmig, enraged
harmlos, harmless
instinktiv, instinctive
ironisch, ironical
lüstern, desirous
lustig, merry

manierlich, mannerly
phlegmatisch, phlegmatic
schamlos, shameless
sorgenvoll, anxious
sorglos, free from care
taktlos, without tact
taktvoll, judicious
talentiert, talented
verschämt, shamefaced
witzig, witty

Derivative Verbs

belustigen, amuse
bereuen, rue, repent

beschämen, put to shame
besorgen, take care of

betiteln, title
charakterisieren, characterize
gelüsten, desire
härmen, grieve
schämen sich, be ashamed

schaudern, shudder
sorgen, care
titulieren, title
versorgen, take care of

B. ADJECTIVES AND ADVERBS

all, all
beste, best
blau, blue
blond, blond, light colored
braun, brown
brav, brave, good
brillant, brilliant
doppelt, double
drollig, droll, funny
elegant, elegant
ernst, earnest
falsch, false
fanatisch, fanatic
faul, foul, putrid, lazy
fein, fine, refined
fern, far
fest, fast, solid
fett, fat
frei, free
frisch, fresh
gelb, yellow
grausam, (gruesome) cruel
grotesk, grotesque
grün, green
gut, good
halb, half
harsch, harsh
hart, hard
hohl, hollow
human, humane

imposant, imposing, impressive
infam, infamous, base
inklusive, inclusively
intelligent, intelligent
intensiv, intensive
interessant, interesting
intern, internal
international, international
intim, intimate
intolerant, intolerant
jovial, jovial
jung, young
kahl, callow, bald
keck, quick, lively, bold
klar, clear
kokett, coquettish
kühl, cool
lahm, lame
lakonisch, laconic
lässig, lazy
laut, loud
letzt, last
lose, loose
mager, meager
mehr, more
meist, most
mild, mild
minder, minus, less
mürrisch, morose
nächst, next

nackt, naked
naiv, naive, ingenuous
netto, net
neutral, neutral
nobel, noble, generous
offiziell, official
originell, original
oval, oval
parallel, parallel
plump, plump, clumsy
populär, popular
privat, private
profan, profane
quer, queer, cross
quitt, quit, released
rar, rare
rasch, rash, quick
reich, rich
reif, ripe
roh, raw
rot, red
rund, round
satt, satiated
sauer, sour
schäbig, shabby
schal, shallow
scharf, sharp
scheu, shy
schier, sheer
schlau, sly

schmal, (small) narrow
schnippisch, snappish
selber, self
selten, seldom, rare
sicher, secure, safe
siech, sick
solid, solid
sonder, sundry, separate
stätig, steady
steif, stiff
stereotyp, stereotyped
stets, steadily, always
still, still
subtil, subtle
tragisch, tragic
treu, true, loyal
trivial, trivial
typisch, typical
vakant, vacant
voll, full
wach, awake
warm, warm
weh, woe, painful
weise, wise
wert, worth
wild, wild
willkommen, welcome
wohl, well
wund, wounded, sore
wüst, waste, desolate

C. VERBS

ätzen, etch
backen, bake
beginnen, begin
bersten, burst
bieten, bid, offer

binden, bind
blühen, blow, bloom
bohren, bore
borgen, borrow
brauen, brew

brechen, break
bringen, bring
brüllen, brawl, roar
bummeln, bum, loaf
dauern, endure, last
deklamieren, (declamation) recite
diktieren, dictate
fahren, fare, move
fallen, fall
fasten, fast
fehlen, fail, be lacking
finden, find
flackern, flicker
flattern, flutter
fliegen, fly
fliehen, flee
florieren, flourish
folgen, follow
frieren, freeze
fühlen, feel
füllen, fill
gähnen, yawn
gebären, (bear) give birth
gellen, yell
gleiten, glide
glimmen, gleam
glitzern, glitter
glühen, glow
gratulieren, congratulate
greifen, gripe, grasp
grinsen, grin
grunzen, grunt
hacken, hack
halten, hold
hangen, hang
hauen, hew
heischen, ask
helfen, help

heulen, howl
hindern, hinder
hinken, (hunch) limp
holen, haul, get
hören, hear
hüpfen, hop
ignorieren, ignore
illuminieren, illuminate
imitieren, imitate
imponieren, impose, impress
infizieren, infect
irren, err

kapitulieren, capitulate
klopfen, club, strike
kommen, come
kosten, cost
krächzen, crow
kratzen, scratch
kriechen, crouch, creep
lachen, laugh
laden, load
lauschen, listen
lecken, lick (tongue)
lehnen, lean
leihen, loan
lenken, (link) turn
lernen, learn
liefern, deliver
liegen, lie, rest
lispeln, lisp
lugen, look
lügen, lie, tell an untruth
lullen, lull
machen, make
mähen, mow
meinen, mean
melken, milk

merfen, mark, remark

mifchen, mix

murmeln, murmur

murren, be morose, growl

muß, must

nagen, gnaw

nähren, nourish, feed

necken, nag, tease

niefen, sneeze

ordnen, (order) arrange

packen, pack, seize

parieren, parry

pfeifen, fife, whistle

pflücken, pluck

picken, pick

placken, plague, tease

plärren, blare

plätfchern, splash

plündern, plunder

pochen, poke

pökeln, pickle

polieren, polish

predigen, (predicate) preach

preifen, praise

preffen, press

prickeln, prickle

puffen, puff

quaken, squeak

quetfchen, squash

quieken, squeak

raffinieren, refine

rafcheln, rustle

rafieren, (razor) shave

rauben, rob

rechnen, reckon

regieren, (regent) govern

reiben, rub

reichen, reach

reiten, ride (on horseback)

rennen, run

reparieren, repair

repetieren, repeat

repräfentieren, represent

revidieren, revise

ringen, wring

rinnen, run (fluids)

röften, roast

rücken, rock, move

rühren, (uproar) stir

rumpeln, rumble

fäen, sow

fagen, say

fammeln, assemble

faugen, soak, suck

fchaben, shave

fchaukeln, shake, oscillate

fcheinen, shine

fchelten, scold

fcheren, shear

fcheuern, scour

fchieben, shift, shove

fchlafen, sleep

fchlagen, slay, slug, strike

fchlingen, sling

fchmauchen, smoke

fchmecken, smack, taste

fchmeicheln, (smicker) flatter

fchmieren, smear

fchmunzeln, smile

fchnappen, snap

fchnarchen, snore

fchnäuzen, (snot) blow one's nose

fchnüffeln, sniff

fchreiben, (scribe) write

fchreien, shriek

ſchwanken, swing, waver
ſchwärmen, swarm
ſchweben, (swift) hover
ſchwenken, swing
ſchwimmen, swim
ſchwingen, swing
ſchwitzen, sweat
ſchwören, swear
ſegnen, sign with the cross, bless
ſehen, see
ſenden, send
ſieden, seethe
ſingen, sing
ſinken, sink
ſitzen, sit
ſoll, shall
ſpähen, spy
ſpannen, span
ſparen, spare, save
ſpedieren, expedite
ſpeien, spit
ſpenden, spend
ſperren, (spar) obstruct
ſpinnen, spin
ſpleißen, split
ſpreizen, spread
ſprießen, sprout
ſpringen, spring
ſputen, speed
ſtauen, stow
ſtaunen, astound
ſtechen, stick, stab
ſtehen, (stay) stand
ſtehlen, steal
ſtocken, be stuck, stop
ſtopfen, stuff

ſtören, stir, disturb
ſtottern, stutter
ſtreben, strive
ſtrecken, stretch
ſtreichen, stroke
ſtreifen, strip
ſtreuen, strew
ſtrotzen, strut
ſuchen, (sought) seek
tättowieren, tattoo
ticken, tick
trampeln, trample
trauen, trust
treten, tread, step
trinken, drink
trollen, troll
tummeln, tumble about
tupfen, tip
vergeſſen, forget
vexieren, vex
wachſen, wax, grow
wägen, weigh
wahren, beware, protect
wandern, wander
warnen, warn
waſchen, wash
waten, wade
wecken, waken, wake
wetzen, whet
wiegen, weigh
wimmern, whimper
winden, wind
wirken, work
wollen, will
wringen, wring
zwitſchern, twitter

D. PREPOSITIONS

an, on
anstatt, (in)stead (of)
auf, up(on)
aus, out (of)
außer, (outer) outside of, besides
außerhalb, (outer half) outside
binnen (b=innen), inside, within
diesseits, (on) this side (of)
entlang, along
für, for
halben, halber, (in behalf of) on account of (half *originally means* side)
hinter, (be)hind

in, in
innerhalb, (inner half) within
jenseits, yon(der) side, on the other side of
längs, (a)long
oberhalb, (over, upper half) above
über, over
unter, under
unterhalb, (under half) below
vor, (be)fore
während, (wearing) during
zu, to
zufolge, (to follow) in accordance with

II. GERMAN WORDS WHICH CAN BE MADE SELF-EXPLANATORY BY THE SUBSTITUTION OF CONSONANTS OR VOWELS

A. CONSONANTS

1. German b, English f (gh, when pronounced f)

der Dieb, thief
halb, half
das Kalb, calf
das Laib, loaf
das Laub, leaf, foliage
ob, if

schnauben, sniff, snuff, pant, breathe heavily
selbst, self
der Stab, staff
taub, deaf
das Weib, wife, woman

2. German b, English p

die Börse, purse, exchange
der Pöbel, people, mob

die Rübe, rape (seed), beet

3. German b, English v

der Abend, eve, evening
der Biber, beaver
eben, even

das Fieber, fever
geben, give
das Grab, grave

haben, have
heben, heave, lift
der Herbst, (harvest) autumn
die Kerbe, (carve) notch
der Knabe, *originally* knave, *now* boy
leben, live
die Leber, liver
lieben, love
der Nabel, navel
der Rabe, raven
die Salbe, salve, ointment
schaben, shave

schieben, shove
das Sieb, sieve
das Silber, silver
der Skorbut, scurvy
der Stab, stave
sterben, starve, die
streben, strive
die Stube, stove room, room
die Taube, dove
übel, evil
über, over
weben, weave

4. German b lost
der Wirbel, whirl

5. German ch, English ch
bleichen, bleach

6. German ch, English f
der Schacht, shaft   die Schicht, (shift) layer, stratum

7. German ch, English g
feucht, foggy, damp

8. German ch, English gh
doch, though   hoch, high
durch, through   der Nachbar, neighbor

9. German cht, English ct
die Pacht, compact

10. German cht, English ght
This does not apply to words in which t is an inflection: er mach=t.

acht, eight   fechten, fight
dicht, tight, dense   die Fracht, freight

die Furcht, fright, fear

der Knecht, *originally* knight, servant of a king, *now* servant

leicht, light (weight)

leuchten, light, shine

das Licht, light

die Macht, might

die Nacht, night

nicht, naught, not

recht, right

die Schlacht, slaughter, battle

schlecht, slight, poor, bad

schlicht, slight, plain

die Sicht, sight

die Tochter, daughter

wichtig, weighty, important

11. German ch, English k

der Becher, beaker, cup

brechen, break

das Buch, book

der Deich, dike

der Lauch, leek, garlic

das Loch, leak, hole

machen, make

die Milch, milk

der Mönch, monk

pochen, poke

die Rache, wreak, revenge

der Rechen, rake

rechnen, reckon, figure

schleichen, (sleek) sneak

schmauchen, smoke

die Sichel, sickle

siech, sick

die Speiche, spoke

stechen, stick, prick

der Storch, stork

streichen, strike

der Strich, stroke

suchen, seek (sought)

der Teich, (dike) pond

das Tuch, (duck trousers) cloth

wach, awake

weich, weak, soft

die Woche, week

12. German ch lost

die Frucht, fruit

13. German ck, English dg

die Brücke, bridge

die Ecke, edge, corner

der Weck, (wedge) roll

die Hecke, hedge

der Rücken, ridge

14. German ck, English g

die Schlacke, slag

schmücken, smug. ador

15. German **ck**, English *tch*

jucken, itch
die Krücke, crutch
strecken, stretch
zwicken, twitch, pinch

16. German **d**, English *t*

der Boden, bottom
die Gardine, curtain
der Hader, hate
die Seide, (satin) silk

17. German **d**, English *th*

das Bad, bath
die Bude, booth
der Dank, thanks
dann, then
das, that
der Daumen, thumb
dein, thine
denken, think
das Ding, thing
dick, thick
der Dieb, thief
dies, this
die Distel, thistle
doch, though
der Donner, thunder
der Dorn, thorn
dort, there
der Draht, thread, wire
der Drang, throng, pressure
drei, three
dreschen, thrash
drohen, threaten
die Drossel, thrush
dünn, thin
durch, through
der Durst, thirst
die Erde, earth
der Faden, fathom
die Feder, feather
fördern, further
die Heide, heath
der Herd, hearth
jeder, either, each
das Kleid, cloth
der Laden, lath
das Leder, leather
leid, loath
nieder, be-neath
der Pfad, path
schaden, scathe, hurt
die Scheide, sheath
der Schmied, smith
sieden, seethe
der Süd, south
wider, (with-stand) against
würdig, worthy

18. German Final **d** where it never occurred in English

fremd, from, foreign
das Kind, kin, relation, child
der Mond, moon
das Pfand, pawn
die Sünde, sin

19. German f, English *b*

prüfen, probe, test

die Tafel, table, tablet

20. German f, English *p*

der Affe, ape, monkey

der Bischof, bishop

das Fell, pelt, skin

greifen, grip

der Hanf, hemp

die Harfe, harp

der Haufen, heap

helfen, help

hoffen, hope

die Hüfte, hip

laufen, leap, run

offen, open

raufen, rip

reif, ripe

der Saft, sap, juice

saufen, sup

das Schaf, sheep

schaffen, shape

scharf, sharp

das Schiff, ship

schlafen, sleep

schleifen, slip over a stone, grind

die Seife, soap

die Staffel, staple

Stief=, step-

streifen, stripe

taufen, dip, christen

tief, deep

triefen, drip

die Waffe, weapon

21. German f, English *v*

die Fahne, vane, flag

der Firnis, varnish

der Hafen, haven, port

liefern, deliver

der Ofen, oven

die Schaufel, shovel

der Teufel, devil

22. German g, English *dg*

hegen, hedge in

23. German g, English *gh*

der Teig, dough

der Trog, trough

wiegen, weigh

24. German g, English *j*

der Gaukler, juggler

der Gimpel, (jump, jumper) simpleton

25. German g, English *y*

gähnen, yawn

das Garn, yarn

gelb, yellow
gellen, yell
gelten, yield, produce

gern, (yearn) gladly
gestern, yesterday

26. German Initial g or ge dropped

gegen, again-st
genug, enough
das Geschwader, squadron
das Gestade, steady land, shore
gesund, sound, healthy

glauben, be-lieve
gleich, like
das Glied, (lith) limb
das Glück, luck

27. German g following Various Vowels

das Auge, eye
der Bogen, bow
eigen, own
fliegen, fly
der Hagel, hail
das Lager, layer
die Lauge, lye
legen, lay, put down
leugnen, lie, deny
liegen, lie (position)
lügen, lie (untruth)
mag, may
der Nagel, nail
nagen, gnaw

die Regel, rule
der Regen, rain
der Riegel, rail, bolt
der Roggen, rye
die Säge, saw
sagen, say
schlagen, slay, strike
das Segel, sail
segnen, sign with the cross, bless
das Siegel, seal
der Tag, day
der Vogel, fowl, bird
der Weg, way
der Ziegel, tile

28. German j, English y

ja, yes
das Jahr, year

jener, yonder, that
das Joch, yoke

29. German k, English c

der Keller, cellar
der Koffer, coffer, trunk
kommen, come

der Krug, crock, jar
die Kuppel, cupola

30. German k, English *ch*

die Bank, bench
die Birke, birch
der Fink, finch
hinken, (hunch) limp
der Kalk, chalk, lime
der Kamin, chimney
die Kammer, chamber
der Kämpe, champion
die Kanzel, chancel
die Kapelle, chapel
das Kapitel, chapter

der Kaplan, chaplain
die Karte, chart
der Käse, cheese
die Kastanie, chestnut
kasteien, chastise
kauen, chew
kichern, chuckle
das Kinn, chin
die Kirche, church
die Kiste, chest, box
die Stärke, starch

31. German l, English *n*
die Orgel, organ

32. German l, English *r*
der Säbel, saber

33. German lg, English *ll*
folgen, follow   der Talg, tallow

34. German Internal l missing in the English Word
die Schalmei, shawm   welch, which
solch, such

35. German mm, English *mb*

dumm, dumb
die Kammer, chamber
der Kummer, encumbrance
die Nummer, number
der Schlummer, slumber

der Trümmer, (thrum) ruin
tummeln, tumble about
der Zimmermann, timberman, carpenter

36. German mm, English *mp*

die Klammer, clamp, clasp
klemmen, clamp
krumm, crumpled, crooked

der Stummel, stump
wimmern, whimper

37. German n missing in English

fern, far
fünf, five
die Gans, goose
der Mund, mouth
sanft, soft

der Sporn, spur
der Stern, star
uns, us
der Wunsch, wish

38. German nn, English *nd*

der Donner, thunder

39. German p, English *b*

die Krippe, crib
das Polster, bolster

die Posaune, bassoon
die Stoppel, stubble

40. German p, English *f*

die Klippe, cliff
platt, flat

die Schärpe, scarf

41. German pf, English *b*

der Knopf, knob, button

der Topf, tub, pot

42. German pf, English *f*

das Opfer, offer, sacrifice
der Schnupfen, (snuff) catarrh

stopfen, stuff

43. German pf, English *p*

der Apfel, apple
der Dampf, (damp) vapor
der Hopfen, hop
hüpfen, hop
impfen, imp, vaccinate
der Karpfen, carp
der Krampf, cramp
das Kupfer, copper
der Pfad, path
der Pfahl, pole
das Pfand, pawn, pledge

die Pfanne, pan
der Pfau, peacock
der Pfeffer, pepper
der Pfeiler, pillar
die Pflanze, plant
das Pflaster, plaster
die Pflaume, plum
die Pflicht, plight, duty
der Pflock, plug
pflücken, pluck
der Pflug, plough

der Pfosten, post
die Pfote, paw
der Pfuhl, pool
der, das Pfühl, pillow
rupfen, rip
schlüpfen, slip
die Schnepfe, snipe

schöpfen, scoop
der Stumpf, stump
der Sumpf, swamp
der Tropfen, drop
der Trumpf, trump
tupfen, tip

44. German r transposed

die Borste, bristle
die Borte, braid
brennen, burn
das Brett, board

heiser, hoarse

das Roß, horse
die Scherbe, scrap

45. German rch, rg, rf, English *rr*

borgen, borrow
die Furche, furrow
das Mark, marrow

morgen, tomorrow
sorgen, (sorrow), care

46. German f, English *r*
der Hase, hare

47. German f, English *sh*

die Drossel, thrush

das Kissen, cushion

48. German f, English *t*

aus, out
beißen, bite
besser, better
daß, that
essen, eat
das Faß, vat, barrel
fassen, (fetter), grasp
die Fessel, fetter
fließen, float, flow
der Fuß, foot
die Geiß, goat
groß, great

grüßen, greet
der Haß, hatred
heiß, hot
der Kessel, kettle, boiler
der Kloß, (cleat) clod
lassen, let
das Los, lot, destiny
der Mörser, mortar
die Nessel, nettle
die Nuß, nut
die Schloße, sleet
schmeißen, smite

die Schüssel, scuttle
der Schweiß, sweat
der Spieß, spit, spear
spleißen, split
sprießen, sprout

die Straße, street
süß, sweet
das Wasser, water
weiß, white

49. German ſ, English z

blasen, blaze

50. German ſch, English ch

das Schach, chess

die Schanze, chance, risk

51. German ſch, English j

der Schakal, jackal

52. German ſch, English s

die Schlacht, slaughter, battle
die Schlacke, slag
der Schlaf, sleep
die Schlange, (slink) snake
schlau, sly
die Schlehe, sloe
schleichen, (sleek) slink, sneak
schleifen, slip over a stone, grind
der Schleim, slime
schleißen, slit
schleppen, (slip) drag
die Schleuse, sluice
schlicht, slight, plain
schlingen, sling
der Schlitten, sleigh
schlitzen, slit
die Schloße, sleet
der Schlummer, slumber
schlüpfen, slip
schmal, small, narrow

schmauchen, smoke
schmecken, smack, taste
schmeicheln, smicker, flatter
schmeißen, smite
schmelzen, smelt
der Schmerz, smart, pain
schmieren, smear
schmuggeln, smuggle
der Schmutz, (smutty) dirt
schnappen, snap
schnarchen, snore
schnaufen, sniff
die Schnauze, snout
der Schnee, snow
die Schnepfe, snipe
schnüffeln, sniff
der Schnupfen, (snuff) catarrh
die Schnur, snare, string
der Schwaden, swath
die Schwadron, squadron

die Schwalbe, swallow

der Schwan, swan

der Schwarm, swarm

die Schwarte, sward

schwarz, swarthy, black

das Schwein, swine, hog

schwellen, swell

das Schwert, sword

schwimmen, swim

schwindeln, swindle

schwingen, swing

schwitzen, sweat

schwören, swear

53. German sch, English sc

schaden, scathe

der Scharbock, scurvy

der Scharlach, scarlet

die Schärpe, scarf

der Schaum, scum

schelten, scold

die Scherbe, scrap

der Schorf, scurf

schrapen, scrape

die Schraube, screw

schreiben, (scribe) write

schrubben, scrub

54. German sch, English sk

das Scharmützel, skirmish

schinden, skin

der Schirm, (skirmish) screen, umbrella

55. German schw, English s

die Schwester, sister

56. German t, English d

alt, old

der Bart, beard

das Beet, flower bed

das Bett, bed

bieten, bid, offer

das Blatt, blade, sheet, leaf

das Blut, blood

breit, broad

das Brot, bread

die Brut, brood

der Draht, thread, wire

eitel, idle, vain

die Falte, fold

die Furt, ford

das Futter, fodder, food

der Garten, garden

gelten, yield

gleiten, glide

der Gott, God

der Gürtel, girdle

gut, good

halten, hold

hart, hard

das Haupt, head

die Haut, hide, skin

hinten, be-hind

der Hirt, herdsman
kalt, cold
die Karte, card
laut, loud
leiten, lead
die Mitte, middle
der Mut, mood, disposition
die Not, need
die Otter, adder
das Rätsel, riddle
reiten, ride
rot, red
die Rute, rod
die Saat, seed
der Sattel, saddle

der Schatten, shade, shadow
die Schulter, shoulder
schütten, shed
das Schwert, sword
die Seite, side
selten, seldom
der Spaten, spade
sputen, speed
stätig, steady
die Stute, (steed) mare
das Tal, dale, valley
der Tanz, dance

tauchen, duck, dive
der Teich, (dike) pond
der Teig, dough
der Teil, deal, part
teuer, dear
tief, deep
das Tier, (deer) beast
der Tisch, desk, table
der Tod, death
toll, dull, mad
das Tor, door, gate
tragen, (draw) carry
die Traufe, drip, eaves
der Traum, dream
traurig, dreary, sad
treiben, drive
treten, tread, step
das Tuch, duck, cloth
tun, do
die Tür, door
unter, under
das Urteil, ordeal, judgment
walten, wield, rule
waten, wade
weit, wide
die Welt, world
das Wort, word

57. German t, English *th*

die Latte, lath
die Motte, moth
die Mutter, mother

der Vater, father
wert, worth
das Wetter, weather

58. German Final t missing in English

dort, there

59. German tz, English t

die Grütze, grit	setzen, set
die Hitze, heat	sitzen, sit
das Netz, net	strotzen, strut
der Schlitz, slit	wetzen, whet
schwitzen, sweat	der Witz, wit

60. German tz, English tch

ätzen, etch

61. German w, English gu

warten, (ward) guard, watch, wait for

62. English w missing in German

der Sumpf, swamp	süß, sweet

63. German z, English c

der Tanz, dance	der Zins, (census) interest

64. German z, English ch

zirpen, chirp

65. German z, English d

spreizen, spread

66. German z, English sch

der Zettel, schedule, sheet of paper

67. German z, English t

beizen, bite, corrode	kurz, curt, short
der Bolzen, bolt	der Lenz, Lent
der Filz, felt	das Malz, malt
grunzen, grunt	die Münze, mint, money, coin
heizen, heat	der Pelz, pelt, fur
das Herz, heart	die Pflanze, plant

das Salz, salt
schmelzen, smelt
der Schmerz, smart, pain
die Schnauze, snout
der Schurz, (shirt) apron
die Stelze, stilt
stürzen, start, rush
die Warze, wart
der Weizen, wheat
Zacken, tack
der Zagel, tail
zähe, tough
zählen, tell, count
zahm, tame
die Zähre, tear
zapfen, tap
der Zaum, team, bridle
die Zehe, toe
zehn, ten
zehren, tear up, consume
das Zeichen, token

zeigen, (be-token) show
zerren, tear, pull
der Ziegel, tile
ziehen, (tug) pull
der Zimmermann, timberman, carpenter
das Zinn, tin
der Zipfel, tip
der Zoll, toll
der Zopf, tuft (of hair)
zu, to, too
der Zuber, tub
der Zug, tug, pull, train
der Zunder, tinder
die Zunge, tongue
zwei, two
der Zweig, twig
der Zwilling, (twin-ling) twin
der Zwirn, (two-yarn) thread
zwitschern, twitter
zwölf, twelve

68. German z, English *th*

schwarz, swarthy, black

B. VOWELS

69. German aa, English *a*

der Saal, (saloon) hall

70. German aa, English *ai*

das Haar, hair   das Paar, pair

71. German aa, English *ee*

der Aal, eel   die Saat, seed
die Nadel, needle

72. German a, English e

dann, then
der Gast, guest
der Hanf, hemp
die Kastanie, chestnut
der Knall, knell, sound
lassen, let
der Nacken, neck

die Rast, rest
der Samen, (semen) seed
die Schale, shell
der Stamm, stem
wann, when
das Wrack, wreck

73. German a, English ea

der Bart, beard
der Draht, thread, wire
der Fasan, pheasant
das Jahr, year
klar, clear
mager, meager
das Mahl, meal

die Masern, measles
die Rache, w-reak, revenge
die Stadt, (stead) town
die Waffe, weapon
das Wappen, weapon, coat of arms

74. German a, English ee

das Schaf, sheep
schlafen, sleep
die Sprache, speech

der Stahl, steel
die Straße, street

75. German a, English ei

acht, eight
die Fracht, freight (fraught)

der Nachbar, neighbor

76. German a, English i

flackern, flicker
der Gram, (grim) anger
die Macht, might

die Nacht, night
der Schnabel, (nibble) beak

77. German a, English ie

die Bahre, bier

78. German a, English o

alt, old
falten, fold

halten, hold
der Kaffee, coffee

der Kakao, cocoa
kalt, cold
der Kamm, comb
knacken, knock, break
lang, long
die Nase, nose
der Pabst, Papst, pope

die Pappel, poplar
der Pfahl, pole
die Rakete, skyrocket
sanft, soft
schnarchen, snore
der Tabak, tobacco
der Wald, wold, woods

79. German a, English *oo*

die Gans, goose

der Haken, hook

80. German a, English *u*

flattern, flutter

81. German a, English *au*

schlachten, slaughter, kill

82. German ä, English *a*

der Lärm, alarm, noise
lässig, lazy
der März, March
plätschern, plash

der Säbel, saber
schäbig, shabby
schwärmen, swarm

83. German ä, English *aw*

gähnen, yawn

die Säge, saw

84. German ä, English *e*

ätzen, etch
nächst, next

die Sphäre, sphere

85. German ä, English *ea*

die Ähre, ear
stätig, steady

währen, wear, last
die Zähre, tear

86. German ä, English *ee*

der Käse, cheese

87. German ä, English *ei*
   wägen, weigh

88. German ä, English *i*
   das Rätsel, riddle

89. German ä, English *ou*
   zähe, tough

90. German ä, English *ow*

blähen, blow   mähen, mow
krähen, crow   säen, sow

91. German ä, English *y*
   spähen, spy

92. German ai, English *ay*
   der Mai, May

93. German ai, English *oa*
   das Laib, loaf

94. German au, English *aw*
   die Klaue, claw

95. German au, English *ea*

der Baum, beam, tree   der Saum, seam, edge
der Haufen, heap   taub, deaf
das Haupt, head   traurig, dreary, sad
laufen, leap, run   der Zaum, team, bridle

96. German au, English *ee*

der Flaus, fleece   der Lauch, leek

97. German au, English *ew*

hauen, hew, cut   schrauben, screw
kauen, chew   der Tau, dew

98. German au, English *i*

die Braut, bride elect   saufen, sip, drink
die Faust, fist   der Strauß, ostrich
die Haut, hide   taufen, (dip) christen
lauschen, listen   die Traufe, (drip) eaves

99. German au, English *ie*

glauben, believe

100. German au, English *o*

rauben, rob   schmauchen, smoke
die Schaufel, shovel   die Taube, dove

101. German au, English *oo*

der Raum, room

102. German au, English *ou*

aus, out   sauer, sour
das Haus, house   die Schnauze, snout
laut, loud   staunen, astound
die Maus, mouse   tausend, thousand

103. German au, English *ow*

braun, brown   der Schauer, shower
die Daune, down   stauen, stow
die Sau, sow   das Tau, tow, rope

104. German au, English *oy*

die Auster, oyster   jauchzen, (joy) exult

105. German au, English u

auf, up

dauern, endure, last

der Daumen, thumb

der Gaukler, juggler

der Gaumen, gum

die Laute, lute

die Mauer, (*Latin* murus) wall

der Schauder, shudder

der Schaum, scum

tauchen, duck, dive

106. German au, English ue

blau, blue

grausam, gruesome, cruel

107. German au, English y

die Lauge, lye

schlau, sly

108. German e, English a

dreschen, thrash

die Esche, ash

der Esel, ass

die Espe, aspen

fern, far

fest, fast, solid

fett, fat

die Herberge, harbor, shelter

der Herbst, (harvest) autumn

der Herd, hearth

das Herz, heart

die Hexe, hag, old woman, witch

die Kerbe, (carve) notch

der Krebs, crab

die Lerche, lark

letzt, last

der Mensch, man, person

merken, mark, notice

die Messe, mass

necken, nag, tease

der Rechen, rake

recken, rack, stretch

der Schenkel, (shank) thigh

schmecken, smack, taste

der Schmerz, smart, pain

sperren, spar, obstruct

der Stempel, stamp

sterben, (starve) die

der Stern, star

die Werft, wharf

die Wespe, wasp

109. German e, English ai

fehlen, fail

der Flegel, flail

preisen, praise

110. German e, English ea

der Becher, beaker, cup

brechen, break

die Erde, earth

ernst, earnest

die Ernte, (earn) crop
essen, eat
die Feder, feather
das Fest, feast
gern, (yearn) gladly
heben, heave, lift,
das Leck, leak
das Leder, leather
lehnen, lean
lernen, learn

das Mehl, meal, flour
die Perle, pearl
scheren, shear
stets, steadily, always
treten, tread, step
weben, weave
das Wetter, weather
zehren, tear up, consume
zerren, tear, pull

111. German e, English *eu*

die Fehde, (foe) feud

112. German e, English *i*

denken, think
eklig, (irk-some) disgusting
der Epheu, ivy
es, it
fechten, fight
geben, give
keck, quick, lively
leben, live
die Leber, liver
lecken, lick
melken, milk
das Pech, pitch
recht, right

die Schnepfe, snipe
schwenken, swing
die Schwester, sister
sechs, six
segnen, sign with the cross, bless
die Sehne. sinew

die Spezerei, spices
stechen, stick, stab
die Stelze, stilt
streben, strive
welch, which

113. German e, English *ie*

das Feld, field

114. German e, English *o*

jener, yonder, that
das Schwert, sword
wehe, woe

die Welt, world
das Werk, work
wert, worth

115. German e, English *oa*

das Brett, board
das Lehen, loan

der Lehm, loam, clay

116. German e, English *oe*

das Reh, roe
die Schlehe, sloe

die Zehe, toe

117. German e, English *u*

bersten, burst

rennen, run

118. German ee, English *a*

der Teer, tar

119. German ee, English *ay*

die Fee, fay, fairy

120. German ee, English *ea*

der, das Schmeer, smear
die See, sea

der Speer, spear
der Tee, tea

121. German ee, English *o*

der Klee, clover

der Schnee, snow

122. German ee, English *ou*

die Seele, soul

123. German ei, English *a*

der Meister, master
heischen, ask

die Seide, (satin) silk

124. German ei, English *ai*

das Heil, (hail) good luck

die Pein, pain

125. German ei, English *e*

das Fleisch, flesh

scheiden, shed, part

126. German ei, English *ea*

bleichen, bleach
die Heide, heath
heilen, heal
heizen, heat
leiten, lead
meinen, mean
reichen, reach

die Scheide, sheath
der Schweiß, sweat
spreizen, spread
der Teil, deal, part
weich, weak, soft
der Weizen, wheat

127. German ei, English *ee*

drei, three
frei, free

das Tier, (deer) beast

128. German ei, English *i*

beißen, bite
der Deich, dike
dein, thine, thy
eitel, idle, vain
die Feile, file
fein, fine
gleich, like
greifen, gripe
kneifen, nip
leicht, light
das Leinen, linen
die Meile, mile
mein, mine, my
pfeifen, fife, whistle
der Pfeiler, pillar
der Preis, price
reich, rich
reif, ripe
rein, (rinse) clean
der Reis, rice

reiten, ride
scheinen, shine
der Schleim, slime
schmeicheln, smicker, flatter
schmeißen, smite
die Seite, side
spleißen, split
steif, stiff
der Streit, strife
der Teich, dike, pond
treiben, drive
das Veilchen, violet
das Weib, wife, woman
die Weile, while
der Wein, wine
weise, wise
die Weise, wise, manner
weiß, white
weit, wide
der Zweig, twig

129. German ei, English *ie*

der Feind, fiend, enemy

130. German ei, English o

beide, both
das Bein, bone, leg
eigen, own
ein, one
der Geist, ghost
das Heim, home

heiß, hot
das Kleid, cloth
die Reihe, row
die Speiche, spoke
der Stein, stone
zwei, two

131. German ei, English oa

breit, broad
die Eiche, oak
der Eid, oath

die Geiß, goat
heiser, hoarse

132. German ei, English u

reiben, (rive), rub

133. German ei, English y

bei, by

die Leier, lyre

134. German eu, English ay

das Heu, hay.

135. German eu, English e

der Teufel, devil

136. German eu, English ea

teuer, dear

137. German eu, English ee

steuern, steer

138. German eu, English ew

streuen, strew

139. German eu, English *i*

das Feuer, fire

leuchten, light

leugnen, lie, deny

die Seuche, sickness

140. German eu, English *ie*

der Freund, friend

141. German eu, English *oi*

die Beule, (bile), boil

142. German eu, English *oo*

die Beute, booty

143. German eu, English *ou*

scheuern, scour

144. German eu, English *ow*

heulen, howl

145. German eu, English *u*

die Meuterei, mutiny

146. German eu, English *ue*

die Reue, rue, regret

treu, true, loyal

147. German eu, English *ui*

die Schleuse, sluice

148. German eu, English *y*

scheu, shy

149. German i, English *a*

der Hirsch, hart, stag

der Schinken, (shank) ham

der Wirt, warden

150. German i, English *ay*

ich, (aye, *16th century*) yes

151. German i, English *e*

frisch, fresh

der Hirt, herdsman

irren, err

die Kiste, chest, box

der Pinsel, (pencil) brush

sicher, secure, safe

die Skizze, sketch

der Tisch, desk, table

152. German i, English *ea*

die Birne, pear

glimmen, gleam

die Hitze, heat

schwitzen, sweat

der Sitz, seat

153. German i, English *ei*

wichtig, weighty, important

154. German i, English *ie*

der Schild, shield

155. German i, English *o*

der Strich, stroke

wirken, work

156. German i, English *ou*

nicht, nought, not

157. German i, English *u*

hinken, (hunch) limp

die Kirche, church

das Kissen, cushion

rinnen, run, flow

158. German i, English *y*

der Spion, spy

159. German ie, English *e*

hier, here

Stief=, step-

160. German ie, English *ea*

nieder, be-neath

quieken, squeak

ſchmieren, smear

das Wieſel, weasel

161. German ie, English *ee*

die Biene, bee

das Bier, beer

fliehen, flee

frieren, freeze

der Grieche, Greek

der Kiel, keel

das Knie, knee

nieſen, sneeze

ſchier, sheer

ſieden, seethe

der Stier, steer

tief, deep

das Vieh, (fee) cattle (in trading)

das Blieſz, fleece

162. German ie, English *ei*

wiegen, weigh

163. German ie, English *i*

bieten, bid, offer

dies, this

das Glied, (lith) limb

liefern, deliver

ſchieben, shift

das Schienbein, shinbone

der Schmied, smith

ſiech, sick

der Spieſz, spit, spear

triefen, drip

der Ziegel, tile

164. German ie, English *o*

lieben, love

165. German ie, English *oa*

flieſzen, float, flow

der Kittel, coat, frock

166. German ie, English *ou*

ſprieſzen, sprout

vier, four

167. German ie, English *y*

fliegen, fly

168. German o, English a

die Brombeere, bramble
die Flocke, flake
die Otter, adder

die Posaune, bassoon
die Torte, tart
der Zobel, sable

169. German o, English ai

die Borte, braid

170. German o, English au

holen, haul, remove, get
der Kohl, cauliflower, cabbage

die Tochter, daughter

171. German o, English aw

die Pfote, paw
roh, raw

das Stroh, straw

172. German o, English e

dort, there
rot, red

das Schrot, shred
wohl, well

173. German o, English ea

die Bohne, bean
das Brot, bread
drohen, threaten
groß, great
das Ohr, ear

der Osten, east
die Ostern, Easter
der Strom, stream, river
der Tod, death

174. German o, English ee

die Flotte, fleet
die Not, need

die Schloße, sleet
die Woche, week

175. German o, English i

die Borste, bristle
hoch, high

ob, if
der Stock, stick

176. German o, English oa

die Kohle, coal

177. German o, English *oi*
das Kloster, cloister

178. German o, English *oo*

der Koch, cook

los, loose

der Mohr, Moor

das Tor, door, gate

die Wolle, wool

179. German o, English *ou*

doch, though

doppelt, double

die Koppel, coupler

die Sonde, sound

180. German o, English *ow*

der Groll, growl, grudge

die Krone, crown

181. German o, English *u*

der Donner, thunder

die Drossel, thrush

der Golf, gulf

der Moder, mud

der Mord, murder

die Nonne, nun

der Onkel, uncle

der Orkan, hurricane

der Pflock, plug

der Rost, rust

solch, such

der Sommer, summer

sonder, asunder, separate

die Sonne, sun

der Sporn, spur

stocken, be stuck

stopfen, stuff

die Stoppel, stubble

stottern, stutter

strotzen, strut

toll, dull, mad

die Tonne, tun

der Topf, tub

die Trommel, drum

der Trost, trust (in God), comfort

voll, full

der Zober (Zuber), tub

182. German o, English *y*
trocken, dry

183. German oo, English *o*
das Moos, moss

184. German oo, English *oa*
das Boot, boat

185. German ö, English *a*
schöpfen, shape

186. German ö, English *e*
die Hölle, hell   zwölf, twelve

187. German ö, English *ea*
hören, hear   schwören, swear

188. German ö, English *eo*
der Pöbel, (people) mob

189. German ö, English *i*
die Föhre, fir   schön, (sheen, shining) fair
der König, king   stören, stir, disturb
der Pökel, pickle

190. German ö, English *o*
der Mörser, mortar

191. German ö, English *oa*
rösten, roast

192. German ö, English *oi*
das Öl, oil

193. German ö, English *u*
die Börse, purse, exchange   der Knöchel, knuckle
fördern, further

194. German u, English *a*
der Hut, hat   der Sturz, (start) rush, fall
der Kuchen, cake   der Sumpf, swamp

195. German u, English *e*
der Jude, Jew   die Kluft, (cleft) chasm
das Juwel, jewel   die Ulme, elm

196. German u, English *ea*
die Brust, breast

197. German u, English *ee*

die Buche, beech
sputen, speed

die Stute, (steed) mare
suchen, seek

198. German u, English *i*

der Durst, thirst
der Dusel, dizziness
die Furcht, fright, fear
der Kuß, kiss

die Runzel, wrinkle
der Schurz, (shirt) apron
der Wunsch, wish
der Zunder, tinder

199. German u, English *o*

der Busen, bosom
das Dutzend, dozen
der Fuchs, fox
die Furt, ford
das Futter, fodder, food
der Jux, joke
der Krug, (crockery) jar
das Kupfer, copper
kurz, short

die Kutte, (coat) frock
die Mutter, mother
die Rute, rod
der Sturm, storm
tun, do
das Urteil, ordeal, judgment
das Wunder, wonder, miracle
der Wurm, worm
zu, to

200. German u, English *oa*

der Aufruhr, uproar

die Kutsche, coach

201. German u, English *oe*

der Schuh, shoe

202. German u, English *oo*

die Blume, (bloom) flower
das Blut, blood
das Buch, book
die Bude, booth
der Flur, floor

der Fuß, foot
gut, good
der Huf, hoof
der Mut, mood, disposition
die Nudel, noodle

der Pfuhl, pool
der Pudel, poodle
die Schule, school
der Spuk, spook

die Spule, spool
der Stuhl, stool, chair
zu, too

203. German u, English *ou*

du, thou
durch, through
der Flunder, flounder
gesund, sound, healthy
der Grund, ground
die Gruppe, group
der Hund, hound, dog
jung, young
die Mulde, mould
der Mund, mouth
der Pflug, plough

das Pfund, pound
rund, round
die Schulter, shoulder
der Sund, sound
die Suppe, soup
die Truppe, troupe
das Turnier, tournament
die Uhr, (hour) clock, watch
die Unze, ounce
die Wunde, wound

204. German u, English *ow*

die Kuh, cow
nun, now

das Puder, powder
der Turm, tower

205. German u, English *ui*
die Frucht, fruit

206. German u, English *y*
der Luchs, lynx

207. German ü, English *aw*
brüllen, brawl, roar

208. German ü, English *e*
schütten, shed   übel, evil

209. German ü, English *ee*
fühlen, feel   grün, green

grüßen, greet

hüten, heed

kühn, keen, fierce, bold

süß, sweet

210. German ü, English *i*

die Brücke, bridge

füllen, fill

das Füllen, filly

fünf, five

der Fürst, (first) ruler

die Grütze, grit

der Gürtel, girdle

die Hüfte, hip

der Krüppel, cripple

die Küche, kitchen

lügen, lie (untruth)

die Münze, mint, coin

der Pfühl, pillow

der Rücken, ridge

schlüpfen, slip

schnüffeln, sniff

die Sünde, sin

211. German ü, English *o*

blühen, blow

die Büchse, box

für, for

glühen, glow

hüpfen, hop

prüfen, probe, test

über, over

würdig, worthy

212. German ü, English *oa*

die Küste, coast

213. German ü, English *oo*

der Kübel, coop

kühl, cool

die Tür, door

214. German ü, English *ou*

der Süden, south

215. German ü, English *u*

die Hütte, hut

die Krücke, crutch

der Küster, custodian, sexton

pflücken, pluck

plündern, plunder

der Plüsch, plush

die Schüssel, scuttle, bowl

der Tüll, tulle

216. A Small List of Words Subject to more than one Change

beide, both

daß, that

der Dieb, thief

doch, though

dort, there

der Draht, thread, wire

durch, through

der Eid, oath

eigen, own

das Faß, vat, barrel

die Geiß, goat

heiser, hoarse

heiß, hot

die Kammer, chamber

das Kleid, cloth

der Pfad, path

das Pfand, pawn

die Pflanze, plant

die Scheide, sheath

die Seife, soap

die Speiche, spoke

der Tanz, dance

taub, deaf

die Taube, dove

taufen, (dip) christen

tief, deep

der Tod, death

triefen, drip

der Zagel, tail

der Zapfen, tap

der Ziegel, tile

das Zimmer, (timber) room

III. DERIVATIVES

1. Adjectives Based on Adjectives

(a) In ig

fettig, greasy

gütig, good, kind

niedrig, low

völlig, entire, whole

(b) In lich

ältlich, elderly

ärmlich, poorly

bläulich, bluish

bräunlich, brownish

eigentlich, proper

gelblich, yellowish

grünlich, greenish

kleinlich, petty, mean

länglich, oblong

löslich, soluble

öffentlich, public

rechtlich, lawful

reichlich, plentiful

reislich, mature

reinlich, clean

rötlich, reddish

rundlich, roundish

säuerlich, sourish, acidulous

schwächlich, infirm, feeble

schwärzlich, blackish

sonderlich, special, particular

süßlich, sweetish

weichlich, weak, effeminate

2. Nouns Based on the above Adjectives. (All Feminine)

Ärmlichkeit, poorness
Fettigkeit, greasiness
Kleinlichkeit, meanness
Löslichkeit, solubility
Öffentlichkeit, publicity

Rechtlichkeit, rectitude, honesty
Reinlichkeit, cleanliness
Schwächlichkeit, infirmity
Weichlichkeit, effeminacy

3. Adverbs

(a) In ens

bestens, in the best manner
eigens, expressly, especially

(b) In lich

ernstlich, seriously
fälschlich, falsely
höchlichst, in the highest degree
kürzlich, lately

neulich, (newly) lately
schwerlich, hardly
sicherlich, surely
treulich, trustily, faithfully
wahrlich, truly
wohlweislich, very wisely

(c) In sam (some)

gleichsam, as it were, as if

4. Nouns Based on Adjectives

(a) In e. (All Feminine)

Bleiche, pallor
Bräune, brown color
Breite, breadth
Dicke, thickness
Dürre, dryness
Ebene, plain
Ferne, distance
Fremde, foreign country
Frische, freshness
Größe, greatness
Güte, goodness, kindness
Härte, hardness
Höhe, height
Kälte, cold, coldness
Kühle, coolness
Kürze, shortness
Länge, length

Liebe, love
Milde, mildness
Nähe, nearness
Platte, plate
Reife, ripeness, maturity
Säure, sourness, acid
Schärfe, sharpness
Schwäche, weakness
Schwere, heaviness
Stärke, strength
Stille, stillness
Strenge, sternness, severity
Tiefe, depth
Treue, loyalty
Wache, watch
Wärme, warmth
Weiße, whiteness
Weite, width

Wunde, wound
Wüſte, desert

(b) In heit (hood). (All Feminine)

Blindheit, blindness
Blondheit, fair-hairedness
Bravheit, bravery, goodness
Dichtheit, density
Dummheit, stupidity
Dunkelheit, darkness
Eigenheit, property
Falſchheit, falsehood
Faulheit, idleness
Feinheit, fineness, delicacy
Frechheit, (fresh) impertinence
Freiheit, freedom
Geradheit, uprightness
Geſundheit, health
Gleichheit, likeness, equality
Grobheit, roughness, rudeness
Halbheit, half-measure
Hoheit, highness
Kahlheit, baldness
Keckheit, quickness, liveliness
Klarheit, clearness
Kühnheit, boldness
Lauheit, lukewarmness
Mehrheit, majority
Minderheit, minority
Nacktheit, nakedness
Neuheit, novelty
Plumpheit, clumsiness
Reinheit, cleanliness
Sanftheit, softness
Schlappheit, slackness
Schlauheit, slyness, craftiness
Schönheit, beauty

Schroffheit, gruffness
Schwachheit, weakness
Seltenheit, rarity
Sicherheit, security, safety
Sonderheit, peculiarity
Steifheit, stiffness
Taubheit, deafness
Trockenheit, dryness, drought
Wahrheit, truth
Weichheit, weakness, softness
Weisheit, wisdom
Wildheit, wildness
Zahmheit, tameness

(c) In igkeit. (All Feminine)

Dichtigkeit, density
Feuchtigkeit, moisture
Kleinigkeit, trifle
Leichtigkeit, facility
Nettigkeit, neatness
Neuigkeit, news
Süßigkeit, sweetness
Zähigkeit, toughness, tenacity

(d) In keit. (All Feminine)

Drolligkeit, drollery
Eitelkeit, idleness, vanity
Grauſamkeit, gruesomeness, cruelty
Heiſerkeit, hoarseness
Läſſigkeit, laziness
Magerkeit, meagerness
Schäbigkeit, shabbiness
Stätigkeit, steadiness
Übelkeit, (evil) nausea
Traurigkeit, dreariness, sadness
Wichtigkeit, weightiness, importance

(e) In ität. (All Feminine)

Genialität, ingeniousness
Humanität, humanity, kindness
Intensivität, intensity
Intimität, intimacy
Jovialität, joviality
Naivität, ingenuity
Originalität, originality
Popularität, popularity
Rarität, rarity
Solidität, solidity
Trivialität, triviality

(f) In nis (ness)

die Wildnis, wilderness
die Wirrnis, confusion

(g) In schaft (ship). (All Feminine)

Barschaft, (bare, nude money) cash on hand
Eigenschaft, property

(h) In tum (dom)

das Eigentum, property
der Reichtum, riches, wealth

(i) In ung (ing). (All Feminine)

Besserung, improvement
Gleichung, (like) equation

Krümmung, curvature, crookedness
Lähmung, lameness, palsy
Lösung, solution, dilution
Quittung, (acquittal) receipt
Rundung, rounding
Trübung, disturbance

(k) Simple Formations

der Ernst, earnest, seriousness
das Fett, fat, grease
das Grün, green color, verdure
das Recht, right
die Scheu, (shy) timidity
das Übel, evil
die Vakanz, vacancy
das Weh, woe, sadness
der Wert, worth, value
der Willkommen, welcome
das Wohl, welfare

(l) Various Formations

das Alter, age
die Blondine, fair woman
die Brillianz, brilliancy
das Dickicht, thicket
der Fanatismus, fanaticism
der Grobian, ruffian
die Hälfte, half
die Jugend, youth
der Typus, type

5. Verbs Based on Adjectives and Adverbs

altern, grow old
bessern, better
bleichen, bleach

blenden, blind, dazzle
dunkeln, grow dark
ebenen, even, level

fälschen, forge
gesunden, recover health
gleichen, be like
grünen, grow green
halbieren, bisect
härten, harden
höhlen, hollow, excavate
klären, clear, clarify
kürzen, shorten
lähmen, lame, paralyze
lieben, love
lösen, loosen, solve
mehren, increase
nahen, approach
nähern, approach
öffnen, open
quittieren, receipt
reifen, ripen
richten, direct
sättigen, satiate

scheuen, shun
schlichten, level
schwächen, weaken
schwärzen, blacken
sichern, secure
siechen, be sick
sondern, separate
stärken, strengthen
steifen, stiffen
stillen, quiet
tollen, act madly
trauen, trust, make true, unite in
  marriage
trocknen, dry
trüben, trouble, disturb
wachen, watch
wärmen, warm
weißen, whiten
weiten, widen
zähmen, tame

6. Nouns Based on the above Verbs

(a) *Masculine*

Fälscher, forger

(b) *Feminine*

Fälschung, forgery
Halbierung, bisection
Höhlung, excavation
Klärung, clarification
Kürzung, abbreviation
Öffnung, opening

Richtung, direction
Sättigung, satiety
Schlichtung, smoothing
Schwächung, weakening
Sicherung, security
Stärkung, strengthening
Stillung, appeasing, stanching
Trauung, wedding ceremony
Zähmung, taming

7. Adjectives Based on Verbs in I, C

(a) In bar

brennbar, combustible
denkbar, conceivable
eßbar, edible
faßbar, comprehensible
fühlbar, sensible
greifbar, graspable
haltbar, durable
heizbar, fit to be heated
hörbar, audible
kostbar, costly
leitbar, manageable
lenkbar, manageable, dirigible
merkbar, noticeable
scheinbar, apparent
trennbar, separable
trinkbar, drinkable
wägbar, ponderable
waschbar, washable

(b) In haft (having)

dauerhaft, durable
flatterhaft, unstable
glaubhaft, credible
habhaft, possessing
lachhaft, ridiculous
lebhaft, lively
nahrhaft, nutritious
schadhaft, harmful
schmackhaft, palatable
schmeichelhaft, flattering
schreckhaft, fearful, terrific
seßhaft, settled, residing
wehrhaft, capable of bearing arms
wohnhaft, residing

(c) In ig (y)

fällig, falling due
giltig, valid
gläubig, believing
klebrig, sticky
lebendig, alive
schläfrig, sleepy, drowsy
willig, willing

(d) In isch (ish)

neckisch, teasing
schwärmerisch, enthusiastic
trügerisch, deceitful

(e) In lich (like, ly)

förderlich, useful
glaublich, credible
hinderlich, hindering
köstlich, costly
lächerlich, ridiculous
merklich, perceptible
ordentlich, orderly
schädlich, hurtful
schmählich, ignominious
schrecklich, terrible
sterblich, mortal
trefflich, (hitting the mark) excellent
trüglich, illusory
tunlich, feasible
üblich, customary
vergeßlich, forgetful
weinerlich, inclined to weep
wirklich, (working) actual

(f) In los (less)

haltlos, unsustained
hilflos, helpless
leblos, lifeless
schadlos, harmless
schlaflos, sleepless

(g) In reich (rich)

hilfreich, helpful
lehrreich, instructive
segensreich, blissful

(h) In sam (some)

folgsam, obedient
lenksam, manageable
sparsam, economical
strebsam, ambitious
wirksam, effective

(i) Showing the Prefix un

unfehlbar, infallible
unleugbar, undeniable
unsäglich, unspeakable

8. Nouns Based on the above Adjectives. (All Feminine)

Brennbarkeit, combustibility
Dauerhaftigkeit, durability
Fälligkeit, maturity (note)
Flatterhaftigkeit, instability
Folgsamkeit, obedience
Giltigkeit, validity
Gläubigkeit, credibility
Haltbarkeit, durability
Haltlosigkeit, untenability
Hilflosigkeit, helplessness
Kostbarkeit, costliness
Lächerlichkeit, ridiculous situation
Lebendigkeit, liveliness
Leitbarkeit, manageability
Lenkbarkeit, manageableness

Lenksamkeit, manageableness
Schädlichkeit, injuriousness
Schlaflosigkeit, insomnia
Schläfrigkeit, drowsiness
Sparsamkeit, thriftiness
Sterblichkeit, mortality
Strebsamkeit, assiduity
Trefflichkeit, excellency
Trennbarkeit, separability
Unfehlbarkeit, infallibility
Unleugbarkeit, undeniableness
Vergeßlichkeit, forgetfulness
Willigkeit, willingness
Wirklichkeit, reality
Wirksamkeit, efficiency

9. Nouns Based on Verbs in I, C

(a) Simple Formations

Masculine

Biß, bite
Bruch, breach, fraction
Diebstahl, (thief's stealing) theft
Fall, fall

Fang, capture
Griff, grip, grasp
Kniff, trick
Pfiff, whistle
Preis, price, prize
Raub, robbery

Ritt, ride
Ruck, move, jerk
Schein, shine
Schlaf, sleep
Schlag, blow
Schlich, trick
Schliff, polish
Schlung, swallow, throat
Schmuck, adornment
Schreck, scare, fright
Schub, shove, push
Schweif, tail
Sitz, seat
Stich, stitch, prick
Stoß, blow
Strich, stroke
Trab, trot
Trieb, driving, impulse
Tritt, step
Trunk, drink
Wuchs, growth
Zug, (tug) draught, train

Feminine

Dauer, duration
Gabe, gift
Hilfe, help
Kunst, ability, art
Lauer, lurking-place
Schau, show
Tat, deed
Tracht, load, charge

(*b*) In e. (All Feminine)

Falte, fold
Folge, succession
Habe, (having) belongings

Hetze, (hate) chase
Irre, error, astray
Klemme, straits
Lache, laughter
Lage, location, site
Lehne, (leaning) back
Lehre, teaching, doctrine
Lüge, lie, untruth
Mühle, mill
Presse, press
Rinne, gutter, channel
Sage, (saw, saying) legend
Scheide, sheath
Schelte, reproach
Schere, shears, scissors
Schleppe, train (dress)
Schmiere, smear, grease
Spinde, cupboard, closet
Spritze, syringe
Strecke, stretch, distance
Stütze, stay, support
Taste, key (piano)
Taufe, christening
Wage, balance, scales
Wäsche, wash, laundry
Wette, bet
Wiege, balance, cradle

(*c*) In ei. (All Feminine)

Brauerei, brewery
Brennerei, distillery
Bummelei, loitering
Raserei, raving
Schmeichelei, flattery
Schnüffelei, spying
Spinnerei, spinning mills

(d) In **el**

Masculine

Hängfel, hanger (cloth)
Hebel, lever
Klöpfel, knocker
Schlägel, mallet

Feminine

Schaukel, swing
Spindel, spindle

(e) In **en**

Masculine

Glauben, belief
Schaden, damage
Segen, blessing
Streifen, stripe

Neuter

Essen, eating, food
Fasten, Lent
Leben, life
Staunen, astonishment
Streben, striving, ambition
Treffen, (hitting) engagement

(f) In **er**

Masculine

Bäcker, baker
Bläser, blower
Bohrer, bore, gimlet
Brauer, brewer
Brenner, burner
Bummler, loafer
Denker, thinker
Fehler, failure, mistake

Finder, finder
Halter, holder
Jauchzer, shout
Klemmer, (pincher) eye-glass
Läufer, runner
Lauscher, listener
Lehrer, teacher
Lenker, manager
Leuchter, candlestick
Müller, miller
Prediger, preacher
Räuber, robber
Reiter, rider
Renner, runner
Richter, (right) judge
Ritter, (rider) knight
Sammler, collector
Sänger, singer
Schaffner, (shaper) worker, conductor
Schläfer, sleeper
Schleicher, sneak
Schlepper, tugboat
Schmeichler, flatterer
Schnüffler, spy
Schöpfer, shaper, creator
Schreiber, writer, copyist
Schwimmer, swimmer
Seufzer, (soft cry) sigh
Späher, spy
Spinner, spinner
Springer, sprinter
Streber, competitor
Taucher, diver
Treffer, (hitter) prize
Trinker, drunkard
Turner, athlete

Wanderer, wanderer
Wärter, guard
Weber, weaver
Weiser, sign (road)
Zeiger, indicator, hand
Zünder, (tinder) fuse

Neuter

Lager, layer
Schalter, sliding window

(*g*) In heit

Vergessenheit, oblivion

(*h*) In ling

der Täufling, child to be christened

(*i*) In nis. (Neuter)

Hemnis, impediment
Hindernis, hindrance, obstacle

(*k*) In t
Masculine

Lieferant, purveyor

Feminine

Fahrt, ride
Glut, glow, heat
Naht, seam
Predigt, sermon

Neuter

Paket, package

(*l*) In tum (dom)

der Irrtum, error
das Wachstum, growth

(*m*) In ung (ing). (All Feminine)

Blähung, (blowing) inflation
Drohung, threat
Fassung, conception
Förderung, furtherance
Geltung, validity
Haltung, attitude, carriage (body)
Heizung, heating
Impfung, vaccination
Infizierung, infection
Ladung, load, cargo
Linderung, mitigation
Mahnung, reminder
Meinung, meaning, opinion
Mischung, mixture
Nahrung, nourishment, food
Ordnung, order
Plünderung, pillage
Prüfung, (probing) examination
Quetschung, bruise
Rechnung, calculation, bill
Regierung, regency, government
Regung, agitation
Reibung, friction
Richtung, direction
Rührung, emotion
Sammlung, collection
Schmähung, abuse
Schöpfung, creation
Schwankung, hesitation
Schwenkung, evolution
Schwingung, vibration
Sendung, shipment
Senkung, depression
Sitzung, sitting, meeting
Spannung, tension
Sperrung, closing

Sprengung, blasting (causing to spring)
Stauung, congestion
Stockung, stopping, stagnation
Störung, disturbance
Trennung, separation
Übung, exercise
Wanderung, migration
Warnung, warning
Waschung, washing
Wendung, (wending) turn
Widmung, dedication
Windung, winding, convolution
Wirkung, (working) effect
Wohnung, residence
Ziehung, drawing

(n) Foreign Words
Masculine

Gratulant, person who congratulates
Ignorant, ignorant person
Repräsentant, representative

Feminine

Deklamation, declamation
Gratulation, congratulation
Ignoranz, ignorance
Illumination, illumination
Imitation, imitation
Kapitulation, capitulation, surrender
Politur, polish
Reparatur, repair
Repetition, repetition, review
Repräsentation, representation
Revision, revision

Spedition, expedition, forwarding office

(o) Increased by the Prefix ge
Masculine

Gebieter, (bidder) commander
Gedanke, thought
Gehalt, (holdings) contents
Gesang, song
Geschmack, taste

Feminine

Geburt, birth

Neuter

Geächs, moaning
Gebäck, pastry
Gebiet, territory
Gebiß, set of teeth
Gebräu, brew
Gebrechen, ailment
Gebrüll, roaring
Gefängnis, (catch) prison
Gefecht, fight, engagement
Geflacker, flickering
Gefühl, feeling
Gegrinse, grinning
Gegrunze, grunting
Gehalt, (holdings) salary
Geheul, howling
Gehör, hearing
Gekicher, chuckling
Geklopfe, continued knocking
Gekrächz, croaking
Gelächter, laughter
Gelage, (clubbing together) banquet

Gelispel, lisping
Gemurmel, murmuring
Gemurr, grumbling
Gepäck, baggage
Geplätscher, splashing
Geplünder, pillage
Gepolter, rumbling noise
Geprickel, prickling
Gequake, croaking
Geranke, shoots of vine
Gerassel, rattling
Gerumpel, continual rumbling
Geschmier, scribbling
Geschöpf, creature
Geschrei, cry, clamor
Geschwirr, whizzing
Gesöff, poor drink

Gespann, team
Gestotter, stuttering
Gesuch, request
Gesudel, scribbling
Getöse, noise
Getrampel, trampling
Getränk, beverage
Getriebe, machinery
Getümmel, din
Gewächs, growth
Gewebe, fabric, texture
Gewehr, gun, rifle
Gewimmer, whimpering
Gewinde, thread (screw), garland
Gewölbe, vault, arch
Gezisch, hissing
Gezwitscher, twittering

10. Inseparable Verbs Based on Adjectives

(a) Prefix be

befestigen, fortify
befeuchten, moisten
befreien, free
befremden, estrange
begleichen, equalize, settle
belieben, like, please
bereichern, enrich
besänftigen, soften
beschönigen, (render fair) excuse
beschweren, burden
bestätigen, (render steady) confirm
betrauen, trust, confide
betrüben, afflict
bewähren, prove, verify
bezähmen, tame, restrain

(b) Prefix ent

entfernen, remove
entfremden, alienate
entwerten, (worth) depreciate
entwirren, extricate

(c) Prefix er

erblinden, grow blind
erfrischen, refresh
erhärten, harden, confirm
erhöhen, heighten
erkälten, expose to cold
erklären, declare
erkühnen sich, make bold
erlahmen, become lame
erlangen, attain

erleichtern, facilitate
erneuern, renew
eröffnen, open
erschlaffen, slacken
erwachen, awake
erwärmen, warm
erweichen, soften
erweitern, widen

(d) Prefix ver

veralten, become obsolete
verarmen, grow poor
verbessern, correct
verbleichen, grow pale
verbreiten, circulate
verbreitern, broaden
verdichten, condense
verdicken, thicken
verdoppeln, double
verdummen, stultify
verdunkeln, darken
verdünnen, dilute
vereiteln, frustrate
verfälschen, adulterate
verfaulen, rot
verfeinern, refine
verfetten, be covered with fat
vergleichen, compare
vergröbern, make coarse
vergrößern, enlarge
vergüten, make good, pay
verhärten, harden

verhehlen, (hollow) conceal
verjüngen, make young
verklären, clarify
verkleinern, reduce
verkrümmen, become crooked
verkühlen, cool, chill
verkürzen, shorten
verlängern, lengthen
verlauten, become aloud, be reported
verlieben sich, fall in love
vermehren, increase
vermindern, diminish
verrohen, turn brutal
versauern, turn sour
verschärfen, render more severe
verscheuchen, scare away
verschmälern, make narrow
verschönern, embellish
versichern, assure, insure
versteifen, stiffen
versüßen, sweeten
verteuern, make dearer
vertiefen, deepen
vertrauen, trust
vertrocknen, dry up
verübeln, take amiss
verwerten, utilize
verwildern, run wild
verwirren, confuse
verwunden, wound, hurt
verwüsten, lay waste

11. Nouns Based on the above Verbs

(a) Simple Formation

der Vergleich, comparison

(b) In en. (Neuter)

Erwachen, awakening
Vertrauen, trust

(c) In **er**. (All Masculine)

Befreier, liberator
Beschwerer, weight (letter)
Verbesserer, reformer
Verbreiter, divulger
Vermehrer, augmenter
Verschönerer, one who embellishes

(d) In **ung**. (All Feminine)

Befestigung, fortification
Befeuchtung, moistening
Befreiung, liberation
Befremdung, estrangement
Begleichung, settlement
Bereicherung, enrichment
Besänftigung, appeasement
Beschönigung, excuse
Beschwerung, incumbrance
Bestätigung, confirmation
Entfernung, distance
Entfremdung, alienation
Entwertung, depreciation
Entwirrung, extrication
Erblindung, turning blind
Erfrischung, refreshment
Erhärtung, confirmation
Erhöhung, elevation
Erkältung, cold
Erklärung, declaration
Erlangung, attainment
Erleichterung, relief
Erneuerung, renewal
Eröffnung, opening
Erschlaffung, relaxation
Erwärmung, heating
Erweichung, softening
Erweiterung, extension

Verarmung, impoverishment
Verbesserung, correction
Verbreitung, circulation
Verbreiterung, broadening
Verdichtung, condensation
Verdickung, thickening
Verdoppelung, duplication
Verdummung, stultification
Verdunkelung, obscuration
Verdünnung, dilution
Vereitelung, frustration
Verfälschung, adulteration
Verfeinerung, refinement
Verfettung, fatty degeneration
Vergleichung, comparison
Vergrößerung, enlargement
Vergütung, compensation
Verhärtung, callousness
Verjüngung, rejuvenation
Verklärung, clarification
Verkleinerung, reduction
Verkrümmung, crookedness
Verkürzung, shortening
Verlängerung, extension
Vermehrung, increase
Verminderung, decrease
Verrohung, loss of refinement
Verschärfung, greater severity
Verschönerung, embellishment
Versicherung, assurance
Verteuerung, raising of prices
Vertiefung, depression
Verübelung, taking amiss
Verwertung, utilization
Verwilderung, demoralization
Verwirrung, confusion
Verwundung, injury
Verwüstung, devastation

12. Inseparable Verbs Based on Verbs in I, C

(a) Prefix be

bedenken, consider
bedrohen, threaten
befahren, pass over
befallen, befall, attack
befassen sich, meddle with
befinden sich, be in a place
befolgen, follow
befördern, further, promote
befühlen, feel, handle
begreifen, grasp, comprehend
begucken, look at
behalten, hold, keep
beharren, persist
behauen, hew, cut
behelfen sich, make shift
behindern, hinder, impede
beklemmen, oppress
bekommen, (come by) get
belachen, laugh at
beladen, load, burden
belassen, let be
belauschen, listen to
beleben, enliven
belegen, lay (on a seat), secure
belehnen, invest with a fief
belehren, instruct
beleuchten, illuminate
belügen, belie
bemerken, remark
benagen, gnaw
bepacken, charge with
berauben, bereave
berechnen, calculate
berennen, assault (fort)
berichten, report

berühren, touch
besäen, sow, seed
beschaben, shave
beschaffen, procure
beschauen, look at
bescheinen, shine upon
beschimpfen, disgrace
beschlagen, nail upon, coat with
beschleichen, sneak upon
beschmieren, besmear
beschnüffeln, snuffle at
beschreiben, describe
beschwören, swear to
besehen, look at
besetzen, occupy
besingen, sing, celebrate
besitzen, possess
bespannen, put horses to
bespeien, spit on
bespinnen, cover with a texture
besprengen, sprinkle
bespritzen, splash
bespülen, wash
bestechen, bribe
bestehen, consist of
bestehlen, steal from
bestreben, strive at
bestreichen, touch in passing
bestreuen, strew, sprinkle
besuchen, seek up, visit
besudeln, soil
betasten, test, touch
betragen, amount to
betrauen, entrust
betreffen, (hit at) concern
betreiben, (drive) carry on

betreten, (tread) step upon
betrinken sich, get drunk
betrügen, betray, deceive
bewahren, guard, protect
bewehren, arm, equip
beweinen, weep for
beweisen, show, prove
bewirken, effect
bewohnen, occupy a house
bezeigen, show, testify
beziehen, draw over

(b) Occurring in the Past
Participle only

berankt, covered with vine
betaumelt, in a stupor
bewachsen, grown over
bewandert, (traveled) experienced
in

(c) Prefix ent

entbieten, bid, command
entbrennen, be inflamed
entfahren, slip off
entfallen, fall from
entfalten, unfold
entfliegen, fly away
entfliehen, flee from
entfließen, flow from
entgelten, pay for
entgleiten, glide from
enthalten, hold off, abstain
entheben, lift from, free
entkommen, come off, escape
entladen, unload
entlassen, let out, dismiss
entlaufen, run away

entleihen, loan from
entrichten, make right, settle
entringen, wring from
entrinnen, run away, escape
entrücken, remove
entsagen, (say off) desist
entscheiden, separate one's ideas,
decide
entschweben, pass away
entsenden, send off, despatch
entsprießen, sprout forth
entstehen, stand out of, arise
entwenden, (wend) turn away,
steal
entwinden, (wind) wrest from
entziehen, withdraw
entzünden, inflame (tinder)

(d) Occurring in the Past
Participle only

entlegen, lying away, remote

(e) Prefix er

erbrechen, break open
erbringen, bring out, produce
erdenken, think out, devise
erfahren, experience (by traveling)
erfassen, take up
erfinden, find out, invent
erfolgen, follow, ensue
erfrieren, freeze to death
ergeben, give up, disclose
erglühen, glow up
ergreifen, grasp
erhalten, keep up, preserve
erheben, (heave) raise

erheischen, ask, request
erholen, overhaul, recover
erhören, hear, grant
erlassen, let go, release
erlauschen, learn by listening
erleben, live through
erlegen, lay down, kill
erlernen, learn
erleuchten, illumine
erliegen, lie down, succumb
ermahnen, remind
ernähren, nourish
erregen, stir up, excite
erreichen, reach
errichten, erect
erringen, get by exertion
ersaufen, drown (animals)
erschaffen, shape
erscheinen, appear
erschlagen, slay
erschleichen, get by sneaking
erschöpfen, scoop out, exhaust
erschrecken, scare
erschüttern, shatter, shake
ersehen, see from
ersparen, spare, save
erspriessen, sprout forth
erstechen, stab
erstehen, stand out, arise
erstreben, strive at
erstrecken, stretch out, extend
ersuchen, seek from, request
ertragen, bear
ertrinken, (drench) drown
erwachsen, grow up
erwägen, weigh, consider
erwarten, await, expect

erwecken, awaken
erwehren, ward off
erweisen, show, prove
erwirken, work out, effect
erwürgen, wreck, strangle
erziehen, draw out, bring up

(f) Prefix ge

gebieten, bid, command
gedenken, think of, remember

(g) Prefix ver

verbieten, forbid
verbinden, bind, connect
verblühen, (bloom away) fade
verbrechen, break (a law)
verbrennen, burn up
verbringen, bring away, spend
verbummeln, loiter away
verdenken, think ill, blame
verfallen, fall off, decay
verfassen, take together, compose
verfechten, fight for, defend
verfliegen, fly off, evaporate
verfolgen, follow, pursue
verfrieren, freeze to death
vergeben, forgive
vergehen, go away, pass
vergelten, repay
verglimmen, cease gleaming
verglühen, cease glowing
verhalten, withhold
verhauen, beat soundly
verheben sich, (overheave) hurt
    oneself by lifting
verhehlen, conceal (put in a hole)
verhelfen, help to

verhetzen, incite (hate)
verhindern, hinder
verhören, hear, examine
verirren sich, err, go astray
verkleben, glue over
verkommen, come off, perish
verkriechen sich, crouch away
verlachen, laugh at
verladen, load
verlassen, let, leave
verlaufen sich, run the wrong way
verleben, live through
verlegen, mislay
verleihen, loan
verleiten, mislead
verlernen, (unlearn) forget
verleugnen, (lie) deny
vermachen, make over, bequeath
vermerken, remark
vermischen, mix
vermögen, (may) be able
verordnen, ordain, command
verpacken, pack up
verrechnen sich, reckon wrongly
verreiben, pulverize (rub)
verrinnen, run off, expire
verrücken, (rock) move away
versagen, refuse
versammeln, assemble
versaufen, spend in drink
verschaffen, shape, procure
verscheiden, separate, die
verschicken, send away
verschieben, (shift over) put off
verschlafen, sleep away
verschleppen, put off
verschlingen, (sling down) devour

verschlucken, swallow
verschmachten, faint away, smack, have a taste for
verschmähen, disdain
verschnappen sich, let out
verschreiben, prescribe
verschreien, decry
verschütten, spill
verschwitzen, sweat out, forget
verschwören sich, swear badly, conspire
versehen, (foresee) provide
versehen sich, see wrongly, err
versenden, send away
versenken, sink
versinken, sink, founder
versparen, spare, reserve
versperren, (spar) obstruct
versprengen, disperse
verspritzen, squirt away
verstehen, understand
verstopfen, stop, constipate
verstoßen, toss off, disown
verstreichen, strike off, elapse
verstreuen, (strew) scatter
versuchen, seek to get, try
vertragen, bear
vertragen sich, bear one another, agree
vertrauen, trust
vertreiben, drive away
vertreten, tread, step into one's place, represent
vertrinken, spend in drinking
verüben, (operate wrongly) commit
verwahren, guard, keep

verwalten, wield, manage
verwarnen, warn
verweben, interweave
verwehren, (war off) forbid
verweisen, show away, reprimand
verwenden, (wend) turn to, apply
verwetten, lose by betting
verzehren, tear up, consume
verzerren, tear off, distort
verziehen, pull off, delay

(h) Special Uses of the Past Participle

verlegen, mislaid, embarrassed
verrückt, unbalanced, crazy
verstorben, deceased
verstört, disturbed
verwachsen, ill-grown
verweint, red with tears

(i) Prefix zer

zerbeißen, bite to pieces
zerbrechen, break to pieces
zerfallen, fall apart
zerfließen, flow apart

zerhacken, hack to pieces
zerhauen, cut to pieces
zerklopfen, beat to pieces
zerkneifen, rip apart
zerlaufen, run apart, melt
zerlegen, lay apart, analyze
zermalmen, (mill) crush
zernagen, destroy by gnawing
zerpflücken, pluck up
zerquetschen, squash
zerreiben, (rub) pulverize
zerrinnen, flow apart, melt
zerrühren, stir
zerschaben, scrape up
zerschlagen, beat to pieces
zerschmettern, (smite) crush
zersprengen, burst into pieces, blow up
zerspringen, fly into pieces, crack
zerstechen, pierce
zerstören, destroy
zerstoßen, pound
zerstreuen, (strew) scatter
zertrampeln, trample down
zertrennen, disjoin
zertreten, tread under foot

13. Adjectives Based on the above Inseparable Verbs

(a) In bar

bemerkbar, noticeable
berechenbar, calculable
besetzbar, fit to occupy
bewirkbar, feasible
bewohnbar, habitable
erfaßbar, conceivable
erhaltbar, obtainable
erlernbar, learnable
erregbar, excitable

erreichbar, attainable
ersehbar, perceptible
verfechtbar, fit to defend
verleitbar, seducible
verschaffbar, procurable
verschiebbar, fit to postpone
versenkbar, sinkable
verwendbar, applicable
zerlegbar, divisible
zerstörbar, destructible

(b) In iſch

betrügeriſch, deceitful
erfinderiſch, inventive

(c) In lich

bedenklich, causing to think, critical
bedrohlich, menacing
begreiflich, comprehensible
beharrlich, perseverant
behilflich, helpful
bemerklich, noticeable
beſchaulich, contemplative
beſtechlich, bribable
entzündlich, inflammable
erheblich, weighty

erſprießlich, profitable
erträglich, tolerable
unbeſchreiblich, indescribable
unentgeltlich, free of charge
unerläßlich, irremissible
unzertrennlich, inseparable
verbindlich, obliging
verläßlich, reliable
verträglich, peaceable
vertraulich, confidential
zerbrechlich, brittle

(d) In ſam

enthaltſam, abstinent

14. Nouns Based on the above Adjectives. (All Feminine)

Beharrlichkeit, perseverance
Beſchaulichkeit, contemplativeness
Beſtechlichkeit, corruptibleness
Enthaltſamkeit, abstinence
Erregbarkeit, irritability
Unerträglichkeit, intolerableness
Unzertrennlichkeit, inseparability

Verbindlichkeit, liability
Verträglichkeit, compatibility
Vertraulichkeit, intimacy
Verwendbarkeit, applicability
Zerbrechlichkeit, brittleness
Zerlegbarkeit, divisibility

15. Nouns Based on the Preceding Inseparable Verbs

(a) Simple Formations
Masculine

Begriff, conception
Bericht, report
Beſchlag, attachment
Beſtand, stock, amount
Beſuch, visit
Betrag, amount
Betrieb, operation
Betrug, fraud

Beweis, proof
Erfolg, result, success
Erlaß, remission
Verband, association
Verfall, decay
Verſand, shipment
Verſtoß, offense
Vertrag, treaty, agreement
Verweis, rebuke

Neuter

Entgelt, compensation
Verbot, prohibition
Verhör, hearing, examination

(b) In **en.**   (Neuter)

Befinden, state of health
Bestreben, aspiration
Betragen, deportment
Verbrechen, crime
Vergehen, misdemeanor
Vermögen, (might) capital
Versehen, mistake
Vertrauen, trust, confidence

(c) In **er.**   (All Masculine)

Gebieter, commander
Verbrecher, criminal
Vertreter, substitute
Verwalter, manager

(d) In **heit.**   (All Feminine)

Betrunkenheit, drunkenness
Entschiedenheit, firmness
Ergriffenheit, deep affection
Erregtheit, excitement
Vergangenheit, past
Verkommenheit, profligacy
Verlassenheit, dereliction
Verlebtheit, decrepitude
Verlegenheit, embarrassment
Verliebtheit, infatuation
Verrücktheit, craziness
Verschlafenheit, drowsiness
Zerfallenheit, state of decay
Zerschlagenheit, complete exhaustion

Zerstreutheit, distraction

(e) In **nis**

die Ersparnis, savings
das Vermächtnis, legacy

(f) In **ung.**   (All Feminine)

Befolgung, observance
Beförderung, promotion
Begleitung, escort
Beklemmung, anguish
Beladung, loading
Belebung, animation
Belegung, engagement
Belehrung, instruction
Beleuchtung, lighting
Bemerkung, remark
Bepackung, load
Beraubung, deprivation
Berechnung, calculation
Berührung, contact
Beschaffung, purchase
Beschreibung, description
Beschwörung, exorcism
Besetzung, setting, cast (play)
Besitzung, property
Bespannung, team
Besprengung, sprinkling
Bestechung, bribery
Beziehung, reference
Entfaltung, unfolding
Enthebung, dispensation
Entladung, unloading
Entlassung, dismissal
Entrichtung, payment
Entsagung, resignation
Entscheidung, decision

Entwendung, theft
Entziehung, withdrawal
Entzündung, inflammation
Erfahrung, experience
Erfindung, invention
Ergebung, surrender
Erhaltung, preservation
Erhebung, promotion
Erholung, recreation
Erhörung, hearing
Erlegung, killing
Ermahnung, reminder
Ernährung, nourishment
Erregung, excitement
Erschaffung, creation
Erscheinung, apparition
Erschöpfung, exhaustion
Erschütterung, concussion
Erwägung, consideration
Erwartung, expectation
Erwirkung, enforcement
Erziehung, education
Verbindung, connection
Verbrennung, combustion
Verfassung, constitution
Verfolgung, persecution
Vergeltung, retribution
Verhinderung, prevention

Verirrung, aberration
Verladung, loading
Verleihung, granting
Verleitung, temptation
Verleugnung, denial
Verordnung, ordinance
Verpackung, package
Versammlung, assembly
Verschiebung, postponement
Verschleppung, mislaying
Verschmähung, disdain
Verschreibung, obligation
Verschwörung, conspiracy
Versenkung, drop (stage)
Verstauung, stowage
Verstopfung, constipation
Versuchung, temptation
Vertreibung, expulsion
Vertretung, substitution
Verübung, perpetration
Verwahrung, safe-keeping
Verwaltung, management
Verwendung, application
Verzehrung, consumption
Zerschmetterung, dashing to pieces
Zerstörung, destruction
Zerstreuung, distraction

IV. WORD-GROUPS

1. alt, old

ältlich, elderly
das Alter, age
das Altertum, antiquity
altertümlich, old-fashioned
altern, show the effects of old age
veraltet, obsolete

2. ander, other

ändern, verändern, change, alter
die Änderung, Veränderung
veränderlich, changeable
die Veränderlichkeit

3. der **Arm**, *arm*

der **Ärmel**, sleeve
umarmen, embrace; die **Umarmung**

arm, *poor*

die **Armut**, poverty
verarmen, become poor
ärmlich, poorly

A possible cognate is **b-arm**
(*with the poor*) in:

barmherzig, charitable
die **Barmherzigkeit**, mercy
das **Erbarmen**, mercy
erbärmlich, miserable

4. die **Asche**, *ashes*

einäschern, incinerate
die **Einäscherung**

5. **aus**, *out (of)*

außer, (outside of) besides
das **Äußere**, exterior
die **Äußerlichkeiten**, appearances
äußern, utter
die **Äußerung**
veräußern, put outside, sell
unveräußerlich
außerordentlich, extraordinary

6. **backen (buk, gebacken)**

der **Bäcker**, baker; die **Bäckerin**
die **Bäckerei**, bakery
das **Gebäck**, pastry

7. das **Bad**, *bath*

baden, bathe

8. die **Bahn**, *road, track, orbit*

bahnen, open a passage
bohnen, polish the floor
die **Bühne**, stage

9. der **Ball**, *ball, sphere*

ballen, clench (fist)
der **Ballen**, bale

10. **bar**, *bare, nude* (referring to
money, *visible, available, ready*)

die **Barschaft**, available cash
entbehren, be deprived of
die **Entbehrung**
unentbehrlich, indispensable

11. **bauen,** (*booth*) *build*

der **Bau** (die **Bauten**), building
das **Gebäude**, building
der **Klavierbauer**, piano builder
der **Bauer**, (boor) farmer; die
Bäuerin
bäu(e)risch, rustic
verbauern, get into boorish ways
der (das) **Bauer**, (bower) bird cage

12. der **Baum**, (*beam*) *tree*

baumeln, dangle, be suspended
from a tree
sich bäumen, prance, stand up like
a tree

13. **befehlen (befahl, be-
fohlen)**, *command, order*

der **Befehl**
empfehlen (**empfahl, empfohlen**),
recommend

die Empfehlung

14. beißen (biß, gebissen), *bite*

verbissen, sarcastic
die Verbissenheit
der Biß, bite
der Bissen, morsel
das Gebiß, set of teeth, bit
der Imbiß, bite
bissig, sarcastic
beizen, corrode, stain
die Beize, caustic

15. der Berg, (iceberg = ice-hill) *hill, mountain*

bergig, hilly, mountainous
bergauf (up), bergab (down)
das Gebirge, range of mountains
das Vorgebirge, promontory
gebirgig, mountainous

16. biegen (bog, gebogen), *bow, bend*

biegsam, flexible; die Biegsamkeit
die Biegung, bend, curve
der Bogen, bow, arc
der Bügel, (bugle, a bent trumpet)
denotes a number of bent objects,
handle, stirrup
das Bügeleisen, pressing iron
bügeln, press clothes; der Bügler
die Bucht, inlet
der Buckel, hump; buckelig
sich bücken, stoop; der Bückling
beugen, bow, incline

vorbeugen, bend forward, (fencing) ward off
sich verbeugen, bow; die Verbeugung

17. bieten (bot, geboten) (bid) *offer*

das Anerbieten, das Angebot, offer
verbieten (verbot, verboten), forbid
das Verbot, prohibition
der Bote, messenger
die Botschaft, message
gebieten (gebot, geboten), (bid) command
der Gebieter, die Gebieterin
gebieterisch, imperious
das Gebiet, jurisdiction, domain, territory
das Gebot, commandment

18. bilden, *frame, form,* especially character and mind, *educate*

die Bildung
bildsam, pliant; die Bildsamkeit
das Gebilde, formation
das Bild, form, likeness, picture, statue

19. ich bin (sein, war, gewesen), (been) *I am*

das Dasein, existence
das Unwohlsein, indisposition
das Wesen, being, essence. character
wesentlich, essential

anwesend, being near, present; ab=
wesend, absent; die Abwesenheit,
die Anwesenheit

verwesen, cease to be, decay; die
Verwesung

verwesen, (be for somebody else)
represent

der Verweser

20. binden (band, gebun=
den), bind

die Binde, cravat
zum Angebinde, as a souvenir
der Band (Bände), volume
das Band (Bänder), ribbon
die Verbindung, connection
der Bund, das Bündnis, alliance,
treaty
der Verbündete, ally
das Bündel, bundle
bändigen, subdue, tame; der Tier=
bändiger

21. bitten (bat, gebeten)
(bid) ask, request

unerbittlich, inexorable
die Bitte, request
beten, ask (in prayer), pray
das Gebet, prayer
betteln, beg (alms); der Bettler, die
Bettlerin
der Bettel, trash
die Bettelei, mendicity

22. das Blatt, (blade) denotes
several objects: blade, edge,
sheet, leaf; die Blätter

blättern, durchblättern, peruse
entblättern, strip of leaves

23. bleiben (blieb, ge=
blieben), remain, stay

unausbleiblich, inevitable
der Verbleib, whereabouts
das Überbleibsel, remnant

24. die Blume, (bloom) flower
das Blümchen, das Blüm(e)lein
blühen, bloom; die Blüte, bloom,
blossom

25. das Blut, blood

blutig, bloody
bluten, bleed
verbluten, bleed to death
von königlichem Geblüt

26. braten (briet, gebra=
ten), (broth, broil) roast, broil, fry

der Braten, (brawn) roast meat
das Wildbret, Wildpret, (wild animal, game)
brodeln, (broth) broil, bubble
die Brühe, broth
verbrühen, scald
brauen, brew; der Brauer, die
Brauerei
das Bräu, Gebräu, brew

27. brauchen, (brook) need

gebrauchen, use; verbrauchen, consume
der Brauch, custom; der Gebrauch,
use

brauchbar, useful; die Brauchbarkeit
gebräuchlich, customary

28. brechen (brach, gebrochen), break

zerbrechen, smash; zerbrechlich, fragile
verbrechen, violate a law
einbrechen, burglarize
unterbrechen, interrupt
das Verbrechen, crime; der Verbrecher, verbrecherisch
der Einbrecher, burglar; der Einbruch
die Unterbrechung, ununterbrochen
das Gebrechen, ailment; gebrechlich
der Bruch, break, breach, fraction
brüchig, brittle
wortbrüchig, treacherous; die Wortbrüchigkeit
der Brocken, morsel, crumb
bröckeln, crumble
das Brachland, field to be broken after the crop

29. breit, broad, wide
die Breite
ausbreiten, spread; verbreiten, scatter
verbreitern, broaden, widen
die Ausbreitung, Verbreitung, Verbreiterung

30. brennen (brannte, gebrannt), burn

der Brenner, burner; die Brennerei, distillery

die Verbrennung, combustion
brennbar, verbrennbar, combustible
der Brand, conflagration
brandmarken, brand
die Brunst, fire, passion
die Inbrunst, fervor, ardor; inbrünstig
branden, move like flames
die Brandung, surf

31. der Bruder, brother

brüderlich, fraternal; die Brüderlichkeit
die Brüderschaft, fraternity
sich verbrüdern, fraternize
die Verbrüderung
Zwei Brüder; Gebrüder Rochlitz, Rochlitz Bros.

32. die Brust, breast

die Armbrust, (arcuballista) crossbow
die Brüstung, (breast support) parapet
sich brüsten, be proud, boast

33. die Burg, (borough) fortified place, town, castle

der Bürger, citizen, commoner
die Bürgerschaft, population
bürgerlich, civil, civic
der Bürge (from borgen, borrow), bondsman
bürgen, vouch; die Bürgschaft, bail
verbürgen, guarantee

34. die Dämmerung, (*dim*)
dusk, dawn

dämmern, dawn; dämmerig, dusky

35. der Dampf, (*damp*)
vapor, steam

der Dampfer, steamer
dampfen, steam; verdampfen, evaporate
dumpf, close, musty, gloomy

36. der Dank, *thanks*

dankbar, die Dankbarkeit
der Undank, ingratitude
danken, thank
sich bedanken, return thanks, decline
   with thanks
verdanken, owe; abdanken, resign
die Abdankung

37. dauern, (*en-dure*) *last*

die Dauer, duration
dauerhaft, durable; die Dauerhaftigkeit
Compare: bedauern, pity, regret
das Bedauern; bedauerlich, deplorable

38. die Decke, (*deck, cover of
a ship*) *cover, blanket, ceiling*

der Deckel, lid; das Gedeck, cover
   (dinner)
decken, cover; abdecken, clear
entdecken, discover; der Entdecker,
   die Entdeckung
das Deck, Verdeck, deck

das Dach, (thatch, cover of a house)
   roof
bedachen, roof
das Obdach, (up-roof) shelter
obdachlos (less), die Obdachlosigkeit

**39. denken (dachte,
gedacht),** *think*

der Denker, thinker; das Andenken,
   souvenir
denkbar, erdenklich, imaginable
der Gedanke, thought
gedankenlos (less), die Gedankenlosigkeit
bedacht, bedächtig, bedachtsam,
   thoughtful
die Bedachtsamkeit
aus Unbedacht, inadvertently
das Gedächtnis, memory
die Andacht, thoughtfulness (religion), devotion, service; andächtig
der Verdacht, (evil thought) suspicion
verdächtig, suspicious; verdächtigen,
   suspect
mit Vorbedacht, purposely, deliberately

40. dicht, *tight, thick, compact*
die Dichtigkeit
verdichten, condense; die Verdichtung

41. dick, *thick*
die Dicke, die Dickheit
verdicken, condense; die Verdickung

42. dienen, serve

verdienen, deserve, earn
der Bediente, der Diener, servant
der Dienst, service; Verdienst, merit
verdienstlich, meritorious
dienlich, serviceable, useful
dienstlich, official

43. doppelt, double

verdoppeln, die Verdoppelung

44. das Dorf, (thorpe, New-dorp) village

der Tölpel, awkward fellow, dunce (cf. villain)
die Tölpelei, tölpelhaft
übertölpeln, overreach, cheat

45. der Draht, (thread) wire

drahtlos (less)
drehen, (throw) turn, twist
die Drehung, Umdrehung, revolution
drechseln, turn, lathe
der Drechsler

46. dringen (drang, ge-drungen), (throng) crowd, press, penetrate

dringend, dringlich, urgent
aufdringlich, zudringlich, obtrusive
die Aufdringlichkeit
eindringlich, impressive
der Eindringling, intruder
der Drang, pressure, impulse
der Andrang, rush
die Drangsal, pression

drängen, press, crowd, urge
bedrängen, oppress, vex
verdrängen, displace
die Bedrängnis, predicament
die Verdrängung, displacement
das Gedränge, crowd

47. drohen, threaten

die Drohung, threat
bedrohlich, threatening

48. drücken, press

ausdrücken, express; bedrücken, oppress
der Druck, pressure
der Ausdruck, die Bedrückung
der Eindruck, impression
drucken, press, print
der Drucker, die Druckerei

49. dulden, (thole) tolerate

duldsam, tolerant; die Duldsamkeit
der Dulder, die Dulderin, sufferer
die Geduld, patience; geduldig
sich gedulden, be patient

50. dunkel, dark

die Dunkelheit, verdunkeln
Compare: der Dünkel (denken), conceit

51. dünn, thin

verdünnen, thin, dilute; die Verdünnung
dehnen, thin out, stretch, extend, expand
dehnbar, extensible; die Dehnbarkeit

52. e b e n, *even, plain, level*

die Ebenheit, evenness; die Ebene, plain

ebenen, level

eben, (*in regard to time*) just now

ebenbürtig (die Geburt, birth)

53. d i e E h e, *matrimony, marriage*

der Ehemann (husband), die Ehefrau; das Ehepaar (pair), husband and wife

ehelich, matrimonial

sich verehelichen, marry

echt, legitimate, genuine; die Echtheit

54. d i e E h r e, *honor*

ehren, beehren, honor

ehrlich, honest; die Ehrlichkeit

ehrenhaft, honorable; die Ehrenhaftigkeit

ehrerbietig (bieten, bid, offer), respectful

ehrgeizig (der Geiz, greed), ambitious

der Ehrgeiz

55. e i n, *one*

einfach, simple

die Einfachheit; vereinfachen, simplify

einsam,(a)l-onesome; die Einsamkeit

vereinsamt, isolated

einmal (das Mal, mark, time), once

einmalig, happening but once

einfältig, (onefold) simple, silly

einzig, existing but once, unique

einst, once; einstig, some time to come

einzeln, (by ones) single

vereinzelt, isolated; die Einzelheiten, particulars

einig, united, agreeing

einigen, die Einigkeit; die Dreieinigkeit, Trinity

die Einheit, unit; einheitlich, uniform

die Einöde, desert

der Verein, union, association, club

vereinen, vereinigen, die Vereinigung

die Vereinigten Staaten

vereinbar, (capable of combination) compatible

vereinbaren, agree; die Vereinbarung

ähnlich (*corruption of* einlich), similar, resembling

die Ähnlichkeit, ähneln; anähneln, assimilate

56. e i t e l, (*idle*) *vain, useless*

die Eitelkeit, vanity

vereiteln, frustrate; die Vereitelung

57. e k (e) l i g, (*irk-some*) *distasteful*

der Ekel, distaste, aversion

ekelhaft, loathsome

anekeln, disgust

58. e m p o r, *upward, onward*

sich empören, rise, rebel

der Empörer, die Empörung

empört, aroused, indignant
der Emporkömmling (kommen), up-
start

59. das Ende, *end*

enden, beenden; verenden, die (animals)
endigen, beendigen, die Beendigung
vollenden, (full) complete; die
Vollendung
endlich, (in the end) at length
unendlich, immense; die Unendlich=
keit
endlos (less), die Endlosigkeit
die Endung, ending, inflection

60. der Erbe, (*orphan*) *heir*

die Erbin, heiress; die Erbschaft,
inheritance
erblich, hereditary; die Erblichkeit,
hereditary character
erben, inherit; beerben, inherit from
enterben, disinherit; die Enterbung

61. die Erde, *earth*

irden, earthen; irdisch, earthly
beerdigen, bury; die Beerdigung

62. erlauben, *allow, permit*

die Erlaubnis
mit Verlaub, with (your kind)
permission
der Urlaub, furlough; beurlauben

**63. essen (aß, geges=
sen), *eat***

eßbar, edible

das Aas (die Äser), carcass
fressen (fraß, gefressen), (fret) eat
(*referring to animals*)
der Fraß, food, prey
gefräßig, gluttonous; die Gefräßig=
keit

64. ewig, (*aye, ever*) *perpetual*

die Ewigkeit; verewigen, perpetuate

65. der Faden, (*fathom*) *thread*

der Bindfaden, twine
einfädeln, thread, contrive
fadenscheinig (scheinen, shine, appear), threadbare

**66. fahren, (*fare, ferry, thor-
oughfare*) *move, travel, ride***

die Fahrt, fare, ride; die Fähre, ferry
fahrbar, befahrbar, practicable
erfahren, (obtain by traveling) find
out, hear, experience
erfahren, experienced; die Erfah=
rung
das Gefährt, vehicle
der Gefährte, fellow-traveler
die Gefahr, fear, danger
gefährlich, dangerous
gefährden, endanger
die Fuhre, cart load
der Fuhrmann, truckman
fertig (fährtig, fit to move), ready
die Fertigkeit, dexterity
anfertigen, verfertigen, produce
die Anfertigung
führen, (cause to move) guide, lead
der Führer, die Führung

die Furt, ford

67. fallen (fiel, gefallen), *fall*

abfallen, desert
anfallen, attack
der Abfall, der Anfall
verfallen, fall apart; der Verfall
der Fall, (*Lat. cadere*, fall, *casus*)
  fall, case
der Beifall, (falling in with) approval; beifällig
der Zufall, accident; zufällig
fällig, falling due; die Fälligkeit
hinfällig, (falling down) frail
die Hinfälligkeit
die Falle, trap
gefallen (gefiel, gefallen), (*from the
  falling of the lot*) please, suit
der Gefallen, favor
gefällig, obliging; die Gefälligkeit

68. falsch, *false*

die Falschheit, falsehood
fälschen, forge
der Fälscher, die Fälschung
verfälschen, adulterate

69. falten, *fold*

die Falte, fold, wrinkle
einfältig, (one-fold) simple
die Einfalt

70. fangen (fing, gefangen), (*fangs*) catch, seize, capture

anfangen, take up, begin

der Anfang; anfänglich, anfangs,
  in the beginning
empfangen, receive
der Empfang
der Fang, catch, haul

71. die Farbe, *color, paint*

der Färber, die Färberei
färben, farbig

72. faul, *foul, rotten, lazy*

die Faulheit
faulenzen, idle; der Faulenzer
faulen, verfaulen, rot, putrefy
die Fäulnis, rottenness

73. fechten (focht, gefochten), *fight*

anfechten, contest; die Anfechtung
verfechten, fight for, advocate
der Fechter, fighter; das Gefecht,
  combat

74. die Feder, *feather, pen, spring*

federn, shed feathers, be elastic
das Gefieder, plumage; gefiedert,
  feathered

75. der Fehler, *failure, mistake, error*

unfehlbar, infallible; die Unfehlbarkeit
fehlen, be absent, be missing
verfehlen, miss

76. die Feier, (*fair*) *cessation of work, rest, celebration*

der Feiertag, holiday
feierlich, solemn; die Feierlichkeit
die Ferien, (*plur.*) vacation

77. feig(e), (*fey*) *cowardly*

der Feigling; die Feigheit

78. fein, *fine, refined*

die Feinheit
verfeinern, refine; die Verfeinerung

79. der Feind, (*fiend*) *enemy*

die Feindin; die Feindschaft, enmity
feindschaftlich, feindselig, hostile
die Feindseligkeiten, (*plur.*)
anfeinden, arouse enmity
sich verfeinden, fall out with
abfinden, get clear of all claims

80. das Feld, *field*

der Feldherr, (*master*) general
das Gefilde, plain, fields

81. fern, (*fer-n*) *far*

die Ferne, distance
entfernen, remove
die Entfernung, distance

82. die Fessel, *fetter*

fesseln, fetter
fassen, anfassen, fetter, seize, touch
vorgefaßt, previously conceived
die Fassung, setting, composition, comprehension wording

fassungslos, disconcerted
die Fassungslosigkeit
faßlich, comprehensible
die Abfassung, wording
die Auffassung, conception
die Verfassung, constitution
der Verfasser, author

83. fest, *fast, solid*

festigen, befestigen, strengthen, fortify
die Festigkeit, die Befestigung
die Festung, fortress

84. feucht, (*fog*) *damp, moist*

anfeuchten, befeuchten, moisten
die Befeuchtung
die Feuchtigkeit, humidity

85. das Feuer, *fire*

die Feuerung, fuel
anfeuern, incite
abfeuern, discharge a gun

86. finden (fand, gefunden), *find*

empfinden, (find within) feel, perceive
empfindlich, sensitive
die Empfindlichkeit
erfinden, (find out) invent
der Erfinder, die Erfindung
erfinderisch, inventive
der Fund, find
der Findling, foundling
findig shrewd; die Findigkeit
das Befinden, state of health
befindlich, present

87. finster, *dark, obscure*

die Finsternis, darkness, eclipse
verfinstern, darken

88. der Fisch, *fish*

der Fischer, die Fischerin, fischen

89. flach, *(fluke) flat, level*

die Fläche, level
die Oberfläche, surface
oberflächlich, superficial; die Ober=
    flächlichkeit
die Flachheit, shallowness
abflachen, level

**90. flechten (flocht, ge=
    flochten),** *twist, plait*

die Flechte, braid
das Geflecht, texture, wicker work

91. das Fleisch, *flesh, meat*

fleischig, der Fleischer
zerfleischen, lacerate

92. der Fleiß, *(flite) diligence,
    industry*

fleißig

**93. fliegen (flog,
    geflogen),** *fly*

verfliegen, evaporate
der Flug, flight
der Flügel, wing, grand piano
das Geflügel, poultry
überflügeln, surpass
flügge, able to fly, fledged

**94. fliehen (floh,
    geflohen),** *flee*

die Flucht, flight
die Ausflucht, excuse
die Zuflucht, refuge
flüchtig, fugitive, flighty, superficial
die Flüchtigkeit
der Flüchtling, fugitive
flüchten, save by flight
verflüchtigen, evaporate

**95. fließen (floß, ge=
    flossen),** *float, flow*

verfließen, flow off, expire
fließend, fluently
das Floß, raft; der Flößer
der Fluß, river
der Einfluß, influence
einflußreich, (rich) influential
beeinflussen, influence
flüssig, fluid, liquid
die Flüssigkeit

96. folgen, *follow*

verfolgen, pursue, persecute
der Verfolger, die Verfolgung
folglich, zufolge, in consequence of
das Gefolge, retinue
folgsam, obedient; die Folgsamkeit
der Erfolg, (the following, result)
    success
erfolgreich, successful
erfolglos, unsuccessful
die Erfolglosigkeit, lack of success
folgern, (cause to follow) infer
die Folgerung, inference

97. forschen, *investigate, search*

der Forscher, explorer; die Forschung
unerforschlich, inscrutable

98. fort, *forth, forward*

fordern, call forth, demand, require
die Forderung
erforderlich, requisite
fördern, further, advance, promote
förderlich, helpful; die Förderung
befördern, transport; die Beförde=
rung

99. fragen, *ask, interrogate*

die Frage, question
fraglich

100. frei, *free*

freiwillig, (willing) voluntary
die Freiheit, freedom, liberty
befreien, free, deliver
der Befreier, die Befreiung

101. der Freund, *friend*

die Freundin; die Freundschaft
freundlich, die Freundlichkeit
sich anfreunden, befreunden mit,
make friends with
sich freuen, (feel friendly) enjoy
oneself, be glad

**102. frieren (fror,
gefroren)**, *freeze*

gefrieren, congeal
der Frost, frostig
frösteln, feel a slight chill

103. frisch, *fresh*

erfrischen, refresh; die Erfrischung

104. fromm, *pious*

die Frommheit
der Frömmler, hypocrite; die
Frömmelei

105. die Frucht, *fruit*

fruchtbar, (bearing) fertile
die Fruchtbarkeit
fruchtlos (less), die Fruchtlosigkeit
fruchten, bear fruit, be productive
befruchten, fertilize; die Befruchtung

106. fühlen, *feel*

befühlen, touch
fühlbar, sensible
feinfühlend, feinfühlig, delicate
das Gefühl, feeling
gefühlvoll, expressive
gefühllos, inexpressive
die Gefühllosigkeit, insensibility

107. füllen, *fill*

erfüllen, fulfil
erfüllbar, realizable; die Erfüllung
die Füllung, das Füllsel, filling
die Füllfeder, fountain pen

108. die Furcht, *fright, fear*

furchtbar, dreadful
furchtlos (less)
furchtsam, timid
die Furchtbarkeit, —losigkeit, —sam=
keit

fürchterlich, terrible, frightful
fürchten, fear; befürchten, apprehend
die Befürchtung

109. der Fürst, (*first*)
leader, sovereign

die Fürstin; das Fürstentum, principality
der Kurfürst, elector
fürstlich, princely
die Fürstlichkeiten, (*plur.*) royalty

110. das Futter,
(*fodder*) food

füttern, feed
die Fütterung

111. ganz, entire, whole

gänzlich, entirely
ergänzen, (make entire) supply
die Ergänzung

112. der Gast, guest

gastfreundlich, hospitable
die Gastfreundschaft, hospitality
gastlich, hospitable; die Gastlichkeit

113. der Gatte, (*gather*) companion, husband

die Gattin, wife
die Gattung, companionship, species

114. das Gatter, lattice

das Gitter, trellis, lattice
vergittern, grate up, lattice

115. der Gaukler, *juggler*

die Gaukelei, vorgaukeln

116. das Gebahren,
(*bearing*) gesture

die Gebärde, Geberde, gesture
sich geberden, gebärden, behave
ungeberdig, refractory, unruly
die Ungeberdigkeit

117. gebären (gebar, geboren), (*bear*) give birth

angeboren, innate
der Eingeborene, native
die Geburt, birth; gebürtig, a native of
ebenbürtig, of equal birth
die Ebenbürtigkeit

118. geben (gab, gegeben), *give*

ergiebig, (giving out) productive
frei(free)gebig, liberal, lavish
die Ergiebigkeit, die Freigebigkeit
das Ergebnis, result
die Gabe, gift; begabt, gifted
die Mitgift, dowry
vergebens, (given away) in vain

119. die Gebühr, (*bear, burden*) dues, fee

es gebührt mir, it is due me
gebührlich, duly; suitable, decent

120. gedeihen (gedieh, gediehen), *be strong, become strong, prosper*

gedeihlich, prosperous
gediegen, sound, substantial
die Gediegenheit

121. gegen, *against*

begegnen, encounter; die Begegnung
entgegnen, reply; die Entgegnung
entgegen, opposite
der Gegner, opponent
gegenwärtig, opposite, present
die Gegenwart, present time
gegenseitig, from opposite sides, mutual
die Gegenseitigkeit, reciprocity
gegenüber, opposite
mein Gegenüber, the person opposite me
die Gegend, land
die Umgegend, surrounding country

122. gehen (ging, gegangen), *go*

das Vergehen, (going wrong) misdemeanor
das Vorgehen, procedure, action
der Gang, (gang plank) gait, passage
der Abgang, departure; Aus—, exit; Durch—, thoroughfare; Ein—, entrance; Her—, progress; Über—, transition, crossing; Um—, intercourse; Unter—,

setting, downfall; Vor—, occurrence; Zu—, access, approach
umgänglich, sociable; die Umgänglichkeit
unumgänglich, inevitable
vergänglich, transitory, perishable; die Vergänglichkeit
die Vergangenheit, past, antecedents
zugänglich, accessible; die Zugänglichkeit
der Fußgänger, pedestrian
gängeln, lead by a string

123. der Geist, *ghost, spirit, mind, intellect*

geistig, intellectual
geistlich, spiritual
geisterhaft, ghostly
der Geistliche, clergyman; die Geistlichkeit
begeistern, inspire; die Begeisterung
vergeistigen, spiritualize; die Vergeistigung

124. das Geld, *(yield, pay, value) money*

gelten (galt, gegolten), yield, be worth
entgelten, compensate
unentgeltlich, free of charge
vergelten, repay
giltig, gültig, valid
gleichgiltig, (of like value) indifferent
die Giltigkeit, Gleichgiltigkeit

125. der Gemahl, *husband*
die Gemahlin, wife
vermählen, give in marriage
die Vermählung

126. gemein, (Lat. communis) *common, vulgar, general*
die Gemein(d)e, community, congregation
die Gemeinheit, vileness
die Gemeinschaft, intercourse
gemeinschaftlich, in company
verallgemeinern, generalize
die Verallgemeinerung

127. genau (nahe, *near, close*), *accurate*
die Genauigkeit

128. genesen (genas, genesen), *recover from illness*
die Genesung

129. genug, *enough*
genügen, be enough, suffice
genügsam, frugal; die Genügsamkeit
sich begnügen, be contented with
das Vergnügen, contentment, pleasure
vergnügt, pleased, happy
genugtun (do), satisfy; die Genugtuung

130. geschehen (geschah, geschehen), *occur, happen*
die Geschichte, occurrences, story, history

geschichtlich, historical
das Geschick, das Schicksal, occurrences, fate
schicklich, (apt to occur) suitable, convenient
die Schicklichkeit

131. gesund, (*sound*) *healthy*
gesunden, recover; die Gesundheit
gesundheitlich, hygienic

132. die Gier, Gierde (*yearn*) *greed, desire*
die Begier, Begierde, greed
gierig, begierig, greedy
die Neu(news)gier(de), curiosity
neugierig
begehren, yearn, desire; das Begehr
begehrlich, covetous; die Begehrlichkeit
gern, (*yearn*) greedily, eagerly
der Geier, (greedy bird) vulture

133. gießen (goß, gegossen), (*gush*) *pour, cast*
der Gießer, foundryman; die Gießerei
der Guß, casting, gust
die Gosse, gutter, sewer

134. der Glanz, *splendor, polish, luster*
glänzen, shine, glitter
glänzend, resplendent, brilliant

135. glauben (g=lauben, be-lieve), believe

der Glaube(n), belief
der Aberglaube, superstition
abergläubisch
gläubig, believing, faithful
der Gläubige, believer
der Gläubiger, creditor
beglaubigen, certify
die Beglaubigung
glaubhaft, authentic; die Glaub=
    haftigkeit
geloben, (make credible) vow
das Gelöbnis, das Gelübde, vow
verloben, betroth
das Verlöbnis, die Verlobung
das gelobte Land, Land of Promise

136. gleich (g=leich) like, equal

gleich, (in regard to time) at once
die Gleichheit, equality
das Gleichnis, simile, allegory
die Gleichung, equation
gleichsam, as it were
gleichwohl, nevertheless
vergleichen (verglich, verglichen),
    compare
der Vergleich, unvergleichlich

137. das Glied (G=lied) lid, member, link

zergliedern, dismember
die Zergliederung
das Mitglied, member

138. das Glück (G=lück) luck, happiness

glücklich, lucky, happy
glücken, turn out luckily
beglücken, make happy
das Unglück, misfortune, accident
verunglücken, meet with an acci-
    dent
der Glückwunsch (wish), congratu-
    lation
beglückwünschen

139. glühen, glow

das Glühlicht, incandescent light
die Glut, glow, heat

140. das Gold, gold

golden, gülden
der Gulden, ducat
vergolden, gild; die Vergoldung

141. der Gott, God

die Göttin, goddess; die Gottheit,
    Deity
der Abgott, idol; Halb—, demi-
    god
gottlos, impious; die Gottlosigkeit
göttlich, divine; die Göttlichkeit
abgöttisch, idolatrous
die Abgötterei, idolatry
die Viel(many)götterei, polythe-
    ism
vergöttern, idolize; die Vergötterung
der Götz(e), idol
der Gottseibeiuns, (God be with
    us) Old Nick

142. g r a b e n (g r u b, g e g r a=
b e n), (*grave*) *dig, delve*

ausgraben, excavate; die Aus=
grabung

begraben, bury; das Begräbnis

der Graben, ditch

das Grab, grave

der Toten(dead)gräber, gravedigger

die Gruft, tomb, sepulcher

die Grube, pit

das Grübchen, (slight impression)
dimple

grübeln, delve, rack one's brain

der Grübler, die Grübelei

143. d e r G r a m, (*grim*)
grief, sorrow

grämlich, sullen; die Grämlichkeit

sich grämen, grieve

vergrämt, sorrowful

der Grimm, grim, rage, wrath

der Ingrimm, anger

grimmig, ingrimmig

ergrimmen, be enraged

144. g r e i f e n (g r i f f, g e=
g r i f f e n), (*gripe*) *grasp, seize,
catch*

greifbar, seizable, palpable

handgreiflich, evident

der Griff, grip, hold, handle

angreifen, attack; der Angriff

begreifen, conceive; der Begriff

abgegriffen, worn out

ergriffen, thrilled

angegriffen, exhausted

die Ergreifung, seizure, arrest

145. g r o b, *rough, coarse, rude*

die Grobheit; der Grobian, boor

146. g r o ß, *great, big, large,
tall, grand*

der Großvater, die Großmutter

die Großstadt, metropolis

der Großstädter, großstädtisch

die Großmut (mood), generosity

großmütig

der Gernegroß (yearn), would-be-
great

die Größe, greatness, size

vergrößern, magnify; die Vergröße=
rung

das Vergrößerungsglas

147. d e r G r u n d, *ground,
soil, foundation*

der Abgrund (off, without), abyss

der Grundsatz (setzen), foundation,
principle

grundsätzlich, on general principles

gründen, begründen, ground, found

der Gründer, die Gründung

begründen, substantiate; die Be=
gründung

gründlich, thorough; die Gründlich=
keit

unergründlich, impenetrable

grundlos, die Grundlosigkeit

148. g r ü ß e n, *greet, salute*

begrüßen, welcome; die Begrüßung

der Gruß, greeting

149. die Gunst, (*kindness*) *favor*

die Misgunst, envy, grudge
die Ungunst, disfavor
günstig, misgünstig, ungünstig
begünstigen, favor
die Begünstigung, discrimination
der Günstling, favorite
gönnen, be kindly disposed, favor
der Gönner, patron, protector

150. gut (besser, am besten), *good*

nichts für ungut, do not feel offended
das Gut, die Güter, goods, estate, farm, merchandise
der Güterzug, freight train
begütert, well to do
gütig, good, kind
begütigen, (make good) appease
sich gütlich tun (do), be good to oneself, pamper oneself
vergüten, (make good) refund
die Vergütung, refunding
die Güte, goodness, kindness
gutmütig (mood), good-natured
bessern, better, improve
ausbessern, repair
verbessern, correct
die Besserung, better health
die Ausbesserung, Verbesserung
unverbesserlich, incorrigible
büßen, (do better) pay for, atone
die Buße, penitence
der Büßer, die Büßerin, penitent

die Verbüßung, serving a term in prison

151. das Haar, *hair*

haarig, behaart, hairy

152. haben (hatte, gehabt), *have*

die Habe, Habseligkeiten, (*plur.*) belongings
die Handhabe, handle; handhaben
wohlhabend, wealthy; die Wohlhabenheit
die Habsucht (siech, sick, mania), covetousness; habsüchtig
vorhaben, (have before one's mind) intend
das Vorhaben, intention, plan

153. der Hader, *quarrel, dispute*

hadern

154. die Haft, (Lat. capio, *captivity*) *custody, imprisonment*

anhaften, (be caught) stick to
verhaften, arrest; die Verhaftung
haftbar, responsible, liable
die Haftung, die Haftbarkeit
heften, (cause to stick) fasten together, stitch
einheften, fasten together, file
das Heft, (stitched) book, file
das Heft eines Schwertes, haft, hilt of a sword
das Heftpflaster, court plaster

155. der Hag, die Hecke, *haw, hedge*

behaglich, (hedged in) peaceful, comfortable; die Behaglichkeit
der Hain, Hagen, grove
das Gehege, enclosure
hegen, (keep enclosed) foster, cherish
einhegen, umhegen

156. hager, *haggard, lean*
die Hagerkeit

157. der Hahn, *(hen) rooster, faucet, trigger*

die Henne, hen; das Huhn, chicken
das Hühnerauge (eye), corn on the foot

158. der Haken, *hook*

haken
häkelig, (hooky) ticklish, critical
häkeln, work in crochet
die Häkelei, crochet work

159. halb, *half*

die Halbinsel, peninsula; die —kugel, hemisphere; der —mond, crescent
die Hälfte, half
halbieren, bisect; die Halbierung

160. hallen, *sound, resound*

der Hall, sound
der Wieder(again)hall, echo
einhellig, (one sound) unanimous

die Einhelligkeit
hell, clear, bright, light, shrill
die Helle, Helligkeit
der Hellseher, clairvoyant
erhellen, become light, evident

161. halten (hielt, gehalten), *hold*

der Halt, hold, support
der Anhalt, (something to hold on to) basis
der Haushalt; die Haushälterin, housekeeper
haushälterisch, economical
haltbar, durable; die Haltbarkeit
sich enthalten (off), abstain
enthaltsam, die Enthaltsamkeit
enthalten, (hold inside) contain
der Inhalt, contents
aufhalten, hold up, detain
unaufhaltsam, uncheckable
sich aufhalten, (detain oneself) stay
der Aufenthalt, detention, sojourn
unterhalten, entertain, converse
die Unterhaltung
der Halter, holder; der Behälter, tank
das Verhalten, action, conduct
das Verhältnis, ratio, proportion
die Haltung, attitude

162. die Hand, *hand*

handlich, handy; die Handlichkeit
aushändigen, einhändigen, hand
handhaben, handle; die Handhabung
behende, handy, quick; die Behendigkeit

der Handel, (handling of merchandise) trade, commerce
der Händler, dealer
die Handlung, store, action, act
handeln, deal, trade; ab—, bargain; be—, treat; ver—, negotiate
die Behandlung, Verhandlung

163. hangen (hing, gehangen), hang, be suspended
abhängen, depend
abhängig, dependent; die Abhängigkeit
der Hang, propensity, inclination
der Abhang, slope
der Anhang, followers, appendix (book)
der Anhänger, adherent
anhänglich, attached to; die Anhänglichkeit
der Vorhang, curtain; Zusammen—, connection
der Henkel, handle
das Gehänge, festoon, garland
hängen, hang, suspend
behängen, cover with; ver—, cover by a curtain
das Verhängnis, fate, destiny
verhängnisvoll, fateful
henken, hang; der Henker, hangman

164. der Harm, harm, grief, sorrow
harmlos, die Harmlosigkeit
sich abhärmen, grieve, pine

165. hart, hard
hartnäckig (neck), stubborn
die Hartnäckigkeit
die Härte, hardness, cruelty
abhärten, harden; er—, confirm; ver—, obdurate
die Abhärtung, Er—, Ver—

166. haschen, snatch, seize
erhaschen; der Häscher, bailiff

167. der Haß, hate, hatred
hassen, hate
häßlich, hateful, homely; die Häßlichkeit
verhaßt, hated, odious
gehässig, malicious; die Gehässigkeit

168. der Hauch, breath
hauchen
keuchen, cough, pant
der Keuchhusten, whooping-cough

169. der Haufe, heap, pile
häufen, heap, pile
häufig, frequent; die Häufigkeit

170. das Haupt (Häupter) (Lat. caput) head
der Hauptmann, captain
der Häuptling, chieftain
enthaupten, behead; die Enthauptung
die Behauptung, statement, assertion

behaupten, state, assert
überhaupt, in general

171. das Haus, house

häuslich, domestic; die Häuslichkeit, home life
hausen, reside; die Behausung, lodging
das Gehäuse, casing, case

172. die Haut, hide, skin

die häutige Bräune, croup
häuten, strip off the skin

173. heben (hob, gehoben) (heave) lift, raise

aufheben, pick up, put in a safe place, lift, suspend
erheblich, (fit to be raised) important, weighty
erhaben, elevated, sublime; die Erhabenheit
der Urheber, (original raiser) author
der Hebel, lever
der Hub, lift, stroke (piston)

174. das Heer, (harry, plunder) army, host

verheeren, devastate; die Verheerung

175. der Heide, heathen, pagan

die Heidin; das Heidentum, paganism
heidnisch

die Heide, das Heideland, heath, forest
die Heidelbeere, bilberry

176. heilen, (heal) cure, save (the soul)

die Heilung, cure
heilbar, curable; die Heilbarkeit
heilsam, wholesome
das Heil, welfare, salvation
heillos (less), mischievous, wicked
der Heiland, Saviour
das Unheil, harm, mischief

177. heilig, holy, saint

der, die Heilige, saint
das Heiligtum, sanctuary
die Heiligkeit, sanctity
Allerheiligen, All Saints' Day
der heilige Abend, Christmas Eve
heiligen, sanctify
entheiligen, desecrate; die Entheiligung
schein(shine, appear)heilig, sanctimonious
die Scheinheiligkeit

178. das Heim, home

einheimsen, bring into the home, garner
anheimeln, remind of home
heimisch, homelike
unheimlich, uncanny
heimlich, relating to the home, private, secret
die Heimlichkeit

verheimlichen, conceal; die Ver=
  heimlichung
geheim, private, secret
das Geheimnis, secret, mystery
geheimnisvoll, mysterious
die Heimat, home, native country
heimatlich, homelike
heimatslos, homeless; die Heimats=
  losigkeit

179. h e i f e r, *hoarse*
die Heiferkeit

180. h e i ß, *hot*
heizen, heat; der Heizer, fireman
die Dampfheizung, steam heat
die Hitze, heat
hitzig, hot-headed
erhitzen, heat

181. h e l f e n (h a l f,
  g e h o l f e n), *help*
der Helfer, die Hilfe
der Gehilfe, assistant
der Not(need)behelf, shift
hilflos (less), die Hilflosigkeit
behilflich, helpful
unbeholfen, awkward; die Unbe=
  holfenheit

182. d e r H e r b f t, (*harvest*)
  autumn, fall
herbftlich

183. d i e H e r d e, *herd, flock*
der Hirt, herdsman

184. d a s H e r z, *heart*
herzhaft, courageous
herzlos (less), die Herzlosigkeit
herzig, lovely, charming
beherzt, bold-hearted
herzen, hug
beherzigen, take to heart

185. h e t z e n (h a f f e n, *hate*),
  stir hatred
aufhetzen, instigate
die Hetze, der Hetzer, die Hetzerei
die Hetzjagd, race hunting

186. h e u d) e l n, *dissemble*
der Heuchler, hypocrite; die Heuch=
  lerin, die Heuchelei, heuchlerisch

187. d i e H e r e, (*hag,
  old woman*), *witch*
die Hexerei, witchcraft
der Hexenmeister (master), wizard
hexen, behexen

188. h i n d e r n, *hinder, prevent*
das Hindernis, obstacle
hinderlich, cumbersome

189. h o d), *high*
die Hoheit, highness
die Höhe, Anhöhe, height
erhöhen, raise; die Erhöhung
höher (higher), höchft (highest)
höchlichft, exceedingly
der Hügel, hill; hügelig

190. hoffen, *hope*

unverhofft, unhoped for
hoffentlich, it is to be hoped
die Hoffnung, hope
hoffnungslos (less), die Hoffnungs=
    losigkeit

191. hohl, *hollow*

die Höhle, hollow, cave
aushöhlen, hollow out
hehlen, verhehlen, (put in a cave)
    conceal
unverhohlen
der Hehler, concealer of stolen goods
die Hehlerei
die Hülle, wrap, cover, veil
die Hülse, hull, husk
hüllen, wrap, cover, veil
in Hülle und Fülle, enough and
    to spare

192. höhnisch, (*heinous*), *scornful, sneering*

verhöhnen, sneer at
der Hohn, sneer, mockery

193. holen, (*haul*) *get, fetch*

abholen, call for
abholen lassen, send for
wieder(again)holen, repeat
erholen, recover from illness
die Erholung, Wiederholung

194. hören, *hear*

erhören, hear grant; die Erhörung
unerhört

von Hörensagen (say)
das Gehör, hearing; hörbar, au-
    dible
horchen, harken, listen
der Horcher
gehorsam, obedient; der Gehorsam

195. die Hose, (*hose, hosiery*) *trousers*

die Hosenträger (tragen, carry;
    plur.), suspenders
die Wasserhose, waterspout

196. der Hof, *yard, court*

der Hofmann, courtier
der Bahnhof, station building
hofieren, court
höfisch, courtly
hübsch, pretty, comely
höflich, courteous, polite
die Höflichkeit
das Gehöft, farm.

197. der Hund, (*hound*) *dog*

die Hündin, hündisch
verhunzen, spoil, run down

198. der Hunger, *hunger*

die Hungersnot (need), famine
hungern, be hungry
aushungern, subdue by hunger
verhungern, starve to death
hungrig
der Heiß(hot)hunger, greediness

199. der Hut, *hat*

der Hutmacher, hatter
hüten, heed
behüten, protect
verhüten, prevent
der Hüter, keeper; die Verhütung
behutsam, cautious; die Behutsamkeit
die Nachhut, rear guard
die Obhut (over), protection, charge

200. in, *in*

das Inland, interior; der Insasse (sitzen), inmate
innewerden, get inside of, become aware of
innen, within
drinnen (da-r-innen), drin, in there
binnen (b-innen), within
das Binnengewässer, inland water
inner, inside, internal
innerlich, cordial; die Innerlichkeit
innig, cordial; die Innigkeit
erinnern, (get from within) remind
sich erinnern, remember
erinnerlich, rememberable; die Erinnerung

201. irren, *err*

sich beirren lassen, allow oneself to be duped
sich verirren, go astray
unbeirrt, without erring
irrig, erroneous

der Irre, madman
der Irrgarten, labyrinth
der Irrsinn (sense), insanity
der Irrtum (Irrtümer), error, mistake
die Abirrung, aberration
die Verirrung, perversion
irrtümlich, erroneous

202. ja, *yes*

jawohl, well yes, certainly
das Jawort, acceptance of a proposal
bejahen, affirm; die Bejahung

203. jagen, *hunt, chase*

der Jäger, hunter
die Jagd, hunt, chase

204. das Jahr, *year*

das Jahrzehnt (ten), decade
das Jahrhundert, century
das Früh(early)jahr, spring; Neu—; Schalt (slide)—, leap year
jährlich, yearly, annual
großjährig, of age
minder(minus)jährig, under age
bejahrt, elderly
verjähren, become outlawed; die Verjährung
Jahr und Tag, a long time

205. jauchzen, *shout, exult*

der Jauchzer

206. das Joch, *yoke*

unterjochen, subdue; die Unter=
jochung

207. der Jude, *Jew*

die Jüdin, jüdisch, das Judentum

208. jung, *young*

verjüngen, renovate
die Verjüngung
jüngst, recently
der jüngste Tag, Doomsday
der Jünger, disciple; der Jüngling,
youth
die Jungfrau, Jungfer, maid
jungfräulich, maidenlike
der Junggesell, bachelor
der Junker (junge Herr), squire
die Jugend, youth
das Jugendalter, die Jugendzeit,
youth
der Jugendstil, modern style
jugendlich, youthful

209. kahl, (*callow*) bald

die Kahlheit, der Kahlkopf (head)
kahlköpfig, die Kahlköpfigkeit

210. der Kahn, *boat*

die Kahnfahrt (ride), kahnen

211. der Kalk, (*chalk*) lime

verkalken, get calcined; die Ver=
kalkung

212. kalt, *cold*

die Kälte, cold
sich erkälten, catch a cold; die
Erkältung

213. die Kammer, *chamber*

der Kämmerer, chamberlain
die Kämmerei, treasury board

214. der Kampf, (Lat. cam-
pus, *field, battle-field*) *combat,
fight, conflict*

der Zweikampf, duel
der Kämpfer, fighter (champion)
kämpfen

215. ich kann (können,
konnte, gekonnt), *I can,
understand, know, am able*

ich kann nicht umhin, I cannot get
around it, I cannot help it
die Kunst, ability, skill, art
der Künstler, die Künstlerin, artist
künstlich, artificial
künstlerisch, artistic
gekünstelt, affected

216. die Kanzel, *chancel,
pulpit*

der Kanzler, chancellor
die Kanzlei, chancery
der Reichs(empire)kanzler
abkanzeln, turn down, scold

217. die Kappe, *cap* (*cape*)

Rotkäppchen, Red Riding Hood

verkappt, disguised
die Kapuze, hood

218. die Karte, *card, chart*

das Kartenhaus, castle in the air
die Ansichts(sight)karte, souvenir
postal card
die Landkarte (map), Post—;
Speise—, bill of fare
abkarten, concert, plot

**219. die Kasse, *cash, ready
money, ticket window***

der Kassier(er), die Kassiererin
einkassieren, collect

**220. der Kasten, *chest,
case, box***

der Brief(letter)kasten; Brust-
(breast)—, chest
die Kiste, case, chest, box
die Kaste, caste

221. die Katze, *cat*

der Kater, male cat

222. kauen, *chew*

zerkauen, chew up
wieder(again)kauen, ruminate
der Wiederkäuer

**223. kaufen, (*cheap*)
*buy, purchase***

abkaufen, buy from
verkaufen, (trade away) sell
der Kauf, Verkauf

der Ausverkauf, bargain sale
der Kaufmann, merchant
kaufmännisch, commercial, mercan-
tile
käuflich, purchasable; verkäuflich,
salable
das Kauffahrteischiff, merchantman
der Käufer, purchaser; Einkäufer,
buyer
der Verkäufer, salesman; die Ver-
käuferin

224. die Kehle, *throat*

der Kehlkopf (head), larynx
die Kniekehle, knee-hollow

225. der Keller, *cellar*

der Kellner, waiter

**226. kennen (kannte,
gekannt), (*ken*) *know***

bekennen, (make known) confess
erkennen, recognize
anerkennen, recognize, appreciate
verkennen, mistake
anerkennenswert (worth), credita-
ble
unverkennbar, unmistakable
das Bekenntnis, die Anerkennung
der Kenner, connoisseur
kenntlich, distinguishable
erkenntlich, appreciative
das Kennzeichen (token), distinctive mark
kennzeichnen, characterize
die Kenntnis, knowledge
bekannt, acquainted, familiar

bekanntlich, it is well known
der Bekannte, die Bekanntschaft,
   acquaintance
der Kunde, die Kundin, business
   acquaintance, customer
die Kundschaft, trade
die Kunde, information
kundig, familiar with
die Urkunde (erkennen), document
urkundlich, by document
kundschaften, (gather information)
   spy
auskundschaften, reconnoiter
der Kundschafter, scout
künden, (give knowledge) announce
ankünden, verkünden, announce
ankündigen, verkündigen, announce
die Ankündigung, Verkündigung
kündigen, give notice of withdrawal
die Kündigung, notice of withdrawal
sich erkundigen, inform oneself, in-
   quire
die Erkundigung
bekunden, demonstrate; die Bekun-
   dung
kundgeben (give), manifest
die Kundgebung

227. der Kerker (Lat. carcer,
   incarcerate), *prison, dungeon*
der Kerkermeister (master), turnkey
einkerkern

228. die Kette, (Lat. catena)
   chain
verketten, link together, concatenate

229. der Kiel, *keel, careen*

das Kielwasser, wake
der Kiel, quill
der Keil, wedge
einkeilen, wedge in
die Keilschrift (script), cuneiform
   characters

230. das Kind, *(kin) child*

die Kindheit, childhood
die Kinderei, childishness
von Kindesbeinen (bone, leg) an,
   from the earliest childhood
kindlich, childlike
kindisch, childish

231. das Kinn, *chin*

der Kinnbacken, jaw-bone

232. die Kirche, *church*

der Kirchhof (yard); —turm
   (tower), steeple
kirchlich, ecclesiastical
die Kirmes (Kirchmesse), anniversary of a church, annual fair

233. klagen, *complain, lament*

anklagen, accuse; be—, deplore;
   sich be—, complain; ver—, sue
die Anklage, die —schrift (script),
   indictment
der, die Angeklagte, defendant
der Kläger, die Klägerin, plaintiff
kläglich, lamentable

234. klar, *clear*

aufklären, enlighten; sich auf—,
clear up; er—, declare, explain;
ver—, glorify
die Aufklärung, Er—, Ver—
die Klarheit, clearness, plainness
aufgeklärt, enlightened; die Aufge=
klärtheit

235. kleben, *paste, stick*

ankleben, post; be—, line with
kleberig, sticky
der Klebestoff, mucilage
der Kleister, paste; kleistern
die Klette, clotbur

**236. das Kleid, *cloth, garment,
gown, dress***

kleiden, dress, fit, become
sich ankleiden, dress; sich aus—, undress; ent—, undress; um—,
redress (change); ver—, disguise; die Verkleidung
die Kleidung, clothing
kleidsam, becoming, fitting

237. klein, *(lean) small, little*

kleinlich, mean, paltry; die Klein=
lichkeit
die Kleinigkeit, small matter, trifle
das Kleinod (Kleinodien), small
jewel, trinket
verkleinern, reduce; die Verkleine=
rung

238. klemmen, *pinch, squeeze*

beklemmen, oppress; die Beklem=
mung
beklommen, anxious; die Beklom=
menheit
in der Klemme, in a fix
der Klemmer, eye-glasses
die Klammer, clamp, clasp
anklammern, fasten with clamps
einklammern, put in brackets

**239. klingen (klang, ge=
klungen), *(clank) sound,
tingle, ring***

verklingen, die away, expire
der Klang, sound, tune
die Klingel, bell; klingeln, ring the
bell

240. klopfen, *knock, beat*

anklopfen, aus—
der Klöpfel, knocker

**241. das Kloster, *cloister,
convent***

klösterlich, monastic
die Klause, (close) cell, hermitage
die Klausur, seclusion
der Klausner, hermit, recluse

**242. die Kluft, *(cleft)
gap, chasm***

zerklüftet, full of fissures

243. klug, *clever, prudent*

altklug, precocious

ftaatšflug, politic, diplomatic
die Klugheit, prudence
ausflügeln, puzzle out
die Klügelei, sophistry

244. der Klumpen
clump, mass

der Klumpatsch, awkward person
flumpig, clumsy

245. der Knabe, (knave) boy

knabenhaft, boyish
das Knabenalter (age), boyhood
der Knappe, esquire
der Bergknappe, miner
die Knappschaft, mining company

246. der Knall, (knell)
clap, report

Knall und Fall, suddenly (report
of a gun and fall of the victim)
fnallen, give a report, crack

247. knarren, (gnarl)
creak, rattle

die Knarre, rattle
knurren, gnarl, snarl, grunt
knurrig, das Geknurr
knirschen, gnash one's teeth

248. der Knecht, (knight, serv-
ant of a liege lord) servant,
farmhand

die Knechtschaft, servitude
fnechtisch, servile
der Hausknecht, porter
fnechten, oppress; die Knechtung

249. kneifen (kniff, ge-
niffen), nip, pinch, squeeze

abfnipsen, clip

250. das Knie, knee

fnieen, kneel

251. der Knochen
(knuckle) bone

der Knöchel, knuckle, ankle
fnochig, bony
verknöchert, ossified, narrow-
minded

252. der Knopf, (knob) button

knöpfen, button
knüpfen, button, connect
die Knospe, bud; fnospen
der Knauf, knob; der Knüppel,
knobby stick

253. der Knoten, knot

der Knotenpunkt, railroad junction
fnotig, knotty; fnoten, knot
der Knödel, dumpling
die Knute, knout; der Knüttel,
knotty stick

254. der Koch, cook

die Köchin, cook
fochen, cook; die Küche, kitchen
der Kuchen, cake

255. die Kohle, coal

der Köhler, collier

kohlraben(raven)schwarz, coal-black
verkohlen, carbonize, char

256. kommen (kam, ge-kommen), *come*

ankommen, arrive; be—, (come by) obtain, receive, agree with; ent—, escape; entgegen-(against)—, meet, treat kindly; überein—, agree; unter—, (under roof) secure a position, find shelter; ver—, go to the bad; vor—, appear, occur; zuvor—, be beforehand, prevent, meet; entgegenkommend, zuvor—, obliging

das Einkommen, income; Unter—, shelter
der Nachkomme, descendant; die Nachkommenschaft, offspring
der Abkömmling, descendant; An—, arrival
das Vorkommnis, occurrence, incident
die Zuvorkommenheit, politeness
willkommen, welcome
das Willkommen, bewillkommnen, die Bewillkommnung
abkömmlich, disengaged
herkömmlich, (coming here from the past) traditional; das Herkommen
die Abkunft, descent, origin; An—, arrival; Her—, descent; Über-ein—, agreement; Unter—, shelter; Zu—, (to come) future

künftig, zukünftig, future
mein Zukünftiger, my intended husband

257. der König, *king*

die Königin, queen
das Königreich (realm), kingdom
königlich, royal

258. der Kopf, (*cup*) *head*

kopflos (less), thoughtless
die Kopflosigkeit
kopfüber, head over heels
köpfen, behead
die Kuppe, der Gipfel, summit
gipfeln, culminate

259. der Körper (*corpse*) *body*

die Körperschaft, organization
körperlich, corpor(e)al
verkörpern, embody; die Verkörpe-rung

260. kosten, *cost*

die Kosten, Unkosten, (*plur.*) cost, expense
kostbar, precious; die Kostbarkeit
köstlich, delicious
kostspielig, expensive

261. kosten, *relish, taste*

die Kost, food, fare
beköstigen, furnish with board; die Beköstigung

262. die Kraft, (*craft*, in a physical sense) *strength, force, power*

die Kraftstation, power-house

kraftlos, weak, feeble; die Kraftlosigkeit

kraftvoll, vigorous

kräftig, strong, powerful

kräftigen, strengthen

bekräftigen, corroborate

die Kräftigung, Bekräftigung

entkräften, debilitate

die Entkräftung, exhaustion

263. krank, (*cranky*, in a physical sense) *ill, sick*

die Krankheit, illness, sickness

krankhaft, morbid; die Krankhaftigkeit

erkranken, fall sick; die Erkrankung

kränken, cause to feel sick, offend

die Kränkung

kränklich, sickly

kränkeln, be ailing

264. der Kranz, (*crown*) *wreath, garland*

das Kränzchen, little wreath, girls' club

bekränzen, wreathe, crown

265. kraus, *curly, crisp*

kräuseln, curl

Krausebeere, gouse(kraus)berry

266. der Kreis, *circle, orbit, district*

kreisförmig, circular

kreisen, circulate

der Kreisel, top, whirligig

267. das Kreuz, *cross*

der Kreuzer, cruiser, penny

der Kreuzfahrer (traveler), crusader

der Kreuzzug (ziehen, march), crusade

kreuzen, cross; die Kreuzung

der Kreuzband (binden), newspaper wrapper

sich bekreuzen, make the sign of the cross

kreuzigen, crucify; die Kreuzigung

die Kreuz und die Quer, crisscross

268. kriechen (kroch, gekrochen), (*crouch*) *creep, crawl*

sich verkriechen, creep into a safe place

der Kriecher, toady; die Kriecherei

krauchen, crouch

269. der Krieg, *war*

der Krieger, warrior

kriegerisch, warlike

der Bürgerkrieg, civil war

bekriegen, make war upon

kriegen, get, obtain; sich —, get each other, be married

270. die Krone, *crown*

der Kronprinz, die Kronprinzessin

krönen; die Krönung, coronation

271. der Krug, (*crock-ery*) *pitcher, jar*

die Kruke, stone bottle
der Krug, (Polish) inn
der Krüger, innkeeper

272. die Kugel, *ball, bullet, globe*

die Halbkugel, hemisphere
kugelig, kugelförmig, globular
das Kügelchen, globule

273. kühl, *cool*

die Kühle, coolness
die Kühlheit, reservedness
abkühlen, cool down; die Abkühlung

274. kühn, (*keen*) *bold, daring*

toll(dull, mad)kühn, audacious
die Kühnheit, Toll—
sich erkühnen, dare

275. der Kummer, (*encumbrance*) *grief*

kümmern, grieve, concern
unbekümmert, unconcerned
kümmerlich, miserable

276. küren (*kor, gekoren*) *choose, elect*

der, die Auserkorene, sweetheart
der Kurfürst (first, prince), elector
das Kurfürstentum, electorate

277. kurz, (*curt*) *short, brief*

kürzlich, recently

abkürzen, ver—, abridge
die Abkürzung, abbreviation
kurzsichtig, near-sighted; die Kurzsichtigkeit

278. der Kuß, *kiss*

küssen, kiss

279. die Kutsche, *coach, carriage*

die Kutschenfahrt (ride)
der Kutscher, driver; der —bock, box
kutschieren, ride in a carriage

280. die Kutte, (*coat*) *cowl*

der Kittel, jumper

281. lachen, *laugh*

der Lacher
lachhaft, lächerlich, ridiculous
das Gelächter, laughter
lächeln, smile

282. laden (*lud, geladen*) *load, charge*

ab(off)laden, auf(on)—, aus(out, un-)—; be—, burden; ein(in)—; ver—, ship
überladen, overdone; die Überladenheit, lavish decoration
die Lade, box for storing things, drawer

283. lahm, *lame*

die Lahmheit, Lähmung, palsy

gelähmt; die Gelähmtheit, lameness

erlahmen, lose strength

die Erlahmung, loss of strength

284. das Land, *land, country*

das Ausland, foreign countries

der Ausländer, ausländisch

die Ländereien, landed property

das Gelände, tract of land

hierzulande, in this country

die Landschaft, landscape

landschaftlich, scenic

die Landenge (narrow), isthmus

der Landmann, farmer

der Landsmann, fellow-countryman

die Landsmännin

der Landwirt (warden), farmer

die Landwirtschaft, farming

ländlich, rural

der Ländler, country dance

landen, land

die Landung, landing

285. lang, *long*

entlang, längs, along

die Länge, length

die Lang(e)weile (while), boredom

sich langweilen, bore oneself

länglich, oblong

verlängern, elongate; die Verlängerung

lange, a long time

langsam, slow; die Langsamkeit

verlangsamen, reduce speed

langen, lengthen, reach, hand

anlangen, reach the goal, arrive

was anbelangt, as regards

hinlänglich, long enough, sufficient

unzulänglich, insufficient

verlangen, long for, demand

das Verlangen

von Belang, of importance

286. lassen (ließ, gelassen), *let, leave*

auslassen, omit; ent—, dismiss; hinter—, leave behind, bequeath, leave word; sich nieder(beneath, down)—, settle; unter—, (leave under) leave alone; ver—, desert, abandon; sich ver—, rely upon; zu—, admit

die Auslassung, Nieder—, Unter—

die Verlassenheit, dereliction

die Hinterlassenschaft, estate

ausgelassen, (let out, *of animals*) exuberant; die Ausgelassenheit

der Anlaß, (let on) instigation, cause

anläßlich, because of

unerläßlich, indispensable

fahrlässig, careless

die Fahrlässigkeit

nachlässig, (leave behind) neglectful

die Nachlässigkeit

vernachlässigen, neglect

die Vernachlässigung

zuverlässig, reliable

die Zuverlässigkeit

lässig, lazy; die Lässigkeit

gelassen, calm; die Gelassenheit

das Gelaß, (place in which to leave things) room, space

287. die Laſt (laden, *load*) *burden*

belaſten, burden; ent(un-) —
läſtig, burdensome, troublesome
beläſtigen, molest; die Beläſtigung

288. das Laſter, *vice*

laſterhaft, vicious
läſtern, slander, defame
läſterlich, der Läſterer, die Läſterung

289. das Laub, (*leaf*) *foliage*

die Laube, arbor, bower (lodge)
belauben, cover with leaves
entlauben, shed the leaves

290. laufen (lief, gelaufen), (*leap*) *run*

der Lauf, run, course
die Laufbahn (track), career
der Läufer, runner
der Ausläufer, foothill; Über—, deserter
beiläufig, (running alongside) by the way
geläufig, fluent; die Geläufigkeit
vorläufig, (running ahead) for the time being

291. die Laune, (*lunacy*) *humor, temper*

launig, humorous
launiſch, launenhaft, freakish

292. laut, *loud, distinct*

lauten, sound, read; ver—, (become loud) be reported·
der Laut, sound
lautlos, silent
läuten, (make a noise) ring a bell
das Geläute, ringing of bells

293. lauter, *pure*

lauter Bücher, (purely) nothing but books
läutern, purify, refine; die Läuterung
erläutern, explain; die Erläuterung

294. leben, *live*

beleben, animate; er—, experience; über—, survive; ver—, spend
abgelebt, effete; die Abgelebtheit
das Erlebnis, experience
lebendig, alive, lively
lebhaft, vivacious
leblos, lifeless
die Lebendigkeit, Lebhaftigkeit
das Leben, life
das Ableben, death; Vor—, antecedents
der Leib, (that which lives) body
leiblich, corpor(e)al, natural
leibhaftig, bodily
beleibt, stout; die Beleibtheit
entleiben, kill, murder
einverleiben, incorporate; die Einverleibung

295. leđen, *lick*

lecfer, dainty; die Lecferei
lecferhaft, lickerish
ungeleđt, untidy

296. lehnen, *lean*

ſich anlehnen, lean against
ſich auflehnen, rebel
der Lehnſtuhl, armchair; die Lehne, back

297. leiđt, *light* (to carry),
easy (to do)

leiđthin, lightly
die Leiđtigfeit, facility
erleiđtern, facilitate
die Erleiđterung
den Anfer liđten; das Liđterſđiff

**298. leiden (litt, gelit=
ten),** (*loathe*) *suffer, endure*

das Leid, suffering, grief
es tut mir leid, it causes me sorrow
leidliđ, tolerable
zu meinem größten Leidweſen (regret)
das Leiden, ailment
das Beileid, Mit—, suffering with
others, sympathy
bemitleiden, pity
beleidigen, (cause to suffer) insult
die Beleidigung
die Leidenſchaft (suffering), passion
leidenſchaftliđ, passionate
in Mitleidenſchaft ziehen, (draw
into fellow-suffering) implicate

**299. leihen (lieh, gelie=
hen),** *loan, lend*

die Anleihe, loan
das Lehen, Lehn, fief, feudal tenure
das Darlehen, loan
belehnen, invest; die Belehnung,
investiture
entlehnen, borrow; die Entlehnung

300. leinen, linnen, *made
of linen*

die Leinwand (das Gewand, gown),
linen
der Leinweber (weaver)

301. leiten, *lead*

die Leitung, guidance, management
das Geleit, escort
der Leitfaden (fathom, string),
guiding line
begleiten, escort, accompany
der Begleiter, die Begleitung

302. lenfen, *bend, govern*

lenfbar, —ſam, manageable, dirigible
der Lenfer, ruler, governor
das Gelenf, (link) joint
das Handgelenf, wrist; Fuß—,
ankle
gelenfig, flexible; die Gelenfigfeit
ungelenf, stiff, clumsy

303. lernen, *learn*

verlernen, forget
erlernbar, learnable
lehren, teach; belehren, inform

die Lehre, apprenticeship; die Belehrung

lehrreich (rich), instructive
gelehrig, docile; die Gelehrigkeit
gelehrsam, gelehrt, scholarly
die Gelehrsamkeit, Gelehrtheit, erudition
der Gelehrte, scholar
der Lehrer, die —in, teacher
der Lehrling, apprentice
die Lehre, doctrine, theory

304. lesen (las, gelesen), read

leserlich, legible
belesen, well read; die Belesenheit
die Vorlesung, lecture
lesen, (col-lect) pick, gather
auflesen, pick up; aus—, pick out
die Auslese, selection
die Weinlese, vintage

305. licht, light, bright, shining

das Licht, light, candle
das Bogenlicht, arc light
das Glüh(glow)licht, incandescent light
das Gasglühlicht, Welsbach light
lichterloh, in full blaze
die Lichtung, clearing
belichten, expose; die Belichtung
leuchten, give light, shine
beleuchten, illuminate; die Beleuchtung
das Leuchtgas
der Leuchter, candlestick

der Kron(crown)leuchter, chandelier
die Leuchte, luminary
erlaucht, illustrious, noble
die Durchlaucht, Serene Highness
durchlauchtig, illustrious, serene

306. die Liebe, love

der Liebling, darling
das Lieblingsbuch, favorite book
die Liebelei, flirtation
der Liebhaber, die —in, amateur
der Liebreiz, charm
liebäugeln (das Auge, eye), flirt
lieblich, lovely; die Lieblichkeit
lieblos, unkind; die Lieblosigkeit
liebevoll, affectionate
liebenswürdig (worthy), amiable
die Liebenswürdigkeit
lieb, dear, beloved, agreeable
lieben, love
sich verlieben, fall in love
die Verliebtheit, infatuation
es beliebt mir, it suits me
nach Belieben, (according to liking) as you please
beliebig, optional; mis—
beliebt, popular; die Beliebtheit
fürlieb, vor— nehmen, (take for love) be pleased

307. liefern, (de-liver) furnish, supply

ausliefern, extradite; die Auslieferung
die Lieferung, delivery, part of a set
der Lieferant, purveyor

308. liegen (lag, gelegen), *lie, be situated*

gelegen, well situated, opportune
die Gelegenheit, opportunity
die Lage, site, situation
das Lager, (layer) couch, store, camp
lagern, camp, store
belagern, besiege; die Belagerung,
    der Belagerer
legen, lay, put, place
belegt, coated
überlegen, superior; die Überlegenheit
überlegt, considerate; die Überlegtheit
überlegen, consider; die Überlegung
verlegen, mislay, embarrass
die Verlegenheit

309. lindern, *alleviate, soften*

die Linderung, alleviation
gelinde, soft, gentle

310. link, *left*

links, on the left
linkisch, awkward; der Linkser

311. die Lippe, *lip*

die Lefze, lip

312. die List, *cunning, trick, craft*

listig, cunning; überlisten, outwit

313. loben, *praise, commend*

löblich, laudable
das Lob, praise

314. das Loch, *hole*

löcherig, porous
durchlochen, durchlöchern, perforate
das Leck, leak; lecken
die Lücke, (leak) gap, breach
lückenhaft, fragmentary

315. locken, *decoy, allure, entice*

verlocken, entice; die Verlockung

316. der Lorbeer, *laurel*

der Lorbeerkranz (crown), wreath

317. los, *loose*

lösen, loose(n), free
ablösen, relieve; auf—, dissolve;
    aus—, redeem; er—, rescue
die Lösung, solution
die Ablösung, Auf—, Er—
der Erlöser, Redeemer
das Lösegeld (money), ransom
aufgelöst, exhausted; die Aufgelöstheit

318. das Los, *lot, share, fate*

losen, draw lots
die Losung, watchword

319. löschen (losch, geloschen), *extinguish*

unauslöschlich, indelible
das Löschblatt, blotter
eine Ladung (cargo) löschen, discharge

320. **das Lot**, *lead, plummet*

löten, solder

loten, sound; **die Lotung**

321. **die Luft**, *(lift, loft) air*

luftig, airy, flighty

lüften, ventilate; **die Lüftung**

den Hut (hat) lüften (lift)

322. lügen (log, gelogen)
tell a lie

die Lüge, der Lug, lie

der Lügner, liar; lügenhaft, lüg=
nerisch

verlogen, given to lying

die Verlogenheit, habit of lying

leugnen, ab—, deny

unleugbar, undeniable

323. der Lumpen, *(lump)*
rag, tatter

der Lump, ragamuffin, blackguard

lumpig, ragged, shabby

zerlumpt, ragged

324. die Lust, *(lust) enjoy-*
ment, pleasure

die Lustbarkeit, diversion, sport

lustig, merry; **die Lustigkeit**

belustigen, amuse; **die Belustigung**

lüstern, desirous; **die Lüsternheit**

das Gelüst, desire, appetite

325. machen, *make*

vermachen, bequeath; **das Ver=**
mächtnis

das Gemachte, die Gemachtheit,
affectation

der Makler, broker

gemach, to one's liking, slowly, by
degrees

gemächlich, comfortable; **die Ge=**
mächlichkeit

das Ungemach, adversity

326. das Mädchen, *maid, girl*

die Maid (*poetical*)

mädchenhaft, girlish

die Magd, maid servant

das Mägdlein, little girl

327. ich mag (mögen,
mochte, gemocht), *I may,*
I like, desire

ich vermag, I may, am able
(mighty)

das Vermögen, might, wealth

vermögend, well-to-do

möglich, (that which may be done)
possible

die Möglichkeit; ermöglichen, enable

die Macht, might, power

die Ohn(un)macht, faint; Voll=
(full)—, power of attorney;
Über—, superiority

mächtig, mighty; ohn—, fainting

sich bemächtigen, take possession
of; bevoll—, authorize; er—,
authorize

die Ermächtigung

machtlos (less), die Machtlosigkeit

328. das Mahl, *meal*

das Mehl, meal, flour; mehlig
die Mühle, mill; der Müller

329. mahnen, (*re-mind, ad-mon-ish*) *remind, warn*

abmahnen, dissuade; er—, exhort
die Mahnung, Er—

330. die Mähr, *phantastic story*

das Märchen, fairy tale
märchenhaft, fictitious

331. die Mähre, *mare, nag*

der Marstall, royal stud

332. das Mal, *mark, blemish*

das Muttermal; Denk(think)—,
    monument
Grab(grave)—, tombstone
malen, (make marks, design) paint
der Maler, die Malerin, artist
die Malerei, art of painting
malerisch, picturesque
das Gemälde, painting
das Mal, (mark for checking off)
    time
einmal, once; zwei—, twice;
    manch(many a)—
damals, at that time, then
damalig, of that time
einmalig, occurring once
das Einmaleins, multiplication
    table

333. der Mangel, *deficiency, defect*

mangelhaft, defective; die Mangel-
    haftigkeit
in Ermangelung von, in default of
mangeln, be in want of; er—, fail,
    neglect
bemängeln, criticize deficiencies
die Bemängelung

334. der Mann (Män-
    ner), *man*

das Männchen, male animal, mani-
    kin, little man
mannshoch, of a man's height
mannbar (bear), adolescent
die Mannbarkeit
männlich, male, masculine; die
    Männlichkeit
bemannen, man; die Bemannung,
    crew
sich ermannen, brace oneself up
übermannen, overpower
die Mannschaft, squad, team
man, one, somebody

335. der Mantel
    mantle, cloak

der Deckmantel, disguise, pretext
bemänteln, palliate, excuse
die Bemäntelung

336. der Markt, *market*

markten, bargain, haggle

337. der Marsch, *march*

marschieren, march

das Marschland, marsh-land, salt marshes

338. die Marter, (*martyr*) *torment, torture*

martern, torment
der Märtyrer, martyr
das Märtyrertum (dom)

339. die Masern, (plur.) *measles*

die Maser, spot, mark
masern, vein

340. matt, (*check-mate*) *tired, faint*

die Mattigkeit, faintness
ermatten, weaken; die Ermattung
abgemattet, exhausted; die Abge= mattetheit

341. die Mauer, (Lat. murus) *wall*

der Maurer, mason; die Maurerei, masonry
mauern, wall in
das Gemäuer, ruins

342. das Meer, (*mere, lake*) *sea, ocean*

die Meerenge (narrow), strait
über dem Meeresspiegel (mirror), level

343. mehr, *more*

mehrere, several, a few
die Mehrheit, majority

mehren, ver—, increase, augment
die Vermehrung

344. meinen, *mean, think*

vermeintlich, (wrongly thought) supposed
die Meinung, opinion

345. der Meißel, *chisel*

meißeln, chisel

346. meist, *most*

meistens, mostly
der Meister, master, employer; meisterhaft
bemeistern, master, control; die Bemeisterung

347. die Menge, (*among, mingle*) *plenty, crowd*

mengen, mingle
das Gemenge, mixture; Hand—, close fight
das Gemengsel, medley

348. der Mensch, (*man*) *human being, man*

der Unmensch, brute, monster
menschlich, (humane); die Mensch= lichkeit
entmenscht, barbarous, cruel
die Menschheit, mankind

349. merken, *mark, note, perceive*

bemerken, remark, observe

die Anmerkung, annotation; Be—, remark

der Vermerk, remark

merklich, perceptible

merkwürdig (worthy), curious

die Merkwürdigkeit

bemerkenswert (worth), noteworthy

das Merkmal, distinctive mark

unbemerkt, unnoticed

aufmerksam, observing, attentive

die Aufmerksamkeit

brand(brand, fire)marken, stigmatize

350. melden, *report, announce*

abmelden, (report off) cancel, resign, withdraw

anmelden, (report on) announce a visitor, enroll

die Abmeldung, An—

der Feuermelder, fire-alarm box

351. messen (maß, gemessen), *measure*

angemessen, (measured on) adequate

unermeßlich, immense; die Unermeßlichkeit

vermessen, (wrongly measured) presumptuous; die Vermessenheit

der Durch(through)messer, diameter

das Maß, measure

das Eben(even)maß, symmetry; Gleich(like)—, proportion, symmetry

maßvoll, moderate; —los, immoderate

die Maßlosigkeit

mäßig, temperate; die Mäßigkeit

gemäß, (measured on to) in conformity with

maßgebend, (giving the measure, standard) authoritative

unmaßgeblich, unpresuming

nach Maßgabe von, in proportion to

einiger(some)maßen, gewisser(certain)—, in a measure, to some extent

352. die Miete, (*meed*) *rent, hire*

der Mieter, tenant; After—, subtenant

der Mietling, hireling, mercenary

mieten, hire, rent; ver—, let

353. mild, *mild*

die Milde, Mildheit, mildness

mildern, mitigate; die Milderung

354. minder, (*minus*) *less, inferior*

minderjährig (year), under age

die Minderheit, minority

mindern, ver—, decrease; die Verminderung

mindestens, at least

355. mischen, *mix*

sich einmischen, interfere; ver—, mingle

die Miſchung, mixture; Ein—, Ver—

der Miſchling, mongrel

das Gemiſch, mixture

die Gemiſchtheit, mingling of social elements

356. die Mitte, *middle, midst*

die Mitternacht (night); der Mittag (day), noon; Mittwoch (week), Wednesday

das Mittel, means, remedy

das Mittelalter, Middle Ages; —lich

mittellos, pennyless

die Mittelloſigkeit, poverty

emittelt, supplied with means

mitten aus, from the midst; — in, in the midst of

unmittelbar, immediate(ly)

rmitteln, (get from the middle) find out

die Ermittelung, investigation

ermitteln, (act as a middleman) mediate

der Vermittler, die Vermittelung

mittels, mittelſt, by means of

vermittelſt, by means of

357. die Mode, *mode, fashion*

altmodiſch, old-fashioned

358. der Mord, *murder*

der Selbſt(self)mord, suicide

der Mörder, murderer; die —in

mörderiſch, murderous; —lich, violent

morden, er—, assassinate

die Ermordung

359. der Morgen, *morning*

die Morgendämmerung (dim), dawn; —röte (red), dawn

das Morgenland, East, Orient

der Morgenländer, morgenländiſch

morgen, tomorrow; über—, day after tomorrow

der Morgen, a morning's work, acre

360. der Mörſer, *mortar*

morſch, (crushed) brittle

die Morſchheit

361. der Mucker, *hypocrite*

die Muckerei

meucheln, plot, cabal

die Meuchelei

der Meuchelmord, assassination; —mörder

362. die Mühe, *trouble, pains*

mühelos, without pains; —voll, troublesome

ſich abmühen, tire oneself

ſich bemühen, endeavor

die Bemühung

mühſam, troublesome; —ſelig, toilsome

die Mühſamkeit, —ſeligkeit

müde, tired

die Müdigkeit, fatigue

ermüden, become tired

unermüdlich, indefatigable

die Unermüdlichkeit

363. der Mund, *mouth*

mundgerecht (right), palatable

mündlich, oral, verbal

es mundet mir, (it suits my mouth) I relish it

die Mündung, mouth of a river, muzzle of a gun

münden, ein—, empty into

364. das Mündel, *(mound, bulwark) ward*

mündig, of age; die Mündigkeit

der Vormund, (protector) guardian

die Vormundschaft (ship)

365. munter, *lively, sprightly*

die Munterkeit

aufmuntern, er—, rouse, encourage

die Aufmunterung, Er—

366. die Münze, *(mint, money) mint, coin*

münzen, mint, coin

auf jemanden abmünzen, (strike a coin for) strike a blow at

der Falsch(false)münzer, counterfeiter; die —ei

367. murren, *grumble, growl*

mürrisch, morose, surly, sulky

368. die Musik, *music*

der Musiker, Musikant, musician

musikalisch, musical

musizieren, make music

die Musikalien, (*plur.*) printed music

369. der Muskel, *muscle*

muskulös

370. die Muße, *leisure, ease*

müßig, idle

der Müßiggang (gehen), idleness

sich bemüßigen, find leisure for

371. das Muster, *(muster) sample, pattern, model*

mustern, review; die Musterung

musterhaft, exemplary

372. der Mut, *(mood) spirit, mind, courage*

die Anmut, (appealing to the mind) sweetness, grace

der Gleich(like)mut, calmness; Groß—, generosity; Hoch(high)—, haughtiness; Sanft(soft)—, gentleness; Wankel—, fickleness; die Weh(woe)—, sadness

anmutig

großmütig, gleich—, hoch—, sanft—, wankel—, weh—; ein—, unanimous

mutig, courageous

ermutigen, encourage; ent—, discourage

die Ermutigung, Ent—

der Mutwille, mischievousness; mutwillig

anmuten, please; ver—, (have in mind) suppose; zu—, (bring to one's mind) expect to do

die Vermutung; Zu—, imputation

vermutlich, supposedly

Wie ist Ihnen zu Mute? (at mood), how do you feel?

hochgemut, high-spirited

mutmaßen, (measure in the mind) conjecture

mutmaßlich, presumptive; die Mutmaßung

das Gemüt, mood, disposition, mind, heart

gemütvoll, full of feeling

gemütlich, (appealing to the mood) congenial, sociable, pleasant

die Gemütlichkeit

373. die Mutter, mother

die Großmutter, mütterlich

die Stief(step)mutter

stiefmütterlich, heartless

bemuttern, treat as a mother would

374. die Mütze, cap

der Mützenschirm (skirm-ish), visor

375. nachahmen, imitate

die Nachahmung

376. der Nachbar, neighbor

die Nachbarin, —schaft (hood)

nachbarlich, benachbart, neighboring

377. die Nacht, night

die Mitternacht; Weih(sacred)—, Christmas

übernachten, stay over night

übernächtig, exhausted by a sleepless night

nächtlich, nocturnal; nachts, during the night

umnachten, surround with darkness

nüchtern (Lat. nocturn-us), sober, uninteresting

die Nüchternheit

ernüchtern, make sober, disillusion

die Ernüchterung

378. der Nacken, neck, nape, shoulders

hartnäckig, stubborn; die Hartnäckigkeit

das Genick, neck, nape

nicken, nod

379. neigen, bow, incline

die Neigung, inclination, propensity

die Abneigung, aversion; Hin—, Zu—, good-will, affection

abgeneigt, disinclined; die Abgeneigtheit

380. nackt, naked, nude

die Nacktheit

381. die Nadel, needle

nähen, sew; an—, stitch on

die Nähmaschine

die Naht, seam

die Näh(t)erin, seamstress

die Nähnadel; Steck(stick)—, pin; Busen—, breastpin

382. nahe, *near*

beinahe (by near), nahezu (near to it), nearly, almost

naheliegend (lying), obvious

unnahbar, inaccessible

die Unnahbarkeit

die Nähe, nearness, proximity

nahen, approach

sich nähern, approach; die Annäherung

annähernd, approximately

der Nächste, (next) fellow-creature

nächstens, in the near future

383. nähren, (*nourish*) *nurse, feed*

ernähren, feed, support; die Ernährung

die Nahrung, nourishment, food

nahrhaft, nutritious; die Nahrhaftigkeit

384. der Name, *name*

der Beiname, surname; Spitz—, nickname; Vor—, initials; Zu—, family name

namenlos (less), anonymous

namhaft, (having a name) reputed

namhaft machen, mention a name

die Namhaftmachung

nämlich, namely, to wit

der nämliche, (before named) the same

namentlich, (by name) notably

benamen, benamsen, name

385. der Narr, *fool*

die Närrin, die Narrheit

närrisch

sich vernarren in, become foolishly fond of

die Vernarrtheit

386. die Nase, *nose*

naseweis, (having a good scent) pert

das Nashorn, rhinoceros

näseln, speak through the nose

387. naß, *humid, moist, wet*

naßkalt, damp and cold

das Naß, liquid; die Nässe, moisture

durchnässen, wet through

netzen, be—, moisten, wet

388. die Natur, *nature*

naturgemäß, according to nature; —getreu (true to)

das Naturell, natural disposition

die Unnatur, unnaturalness

natürlich, natural; of course

die Naturalien, natural curiosities

389. der Nebel, (*nebulous*) *mist, fog, haze*

das Nebelhorn, neb(e)lig

benebeln, cloud, intoxicate

390. nehmen (nahm, genommen), *take*

abnehmen, take off, decrease; an—, accept, take for granted; auf—,

admit; aus(out)—, except; sich
be—, behave; ein—, receive; ent=
—, perceive from; fest(fast)—,
arrest; ver—, perceive; vor(to
the front)—, select; wahr=
(aware)—, observe; zu(to-
wards)—, add, increase
das Benehmen, conduct
dem Vernehmen nach, according to
a rumor
die Vernehmung, examination of
witnesses
die Wahrnehmung
die Abnahme, An—, Auf—, Aus—,
Ein—, Fest—, Zu—
genehmigen, accept, approve; die
Genehmigung
angenehm, acceptable, agreeable
die Annehmlichkeit, pleasant condition
voreingenommen, captured in advance, prejudiced
die Voreingenommenheit
vornehm, (taken to the front)
picked, stylish, haughty
die Vornehmheit
die Vernunft, (taking up through the
mind) perception, reason, sense
die Unvernunft, nonsense
vernünftig, reasonable, rational
die Vernünftigkeit, rationality

391. der Neid, envy, grudge

der Neider, envious person
neidisch, envious; —los (less)
beneiden, envy; —swert (worth),
enviable

392. nein, no

verneinen, answer in the negative
die Verneinung

393. nennen (nannte, ge= nannt), name

benennen, denominate; er—, appoint
die Benennung, Er—
der Nenner, denominator
nennenswert, worth mentioning

394. das Nest, nest

nisten, build a nest
sich einnisten, settle at a place

395. nett, neat, fair, pretty

die Nettheit, Nettigkeit

396. neu, new

neulich, (newly) lately, recently
neuerdings, (a new thing) of late
die Neuheit, novelty; Neuigkeit,
news
die Neuerung, innovation
das Neujahr; der Neuling, novice
erneuen, renovate; erneuern, renew
die Erneuerung

397. nicht, (naught) not

nichtig, invalid, void; die Nichtig=
keit
vernichten, destroy; die Vernich=
tung
nichts, nothing
nichtswürdig (worthy), vile
die Nichtswürdigkeit

398. nieder, (*be-neath*) *low*

niedergeſchlagen (cast), dejected
die Niedergeſchlagenheit
ſich niederlaſſen, (let oneself down)
   settle; die Niederlaſſung
niederträchtig, (dragging down)
   vile
die Niedertracht
niedrig, low; die Niedrigkeit
die Niederung, lowland
erniedrigen, lower; die Erniedrigung,
   humiliation
niedlich, small, nice; die Niedlich=
   keit
die Gnade (Ge=nade), (lowering
   towards the person that offers
   prayer) grace, mercy
gnädig, gracious, merciful
gnädige Frau, —es Fräulein,
   Madam
begnadigen, pardon; die Begnadi=
   gung

399. die Niete, *nut, rivet*

nieten, rivet
die Niete, blank (lottery)

400. die Not, *need, neces-
   sity, misery*

nötig, needy, necessary
nötig haben, be in need of
nötigen, necessitate, compel; die
   Nötigung
notwendig, necessary; die Notwen=
   digkeit

401. die Note, *note,
   printed music*

notieren, auf—, make a memorandum
die Notiz, memorandum; das —=
   buch (book)

402. der Nutzen, *use,
   profit, benefit*

abnutzen, wear out by use; aus—,
   get the best of; be—, use
die Abnutzung, Aus—, Be—
nutzlos (less), die Nutzloſigkeit
nütze, nützlich, useful; die Nützlichkeit
genießen (genoß, genoſſen), benefit
   by, enjoy
genießbar, eatable; die Genießbarkeit
der Genoß, (co-user) companion
der Bundes(bond)genoß, ally
die Genoſſenſchaft, association
der Genuß, enjoyment, profit
der Nießbrauch, Nießnuß, usufruct

403. oben, *above*

ober, over, upper, chief
die Oberin, prioress
der Oberſt, Obriſt (*obsolete*), colonel
die Obrigkeit, government
erobern, (get on top) conquer
der Eroberer, die Eroberung

404. offen, *open, frank*

die Offenheit
offenbar, evident; die Offenbarung,
   revelation; offenbaren, reveal,
   disclose
öffnen, open; er—, reveal, disclose

die Öffnung, Er—

öffentlich, public; die Öffentlichkeit, public

veröffentlichen, publish; die Ver=öffentlichung

405. das Öl, *oil*

ölig, oily

ölen, ein—, oil, smear

die letzte Ölung, extreme unction

406. ordnen, *order, arrange, dispose*

abordnen, delegate; an—, arrange; unter—, subordinate; ver—, prescribe

die Ordnung, order, arrangement

die Anordnung, Unter—, Ver—

ordentlich, ordinary; außer= (extra-)—

die Ordentlichkeit, tidiness

der Abgeordnete, delegate

der Stadtverordnete, member of the common council

407. die Orgel, *organ*

der Organist, orgeln

408. orientieren, (*find the East, get one's bearings*) *give a general idea*

sich orientieren, see one's way

die Orientierung

409. der Ort, *place, region*

der Vorort, suburb

die Ortschaft, village, township

örtlich, local; die Örtlichkeit

erörtern, (dissolve into places, topics) discuss; die Erörterung

410. der Pabst, Papst, *pope*

das Pabsttum, popedom

päbstlich, päpstlich, papal

411. die Pacht, (*com-pact*) *tenure, lease*

pachten, take on lease; ver—, let on lease

die Pachtung, Ver—

der Pächter, tenant, farmer

412. packen, *pack*

die Verpackung, packing

das Gepäck, baggage

das Paket, Packet, parcel

packen, pick, grasp; an—, grasp

das Pack, rabble

413. passen, *fit, be convenient*

anpassen, try on; sich an—, adapt oneself; die Anpassung

es paßt sich nicht, es ist unpassend, it is improper

unpäßlich, indisposed; die Unpäß=lichkeit

414. das Pech, *pitch*

erpicht auf, (stuck on) greedy

die Erpichtheit

415. die Pein, *pain, torture*

peinigen, torment; der Peiniger, die Peinigung

peinlich, painful; die Peinlichkeit

416. die Peitsche, *whip*

peitschen

417. die Person, *person*

persönlich, die Persönlichkeit
personifizieren

418. die Pest, *pestilence, plague*

verpesten, infect; die Verpestung

419. der Pfad, *path*

pfadlos (less), der Pfadfinder

420. das Pfand, *pawn, pledge*

das Unterpfand, pledge, mortgage
pfänden, seize; ver—, pawn
die Pfändung, Ver—
das Pfänderspiel, forfeit game
pfändbar, distrainable

421. der Pfarrer, *parson*

die Pfarre, Pfarrei, parsonage
das Pfarrkind (child), parishioner

422. pfeifen (pfiff, ge=
pfiffen), *(fife, pipe) whistle,
pipe*

auspfeifen, hiss
die Pfeife, pipe, whistle
der Pfeifer
pfiffig, (pointing the lips as if to
whistle) cunning, crafty
die Pfiffigkeit, der Pfiffikus

423. die Pflanze, *plant*

der Pflanzer, planter

pflanzen, plant; an—, lay out; fort=
—, propagate; ver—, transplant
die Pflanzung, An—, Ver—, Fort—
das Pflänzchen, spoiled child

424. das Pflaster, *plaster*

pflastern
das Straßenpflaster, pavement
der Pflasterstein, flagstone
pflastern, pave; die Pflasterung

425. pflegen, *handle, nurse,
cultivate a habit*

verpflegen, nurse; die Verpflegung
die Pflege, care, nursing
der Pflegevater, foster-father
der Pflegling, foster-child
der Krankenpfleger, die —in,
trained nurse

426. die Pflicht, *(plight) duty*

verpflichten, oblige; die Verpflich=
tung

427. der Photograph
photographer

die Photographie, photographieren

428. der Pinsel, *(pencil)
paint brush*

pinseln, paint
die Pinselei, daubing

429. die Plage, *plague,
vexation*

plagen, plague; sich ab—, drudge
die Plagerei, toil, vexation

placen, sich ab—; die Placerei, toil, vexation

430. der Plan, *plan, design*

planen, plan, design
die Plane, cloth cover
der Planwagen, prairie schooner

431. platt, *flat, level, plain, even*

die Platte, plate; die Plattheit, platitude, insipidity
Plattdeutsch, Low German
der, die Plattdeutsche
platterdings, flatly, absolutely
plätten, flatten, iron
die Plätterin, ironing woman

432. der Platz, *place, square* (city)

Platz nehmen, take a seat
platzen, (explode) burst, crack
der Platzregen (rain), shower

433. plaudern, *chat, prattle*

ausplaudern, give away; ver—, prattle away
die Plauderei, chat
plauderhaft, talkative; die Plauder=haftigkeit
das Geplauder, continual tattling

434. plündern, *plunder*

der Plünderer, die Plünderung
der Plunder, worthless stuff

435. der Pöbel, (*people*) *mob, rabble*

pöbelhaft, plebeian, vulgar

436. polieren, *polish*

der Polierer, die Politur

437. die Politik, *politics*

der Politiker, politisch

438. die Polizei, *police force*

der Polizist, policeman
der Geheim(secret)polizist, detective

439. das Polster, *bolster, cushion*

der Polsterer, upholsterer
der Polsterstuhl, stuffed chair
polstern, die Polsterung

440. die Posaune, (*bassoon*), *trumpet*

auspofaunen, trumpet forth, divulge

441. die Posse, (*boss, em-boss*) *jest, farce, comedy*

der Possenreißer (reißen, write), buffoon
possenhaft, farcical
possierlich, ludicrous

442. die Post, *post, post-office, mail*

das Postamt (office), die —karte (card), der —zug (train)

der Weltpostverein, universal postal union

postlagernd (liegen, lie), general delivery

der Postillion

postalisch, postal

143. prächtig, *brilliant, splendid*

die Pracht, splendor

prachtvoll, splendid

prunken, prink, parade; der Prunk, ostentation

prunkhaft, showy

444. prägen, *mint, coin*

ausgeprägt, well-developed; ein= prägen, imprint, impress

die Prägung, coinage; das Gepräge, stamp

445. prahlen, (*brawl*) *brag, boast*

der Prahler, braggard; die Prah= lerei

prahlerisch, boastful

446. der Prediger *predicant, preacher*

die Predigt, sermon

predigen, preach

447. der Preis, *price, prize*

preisgeben, (give as a prize) give up

preisen (pries, gepriesen), praise

anpreisen, advertise; die Anpreisung

preisgekrönt (crown), having been awarded a prize

448. die Presse, *press*

auspressen, er—, extort

die Erpressung

449. der Priester, *priest*

die Priesterin, priesterlich

das Priestertum, priesthood

450. die Probe, (*probe*) ex- periment, trial, rehearsal

probieren, try, taste; an—, try on

451. der Professor *professor*

die Professur, professorship

452. der Prophet, *prophet*

die Prophetin, prophetisch

prophezeien, die Prophezeiung

453. der Proviant, *provi- sions, stores*

verproviantieren, provision

454. der Prozeß, *process, trial, lawsuit*

prozessieren, litigate

455. prüfen, (*probe*) *test, examine*

die Prüfung

456. die Pumpe, *pump*

pumpen, pump

457. der Punkt, (*punct-ual*) *point, dot, period*

punktieren, dot
pünktlich, punctual; die Pünktlichkeit
die Interpunktion, punctuation
interpunktieren

458. putzen, *clean, polish, adorn*

der Putz, finery
die Putzmacherin, milliner

459. die Qual, *pain, torment, affliction*

qualvoll, painful
quälen, torture, vex
die Quälerei, torture

460. das Quecksilber *quicksilver*

erquicken, (quicken, enliven) refresh
die Erquickung, refreshment
unerquicklich, uncomfortable
verquicken, amalgamate; die Verquickung
die Quecke, quick-grass
keck, quick, pert; die Keckheit

461. die Quelle, *well, spring, fountain, source*

quellen (quoll, gequollen), spring from, well

462. quer, (*queer*) *cross, oblique*

verquer, obliquely
der Querkopf (head), queer fellow

durchqueren, traverse
in die Quere kommen, interfere

463. quetschen, *squeeze, squash, bruise*

zerquetschen, crush, squash
die Quetschung, bruise, contusion

464. quitt, *quit, rid*

quittieren, receipt; die Quittung

465. der Rabe, *raven*

der Rappe, black horse

466. die Rache, (*wreak*) *revenge, vengeance*

rächen, der Rächer

467. das Rad (Räder) *wheel*

das Fahrrad (ride), bicycle
der Radler, Radfahrer, cyclist
radeln, ride a wheel
ein zweiräderiger Wagen
rädern, break on the wheel
radebrechen (reden, talk), have a smattering of a foreign language

468. radieren, *erase, etch*

die Radierung, etching
das Radiergummi, eraser

469. das Radieschen *radish*

der Rettig, large black radish

470. r a g e n, *tower, be prominent*

regen, (cause to be erect) stir, agitate

anregen, incite; auf—, er—, excite

die Regung, movement, emotion, agitation

regsam, agile; die Regsamkeit

regungslos, motionless

die Anregung, inspiration; die Auf—, Er—

erregbar, irritable; die Erregbarkeit

471. d e r R a n d (R ä n d e r)
(*rim*) *edge, border, margin*

berändern, um—, border, edge

die Rinde, rind, bark, crust (bread)

abrinden, take off the bark

472. r a ſ ch, (*rash*) *speedy, swift*

die Raschheit

überraschen, surprise; die Über= raschung

473. r a ſ e n, *rave, rage*

die Raserei, madness, frenzy

474. d i e R a ſt, *rest, repose*

raften; raftlos (less), die Raftloſig= keit

475. r a t e n (r i e t, g e r a t e n),
(*read riddles, interpret Runes,*
hence) *suggest meanings, discuss, advise*

abraten, disadvise; an—, advise;

be—, give advice; ſich be—, advise each other, consult; ver—,
advise wrongly, betray

der Berater, adviser; die Beratung,
consultation

der Berrat, treason; der Berräter

verräteriſch, treacherous

ratſam, advisable; die Ratſamkeit

das Rätſel, riddle, puzzle

erraten, guess; rätſelhaft, puzzle-
some

enträtſeln, decipher; die Enträtſelung

der Rat (Räte), counselor, adviser

der Rat, (*as a body*) council

der Bundes(bond)rat, federal council

der Rat (Ratſchläge), advice

beratſchlagen, deliberate; die Be=
ratſchlagung

das Rathaus, city hall

rat, *in the following compounds,
means* thing, matter

der Hausrat, furniture

der Unrat, garbage; der Vor—,
things before one, provisions

vorrätig, in store, on hand

das Gerät, tools

die Gerätſchaften, (*plur.*) imple-
ments

476. r a u b e n, *rob*

berauben, deprive

der Raub, robbery, prey; der
Räuber; der See(sea)räuber, pi-
rate

räuberiſch, rapacious

477. rauh, *rough, hoarse*
die Rauhigkeit, Rauheit
die Rauchwaren, (rough wares) furs

478. der Raum, *room, space*
der Zwischen(between)raum, interval
räumen, make room, evacuate
einräumen, (make room) concede
die Einräumung, concession
anberaumen, make room for, fix
a date
die Anberaumung
aufgeräumt, (cleared) cheerful
die Aufgeräumtheit
der Räumer, cleanser
räumlich, roomy; die Räumlichkeit,
locality
geräumig, spacious; die Geräumig=
keit

479. rechnen, *reckon, calculate, figure*
die Rechnung, calculation, bill
die Rechenschaft, account
berechnen, calculate; die Berechnung
berechnend, mercenary
unberechenbar, incalculable

480. recht, *right*
aufrecht, upright, erect; ge—, just;
un—, wrong
die Gerechtigkeit, justice
das Recht, right, claim, title
die Rechte, (*plur.*) law
das Unrecht, wrong; Vor—, privilege

der Rechthaber, quarrelsome person
die Rechthaberei, rechthaberisch
rechten, contest, dispute
rechtfertigen, justify; die Rechtfer=
tigung
rechtlich, legitimate, honest
die Rechtlichkeit, rectitude, honesty
rechtmäßig, (measured by law)
lawful
rechtlos, lawless; die Rechtlosigkeit
berechtigen, entitle, authorize
die Berechtigung
der Rechtsanwalt (walten, wield,
govern), attorney
das Gericht, court of justice, tribunal
gerichtlich, legal; außer—, out of
court
das Kriegs(war)gericht, court-
martial
der Richter, judge
der Scharf(sharp)richter, execu-
tioner
richten, hin—, string up, execute;
die Hinrichtung
richtig, right, correct; die Richtig=
keit
berichtigen, correct; die Berichtigung
aufrichtig, sincere; die Aufrichtigkeit
richten, direct; die Richtung
berichten, (make right, prepare)
report
der Bericht, report
die Nachricht, (direction to) noti-
fication
benachrichtigen, die Benachrichtigung
unterrichten, instruct

der Unterricht, instruction
das Gericht (put up), dish
einrichten, (prepare the interior)
  furnish
die Einrichtung

481. reden, *talk, speak*

anreden, talk to; be—, über—,
  zu—, persuade; sich unter—, talk
  among each other, converse;
  verab—, agree
die Anrede
die Überredung, Unter—, Verab—
die Rede, speech
der Redner, speaker, orator
rednerisch, oratorical
redselig, loquacious; die Redselig=
  keit
beredt, eloquent; die Beredtsamkeit
redlich, (inclined to talk) frank,
  honest
die Redlichkeit
die Rederei, gossip

482. die Regel, (*regul-ate*) *rule*

regellos (less), irregular
regelmäßig, (measured by rules)
  regular
regeln, regulate; die Regelung
regulieren, die Regulierung

483. der Regen, *rain*

der Regenbogen (bow)
regnerisch, rainy
regnen, rain; ver—, be spoiled by
  rain

484. der Regent, *regent*

die Regentschaft, regency
regieren, govern; die Regierung

485. reiben (rieb, gerie=
ben), *rub* (*rive*)

ab(off) reiben,   ein(in)—;   zer—,
  grind
die Reibung, friction; Ab—, Ein—
die Reiberei, friction, falling out
gerieben, shrewd; die Geriebenheit

486. reich, *rich*

der Reichtum, riches
reichlich, copious; —haltig (holding), abundant
die Reichlichkeit, Reichhaltigkeit
bereichern, enrich; die Bereicherung

487. das Reich, (Cf. Lat. rex,
king) *kingdom, empire, realm*

das Kaiserreich, empire; König—,
  kingdom; Pflanzen—, vegetable
  kingdom; Tier—, animal kingdom

488. reichen, *reach*

ausreichen, (reach out) be sufficient; er—, reach, attain; über=
  —, hand over
hinreichend, (reaching there) sufficient
die Überreichung
erreichbar, attainable; die Erreich=
  barkeit

es gereicht mir zur Ehre, I consider
it an honor
der, das Bereich, reach, extent,
range, realm, field
recken, stretch, rack
das Reck, rack, wooden horse

489. reif, *ripe, mature*

früh(early)reif, premature
reiflich, mature(ly)
die Reife, ripeness, maturity
reifen, mature, ripen
gereift, mature; die Gereiftheit

490. die Reihe, *row, array*

die Reihenfolge (follow), succession
reihen, rank, file; ein—, insert
die Einreihung
der Reihen, Reigen, dance in long
rows

491. der Reim, *rhyme*

der Stab(stave)reim, alliteration
reimen, rhyme, agree
reimlos (less), blank; ungereimt

492. rein, (*rin-se*) *clean, pure*

die Reinheit, cleanliness
reinlich, cleanly; die Reinlichkeit
reinigen, clean; die Reinigung
verunreinigen, soil; die Verunreini=
gung

493. reisen, (*rise*) *travel*

abreisen, depart; ver—, leave town
der Reisende, traveler

die Reise, trip, journey
der Reisige, trooper, horseman

494. reißen (riß, geris=
sen), (*write, scratch characters*)
tear, pull

das Reiß(writing)brett, drawing
board
der Riß, rent, crevice
der Abriß, (tear off) fragment,
brief summary; Um(about)—,
outline; Schatten—, silhouette
reizen, irritate, stimulate
reizend, charming
anreizen, instigate; auf—, incite
die Anreizung, Auf—
gereizt, reizbar, sensitive, irritable
die Gereiztheit, Reizbarkeit
der Reiz, stimulus, charm
reizvoll (full), attractive; —los,
unattractive
die Reizlosigkeit
ritzen, scratch, cleave
der Ritz, die Ritze, crack, fissure

495. reiten (ritt, gerit=
ten), *ride* (*on horseback*)

der Reiter, die Reiterin
die Reiterei, cavalry
der Ritt, ride; Be—, squad
rittlings, astraddle
der Ritter, knight; das —gut
(goods), knight's fee, manor
beritten, mounted
ritterlich, chivalrous; die Ritterlich=
keit

496. renken, *wrench, bend*

ausrenken, dislocate; ein—, put in;
ver—, sprain
die Verrenkung
die Ränke, (*plur.*) crookedness, intrigue
der Ränkeschmied (smith), schemer,
plotter

497. rennen (rannte, gerannt), *run*

das Rennen, Wett(bet)—, race
die Rennbahn (track)
rinnen (rann, geronnen), (run) flow,
leak
gerinnen, coagulate
die Rinne, der Rinnstein (stone),
gutter
blutrünstig, bleeding, bloody

498. die Restauration
restaurant

der Restaurateur, caterer

499. retten, (*rid*) *free,
save, rescue*

erretten, rescue
der Retter, Er—, rescuer
die Rettung, Er—, rescue, salvation
das Rettungsboot, life-boat; der
—gürtel (girdle), life-preserver
rettungslos (less), past help

500. die Reue, (*rue*) *repentance*

reuig, reumütig (der Mut, mood),
—evoll, rueful, repentant
reuen, bereuen, repent

501. die Revanche, *revenge*

sich revanchieren, reciprocate a
favor

502. riechen (roch, gerochen), (*reek*) *smell*

beriechen, smell at
der Geruch, odor
rauchen, reek, smoke
der Raucher, smoker; Nicht—,
non-smoker
räuchern, fumigate
räucherig, smoky

503. der Riegel, (*rail*)
bar, bolt

riegeln, ver—, bolt

504. der Riese, *giant*

riesig, gigantic

505. rieseln, *drizzle*

berieseln, irrigate; die Berieselung

506. der Ring, *ring*

ringeln, curl
der Ringkampf (fight), wrestling
match
der Ringkämpfer

507. ringen (rang, gerungen), *wring, wrestle, struggle*

erringen, obtain by exertion
die Errungenschaft, achievement
ranken, ramp
die Ranke, shoot of vine

508. bie **Rippe,** *rib*
bas **Gerippe,** skeleton

509. r o b e n (reuten), a u s —
(*rode*) *root up*
bas **Robeland,** woodland turned
into arable
zerrütten, shatter; bie **Zerrüttung**
rütteln, auf —, shake, jolt
ausrotten, exterminate; bie **Aus-**
rottung

510. r o l l e n, *roll*
bie **Rolle,** roll, part (play)

511. bie **Rofe,** *rose*
rofig, rosy
bie **Windrofe,** compass card
rofa, rose-colored
Compare: bas **Roß** (**Roffe**), horse
bie **Rofe,** erysipelas

512. b e r **Roft,** *rust*
roftig, rusty; verroften, get rusty
ber **Brat**(fry)**roft,** gridiron
röften, roast, grill

513. r o t, *red*
bie **Röte,** redness, red color
rötlich, reddish
ber **Rötel,** red crayon
bie **Röteln,** red measles
erröten, turn red, blush

514. bie **Rotte,** *rout,*
band, gang
fich zufammenrotten, band together

515. r ü c e n, (*rock, rocking-*
chair) *move, advance*
vorrücen, advance
verrückt, unbalanced, crazy
ber **Verrückte,** bie **Verrücktheit**
ber **Ruck,** jerk, jolt
ruckweife, by jerks

516. b e r **Rücken,** (*ridge*) *back*
rücklings, backward; —wärts,
backward
hinterrücks, from behind
zurück, back
ber **Berg**(mountain)**rücken,** ridge

517. bas **Ruber,** (*rudder*) *oar*
ber **Ruberer,** rower; **Drei**—, trireme
rudern, row
bas **Wett**(bet)**rudern,** rowing race

518. r u f e n (r i e f, g e r u -
f e n), *call*
ber **Ruf,** call, reputation
ber **Beruf,** vocation; beruflich, vo-
cational
bie **Berufung,** appointment, appeal
verrufen, ill-reputed
bas **Gerücht,** rumor
gerüchtweife, by way of rumor
ruchbar, notorious
anrüchig, ill-reputed
berüchtigt, notorious

519. bie **Ruhe** (**Raft,** *rest*)
repose, rest, quiet, tranquillity
ruhen, rest, sleep
fich ausruhen, take a rest; be—

auf, be based upon; ge—, (have a care for) deign (reck)

ruhelos, restless; die Ruhelosigkeit

ruhig, quiet, peaceful

beruhigen, calm, reassure; die Beruhigung

beunruhigen, alarm; die Beunruhigung

520. der Ruhm, *glory, fame, renown*

rühmlich, glorious

rühmen, glorify

berühmt, famous; die Berühmtheit

521. rühren, *(up-roar) stir, move*

aufrühren, stir up; be—, touch; um—, stir; zer—, pulverize

rührend, moving, touching

rührig, active; die Rührigkeit

rührsam, emotional; die Rührsamkeit

die Rührung, Gerührtheit, emotion

Berührung, touch

die Ruhr, (stirring of the bowels) dysentery

der Aufruhr, uproar, rebellion

der Aufrührer, aufrührerisch

522. rund, *round*

rundlich, roundish

runden, round; ab(off)—

die Rundung, Ab—

523. die Runzel, *wrinkle*

runzeln, wrinkle, knit one's brow

524. rüsten, *prepare, fit, equip*

ausrüsten, fit out; zu—, prepare

die Rüstung, armamant

die Ausrüstung, Zu—

die Rüstkammer (chamber), armory

das Gerüst, scaffold, stage

entrüstet, (disarmed, embarrassed) indignant

die Entrüstung

rüstig, robust

die Rüstigkeit

525. die Sache, *(sake) thing, matter, affair*

sachlich, to the point, business-like

sächlich, neuter (gender)

die Haupt(head)sache, principal thing

die Neben(side)sache, subordinate matter

hauptsächlich, principal(ly)

nebensächlich, immaterial

die Ursache, (original matter) cause

verursachen, cause

sachkundig (kennen, know), expert

sachverständig (verstehen, understand), expert

der Sachverständige, expert

526. der Sack, *sack, bag*

einsacken, einsäckeln, (put into a sack) pocket

527. säen, *sow*

der Sämann, sower

die Saat, seed; Aus—, seed corn

der Samen, seed
die Sämerei, nursery

528. der Saft, *sap, juice*

saftig, juicy; die Saftigkeit
saftlos (less), die Saftlosigkeit

529. sagen, *say, tell*

absagen, countermand; auf—, recite; aus—, declare, state; ent—,
renounce; gut—, approve; her—,
recite; unter—, interdict, forbid;
ver—, refuse; voraus—, predict;
weis—, prophesy; zu—, promise
die Absage
die Entsagung, Unter—, Ver—,
Voraus—, Weis—
der Weissager, (wiseacre) prophet
die Sage, saga, tradition, legend
sagenhaft, mythical, fabuluos
unsagbar, unsäglich, unspeakable
besagt, before mentioned

530. sägen, *saw*

die Säge, saw

531. die Salbe, *salve,*
ointment

die Salbung, anointment
salbungsvoll, unctuous, pathetic
salben, ein—, anoint, embalm
die Einsalbung

532. sammeln, *gather*

der Sammler, collector
die Sammlung, collection
zusammen, together

samt, together with
sämtlich, complete; jointly
gesamt, collected, aggregate
die Gesamtheit, sum total

533. der Sand, *sand*

sandig, sandy
versanden, be choked up with sand
die Versandung

534. sanft (sa=n=ft, sacht,
soft) gentle

die Sanftheit, gentleness
die Sanftmut (mood), meekness
sanftmütig, gentle, meek
besänftigen, appease; die Besänftigung
die Sänfte, sedan-chair
sacht, soft, slow, not loud

535. der Sarg, (*sarcophagus*)
coffin

einsargen, put into the coffin

536. satt, (*sad, sat-iate*) *satisfied*

sattsam, sufficiently, enough
die Sattheit, satiety
sättigen, satiate
die Sättigung
übersättigen, surfeit
unersättlich, insatiable; die Uner-
sättlichkeit

537. der Sattel, *saddle*

der Sattler, die —ei (shop)
satteln, auf—; um—, change one's
course

538. ſauber, (*sober*) *clean, neat, elegant*

die Sauberkeit
ſäuberlich, softly, properly
ſäubern, clean; die Säuberung

539. ſauer, *sour*

der Sauerſtoff (*stuff*), oxygen
verſauern, get rusty
ſäuerlich, acidulous
die Säure, acid

**540. ſaugen (ſog, ge=
ſogen),** *suck, soak*

aufſaugen, ein—, absorb; aus—,
exhaust
ſäugen, (*cause to suck*) suckle
der Säugling, infant; das —ſalter
(*age*), infancy
das Säugetier (*animal*), mammal

541. der Saum, *seam,
hem, border, edge*

ſäumen, hem, border, put to the
border, delay, tarry
einſäumen, hem; ver—, put off,
neglect, miss
das Saumtier, beast of burden

542. ſchaben, *shave,
scrape, rub*

ſchäbig, shabby; die Schäbigkeit
die Schuppe, scale, scurf

543. der Schacht, *shaft, pit*

ausſchachten, excavate

544. ſchaden, (*scathe*) *hurt,
injure*

ſchadhaft, defective; die Schadhaf=
tigkeit
ſchädlich, injurious; die Schädlichkeit
ſchadlos, without loss
die Schadloshaltung (*hold*), compensation
der Schadenerſatz (erſetzen, offset),
damages
ſchadenfroh (*glad*), malicious
die Schadenfreude
beſchädigen, damage; ent—, indem-
nify
die Beſchädigung, Ent—

545. das Schaf, *sheep*

der Schäfer, die —in

**546. ſchaffen (ſchuf, ge=
ſchaffen),** *shape, create*

erſchaffen, create; die Erſchaffung
beſchaffen, (*shaped*) constituted
die Beſchaffenheit, quality
der Schaffner, steward, railroad
guard
das Geſchäft, business
geſchäftlich, on business, business-
like
geſchäftig, active; die Geſchäftigkeit
beſchäftigen, employ; die Beſchäfti=
gung
ſchaffen, (*reg.*) shift, remove
ab(off)ſchaffen, abolish; an—, be=
ver—, procure; fort—, weg—,
remove

die Abschaffung, An—, Be—, Fort—, Weg—
schöpfen, shape, create
der Schöpfer, creator; die Schöpfung
das Geschöpf, creature
schöpfen, scoop, draw
erschöpfen, scoop out, exhaust
die Erschöpfung, exhaustion

547. schal, *stale, insipid*
die Schalheit

548. die Schale, *shell, scale, peel, cup, bowl*
verschalen, furnish with a shell or cover
die Verschalung
schälen, ab—, shell, peel

549. der Schall, *sound, ring*
erschallen, ring out
verschollen, (rung out, not heard of) considered dead

550. schalten, *insert*
einschalten, insert; die Einschaltung
das Schaltjahr, leap-year
der Schalter, little sliding window

551. die Scham, *shame*
die Schande, disgrace, infamy
schändlich, shameful; die Schändlichkeit
schänden, dishonor

schamhaft, bashful; die Schamhaftigkeit
schamlos, impudent; die Schamlosigkeit
sich schämen, be ashamed
beschämen, make ashamed
verschämt, bashful; die Verschämtheit
unverschämt, impudent; die Unverschämtheit

552. scharf, *sharp, keen*
die Schärfe, sharpness, severity
schärfen, sharpen, whet
einschärfen, impress; ver—, render more severe
die Verschärfung

553. scharren, *(plough-share) rake, scrape*
ausscharren, dig up; ein—, bury
anschirren, harness; ab—, unharness
das Geschirr, harness
das Geschirr, vessel, crockery

554. die Scharte (scheren, *shear), notch, fissure*
schartig, jagged, full of notches

555. der Schatten
shadow, shade
schattig, shady
beschatten, shade, shadow; die Beschattung
schattieren, shade, shadow; die Schattierung

556. der Schatz, *treasure*

der Schatz, das Schätzchen, (endeared treasure) sweetheart

schätzen, esteem, value

abschätzen, estimate; ein—, assess; über—, overvalue; unter—, undervalue

die Schätzung, Ab—, Ein—, Über—, Unter—

schätzbar, estimable

brandschatzen, damage by fire

die Brandschatzung

557. der Schauder *shudder, horror*

schauderhaft, horrible

schaudern, shudder, shiver

558. schauen, (*show*) *view, look, see*

an(at)schauen; be—, view; durch= (through)—, penetrate; um= (about)—; zu—, watch

die Schau, view, show

das Schaufenster (window); —spiel, play

der Schauspieler, actor; die —in

die Ausschau, outlook; Um—, review

anschaulich, clear, vivid, evident

beschaulich, contemplative; die Beschaulichkeit

559. der Schaum, (*scum*) *foam, froth*

schäumen, scum, skim, foam, sparkle

560. die Scheibe, (*shive*) *slice, disk, target, pane*

die Fensterscheibe, window-pane

561. die Scheide, *sheath, scabbard*

scheiden (schied, geschieden), shed, separate, divorce

entscheiden, separate dissimilar plans, decide; ver—, die; unter—, distinguish

der Abschied, departure

verabschieden, dismiss

abgeschieden, retired

die Abgeschiedenheit

die Ausscheidung, secretion

bescheiden, secretive, modest

die Bescheidenheit

der Bescheid, keeping things apart, finding the right way, giving correct information

die Entscheidung, decision

entschieden, resolute; die Entschiedenheit

der Unterschied, difference

die Unterscheidung, distinction

verschieden, different; die Verschiedenheit

die Scheidung, separation, divorce

der Schiedsrichter, (deciding judge) arbiter

der Scheit, (shide) piece of wood

der Scheiterhaufen (heap), pyre

der Scheitel, parting line (hair), vertex

scheiteln, part the hair

gescheit, discriminating, clever

die Gescheitheit
scheitern, (shatter) be wrecked, miscarry

562. scheinen (schien, ge=
schienen), *shine, appear, seem*
bescheinen, illuminate; er—, appear
der Schein, shine, appearance, evidence, certificate, banknote, bill
der Anschein, appearance; Augen=
(eye)—, inspection
anscheinend, apparently
augenscheinlich, evidently
scheinbar, ostensible; un—, unassuming
bescheinigen, make evident, certify
die Bescheinigung
der Scheinwerfer (throw), searchlight

563. schelten (schalt, gescholten), *scold*
die Schelte, scolding
unbescholten, irreproachable

564. schenken, *pour out* (in a general sense), *give a present*
die Schenke, tavern
der Verschank, serving of a drink
schenken, be—, present with; ver—, give away
die Schenkung, donation
das Geschenk, present

565. scheren (schor, ge=
schoren), *shear*
die Schere, shears, scissors

die Schere, shafts of a carriage

566. scheu, *shy, timid*
die Scheu, shyness
der Abscheu, horror; die Wasser—, hydrophobia
abscheulich, abominable
verabscheuen, abominate
scheuen, be shy, shun, avoid
das Scheusal, monster
scheußlich, hideous; die Scheußlichkeit
scheuchen, ver—, scare away
schüchtern, timid
einschüchtern, intimidate; die Ein=
schüchterung

567. schieben (schob, ge=
schoben), *shove, shift, push*
aufschieben, put off; ein—, insert;
ver—, put off, move out of place
der Aufschub, das Einschiebsel, die
Verschiebung
der Vorschub, (push forward) assistance
der Heuschober, stack of hay
der Schub, push; —karren, pushcart

568. schießen, (schoß,
geschossen), *shoot*
vorschießen, push forward (advance money)
der Schuß, shot
der Ausschuß, refuse; Über—, surplus; Vor—, advance
abschüssig, (shooting down) precipitous

das Geschoß, projectile

der Schütz(e), rifleman; das Geschütz, cannon

569. das Schiff, *ship*

der Schiffbruch (brechen, break), wreck

schiffbar, navigable; die Schiffbarkeit

schiffen, navigate

ausschiffen, disembark; ein—, embark; ver—, despatch

die Ausschiffung, Ein—, Ver—

570. schinden (schund, geschunden), (*skin*) *flay*

der Schinder, flayer, oppressor

der Schund, trash

571. schirmen, (*skirm-ish*) *guard, protect*

beschirmen; der Schirmherr, protector

der Lampenschirm (shade), Ofen— (screen); Regen—, umbrella: Sonnen—, parasol

572. schlafen (schlief, geschlafen), *sleep*

sich verschlafen, oversleep oneself

verschlafen, drowsy; die Verschlafenheit

schlaflos; die Schlaflosigkeit, insomnia

der Schlaf, sleep

schläfrig, drowsy; die Schläfrigkeit

einschläfern, lull to sleep

das Schläfchen, nap; der Schläfer, sleeper

schlaff, schlapp, loose, lax

die Schlaffheit, Schlappheit

die Schlappe, defeat

erschlaffen, languish; die Erschlaffung

die Schläfe, (seat of sleep *according to popular belief*) temple

573. schlagen (schlug, geschlagen), (*slay, slug*) *beat, strike*

der Schlag, stroke, blow

der Schlägel, mallet

schlachten, slaughter

der Schlächter, butcher; die —ei

die Schlacht, battle

nach einem schlachten, schlagen, (*origin unknown*) take after a person

der Schlag; Menschen—, race

das Geschlecht, race, sex, gender

geschlechtlich, sexual

ungeschlacht, uncouth, rude

574. der Schlamm, *mud, mire*

schlammig, slimy, muddy

der Schleim, slime, phlegm

verschleimt, obstructed with slime

575. die Schlange, (*slink*) *serpent, snake*

sich schlängeln, wind, meander

576. schlau, *sly, cunning, crafty*

die Schläue, Schlauheit, craftiness

577. ſ ch l e ch t, (*slight, worthless*) *mean, poor, bad*

ſchlechthin, —weg, simply, plainly
die Schlechtigkeit, meanness, baseness
verſchlechtern, impair; die Verſchlechterung
ſchlicht, (slight) plain, simple
die Schlichtheit
ſchlichten, plane, adjust; die Schlichtung

578. ſ ch l e i ch e n (ſch l i ch, ge= ſ ch l i ch e n), (*sleek*) *sneak*

der Schleicher, die —ei
der Schlich, trick

579. d e r S ch l e i e r, *veil*

ſchleierhaft, mysterious
verſchleiern, veil

580. ſ ch l e i f e n (ſch l i ff, ge= ſ ch l i ff e n), (*slip,* as on a whetstone) *grind, polish*

ungeſchliffen, coarse
der Schliff, polish, good manners
ſchleifen, (*reg.*) drag
ſchleppen, (slip) drag
verſchleppen, drag along, put off
die Schleppe, train (dress)
der Schlepper, Schleppdampfer, tugboat

581. ſ ch l e u d e r n, *sling*

die Schleuder, sling; der —er

582. ſ ch l i e ß e n (ſch l o ß, ge= ſ ch l o ſ ſ e n), (Cf. slot, bar, bolt) *close, shut, conclude*

beſchließen, ſich ent—, decide, resolve
der Schluß, close, conclusion
der Beſchluß, Ent—
ſchließlich, at length; aus—, exclusively; ein—, including
entſchloſſen, resolute; die Entſchloſſenheit
ſchlüſſig, determined; die Unſchlüſſigkeit
das Schloß (Schlöſſer), lock, (guarded building) palace, manor
der Schloſſer, locksmith
der Schlüſſel, key

583. ſ ch l i m m, (*slim, unsubstantial*) *bad, evil, sore*

verſchlimmern, make worse

584. ſ ch l u m m e r n, *slumber*

der Schlummer

585. ſ ch l ü p f e n, *slip*

ſchlüpferig, slippery
der Schlupfwinkel (corner), hiding-place
der Unterſchlupf, hiding-place
die Schlucht, deep valley, ravine

586. ſ ch m a l, (*small*) *narrow*

ſchmälern, lessen; die Schmälerung

587. ſchmaroʒen, *live on others*

der Schmaroʒer, parasite

588. ſchmecken, *(smack) taste, savor*

der Geſchmack, taste
geſchmacklos (less), —voll (full)
die Geſchmackloſigkeit
abgeſchmackt, absurd; die Abge=
  ſchmacktheit
ſchmackhaft, tasteful; die Schmack=
  haftigkeit
ſchmachten, (long for) pine; an—,
  look longingly at; ver—, be
  parched with thirst
ſchmächtig, (languishing) slender
ſchmaʒen, ab—, kiss heartily
der Schmaʒ, hearty kiss

589. ſchmeicheln, *(smicker) flatter*

der Schmeichler, die —in, die
  Schmeichelei
ſchmeichelhaft, ſchmeichleriſch

**590. ſchmeißen (ſchmiß, ge=
  ſchmiſſen),** *(smite, smash) throw, fling*

der Schmiß, (thrust) stroke, scar

**591. ſchmelʒen (ſchmolʒ,
  geſchmolʒen),** *smelt, melt*

ſchmelʒbar, fusible
der Schmelʒ, enamel
die Schmelʒerei, smelter

das Schmalʒ, (melted fat) grease,
  lard

592. der Schmerʒ, *(smart) pain, ache*

ſchmerʒhaft, —lich, painful
ſchmerʒen, pain, hurt
die Kopf(head)ſchmerʒen; Zahn—,
  toothache

593. der Schmied, *smith*

die Schmiede, smithy, forge
ſchmieden, forge, frame, concoct
geſchmeidig, malleable; die Ge=
  ſchmeidigkeit
das Geſchmeide, (goldsmith's work)
  trinkets

594. ſchmuck, *(smug) neat, spruce*

ſchmücken, aus—, adorn, decorate
die Ausſchmückung
der Schmuck, ornament, finery
ſchmucklos, unadorned

595. der Schmuʒ, *(smut) dirt, soil, filth*

ſchmuʒig, dirty
beſchmuʒen, soil

596. der Schnabel, *(neb, nib) beak, bill*

ſchnäbeln, bill and coo

597. ſchnarchen, *snore, snort*

ſchnarren, snarl, rattle
ſchnurren, rattle
der Schnurrbart (beard), mustache

598. ſchnauben, (*sniff*)
puff and blow

die Naſe (nose) ausſchnauben (blow)
ſchnaufen, breathe hard, snort
ſich verſchnaufen, stop for breath
ſchnüffeln, snuffle, sniff
der Schnüffler, sneak; die Schnüffe=
lei
der Schnupfen, (snuff) cold in the
head
verſchnupft, offended

599. der Schnee, *snow*

ſchneien, snow
einſchneien; ver—, be snowbound

**600. ſchneiden (ſchnitt,
geſchnitten),** *cut*

die Schneide, edge
ſchneidig, smart, stylish
der Schneider, tailor; die —in,
dressmaker
der Schnitt, cut, style; Ab—, section
die Schnitte (Brot, bread), slice
der Schnitter, reaper
der Durchſchnitt, (cross-cut) average
durchſchnittlich, on an average
ſchnitzen, ſchnitzeln, carve
der Schnitzer, (wrong cut) blunder
das Wiener Schnitzel, Vienna cutlet

601. ſchnell, *quick, fast,
speedy*

ſchnellen, move quickly, let fly
die Strom(river)ſchnelle, rapids

die Schnalle, buckle
ſchnallen, buckle
ſchnalzen, smack

602. die Schnur, (*snare*)
twine, lace, cord

ſchnüren, lace, string

603. ſchön, (*sheen*) *beautiful,
handsome, fair*

die Schönheit, beauty
verſchönern, embellish; die Ver=
ſchönerung
beſchönigen, consider fair, excuse
die Beſchönigung
ſchonen, treat fairly, spare, save
die Schonung, indulgence, reserva-
tion (forest)
verſchonen, spare, exempt from
ſchonungsvoll, gentle; —los, re-
lentless

604. ſchräg, *oblique, slanting*

der Schragen, trestle
abſchrägen, slope, bevel

605. der Schrank, *closet,
cupboard*

die Schranke, (*shrink*) barrier,
limit
ſchrankenlos, boundless
beſchränken, ein—, restrain
die Beſchränkung, Ein—

606. die Schraube, *screw*

ſchrauben, screw
verſchroben, eccentric, queer

607. der Schreck, *fright, terror*

schreckhaft, fearful, easily frightened
schrecklich, terrible, dreadful
erschrecken (erschrak, erschrocken), be frightened
schrecken, frighten
unerschrocken, intrepid; die Unerschrockenheit

608. der Schrei, *cry*

der Aufschrei, outcry
das Geschrei, shriek; Feld(field)—, warwhoop
schreien (schrie, geschrieen), cry
verschrieen, decried, notorious

609. schreiben (schrieb, geschrieben), *(script) write*

der Schreiber, copyist
beschreiben, (write about) describe
die Beschreibung, description
die Schrift, writing, script, type
die Abschrift, copy; Druck—, print; In—, inscription; Über—, headline; Unter—, signature; Vor—, prescription; Zeit(time)—, periodical
der Schriftsteller, author
schriftlich, in writing

610. schreiten (schritt, geschritten), *stride, step, proceed*

das Einschreiten, interference
die Ausschreitung, excess; Über—, violation of a law

der Schritt, step, stride; Fort—, progress
der Fortschrittler, fortschrittlich

611. der Schuh, *shoe*

der Gummi(rubber)schuh; Hand—, glove; Schlitt(slide)—, skate
der Schuster, Schuhmacher, shoemaker
beschuhen, furnish with shoes

612. die Schuld, *guilt, fault, debt*

die Unschuld, innocence
schuldig, un—
das Verschulden, die Verschuldung, fault
beschuldigen, accuse; ent—, excuse
die Beschuldigung, Ent—
die Schuld, debt
schuldig, indebted; schulden, owe

613. die Schule, *school*

schulpflichtig (pledge), compelled to attend school
der Schüler, die —in, pupil
der Mitschüler (fellow); Vorschule (primary)
einschulen, train; die Schulung

614. die Schulter, *shoulder*

das Schulterblatt (blade)
breitschulterig

615. der Schurz, die Schürze, *(shirt, cover) apron*

schürzen, auf—, truss up, pin up

616. ſ ch ü t t e n, *shed*
der Schutt, rubbish, refuse
ſchütteln, shake, toss
der Schüttelfroſt (frost), shivers
erſchüttern, shake, affect strongly
die Erſchütterung, concussion, shock

617. ſ ch ü z e n, (*shut*) *protect*
der Schuz, protection
ſchuzlos, defenseless; die Schuz=
losigkeit
der Schützling, protégé

618. ſ ch w a ch, *weak, feeble, faint*
die Schwäche, der Schwächling
die Schwachheit, frailty
ſchwächen, weaken; ab—, extenuate

**619. d e r Sch w a g e r (Schwe=
ſt e r,** *sister*), *brother-in-law*
die Schwägerin, sister-in-law
die Schwägerschaft, affinity by
marriage
verſchwägert, related by marriage
die Verſchwägerung
der Schwäher (*obsolete*), father-
in-law
der Schwiegervater, father-in-law;
—ſohn
die Schwiegermutter, —tochter;
—eltern, parents
der Schwager, postillion

620. ſ ch w ä r e n, *fester*
die Schwäre, das Geſchwür, abscess

621. d e r S ch w a r m, *swarm*
ſchwärmen, (let one's imagination
run wild) be enthusiastic

der Schwärmer, enthusiast; die —ei
ſchwärmeriſch

622. ſ ch w a r z, (*swarthy*) *black*
ſchwärzlich, blackish
ſchwärzen, blacken; an—, slander
die Drucker(printer)ſchwärze(ink)

623. ſ ch w a z e n, *chatter,
prattle*
der Schwätzer
ſchwazhaft, talkative; die Schwaz=
haftigkeit
das Geſchwäz, prattling, gossip
geſchwäzig, talkative; die Ge=
ſchwäzigkeit

624. ſ ch w e b e n, (*swif-t*) *be
suspended, soar*
die Schwebe, suspense

625. ſ ch w e i f e n, (*sweep,
swoop*) *stray, ramble*
ausſchweifen, digress, debauch;
ab—, deviate; umher—
die Abſchweifung, Aus—
der Schweif, tail
ohne Umſchweife, (without swaying
about) directly
der Schwibbogen (bow), arch,
vault

**626. ſ ch w e i g e n (ſ ch w i e g,
g e ſ ch w i e g e n),** *be silent*
das Schweigen, der Schweiger
ſchweigſam, taciturn; die Schweig=
ſamkeit

verſchwiegen, discreet; die Ver=
ſchwiegenheit
beſchwichtigen, soothe, appease
die Beſchwichtigung

627. der Schweiß, *sweat,*
perspiration

ſchwißen, sweat; aus—, exude;
ver—, forget

628. ſchwelen, *(sultry)*
smolder

ſchwül, sweltering, sultry; die
Schwüle

629. ſchwelgen, *(swallow)*
revel

der Schwelger; die —ei, gluttony

630. ſchwellen (ſchwoll,
geſchwollen), *swell*

die Schwiele, callus; ſchwielig
die Schwulſt, Ge—, tumor
ſchwülſtig, bombastic; die Schwül=
ſtigkeit
der Schwall, heaving mass

631. ſchwer, *heavy* (to carry),
difficult (to perform)

die Schwere, heaviness, gravity
der Schwerpunkt, center of gravity
ſchwerfällig, (falling heavily)
clumsy
die Schwerfälligkeit
beſchweren, weight ḋown; er—,
aggravate
beſchwerlich, burdensome

ſchwierig, difficult; die Schwierigkeit
ſich beſchweren, complain
die Beſchwerde, complaint

632. die Schweſter, *sister*

die Geſchwiſter, brothers and sisters

633. ſchwimmen (ſchwamm,
geſchwommen), *swim*

verſchwimmen, be blurred; die Ver=
ſchwommenheit
der Schwimmer, die —in
ſchwemmen, cause to swim, float,
water
anſchwemmen, form by alluvion;
über—, flood
die Anſchwemmung, Über—
die Schwemme, horse pond

634. ſchwinden (ſchwand,
geſchwunden), *disappear,*
vanish

entſchwinden, ver—, disappear
die Schwindſucht (ſiech, sick), consumption
ſchwindſüchtig, consumptive
der Schwund, extinction
ſchwenden, ver—, cause to disappear, waste, squander
der Verſchwender, die —ung, ver=
ſchwenderiſch
der Schwindel, swoon, dizziness
ſchwind(e)lig, dizzy
der Schwindel, swindle
der Schwindler, die —elei
ſchwindeln

635. ſchwingen (ſchwang, geſchwungen), *swing*

die Schwingung, vibration
unerſchwinglich, unattainable
die Schwinge, swing
der Schwengel, handle
überſchwenglich, enthusiastic
die Überſchwenglichkeit
der Schwung, vibration, rapture
der Aufſchwung, elevation; Um—, revolution
ſchwungvoll, animated, enthusiastic
ſchwenken, cause to swing, shake, rinse
die Schwenkung, wheeling, evolution
ſchwanken, waver, hesitate
die Schwankung
ſchwank, slender, flexible
der Schwank, joke, farce
der Schwanz, (that which swings) tail
ſchwänzeln, wag the tail
die Schule ſchwänzen, play truant, "cut recitation"

636. ſchwören (ſchwur, ſchwor, geſchworen), *swear*

beſchwören, conform by oath, recite a magic formula, conjure up; ſich ver—, conspire
die Beſchwörung, Ver—, der Verſchwörer
der Geſchworene, member of a jury
der Schwur, oath

637. die Seele, *soul*

Allerſeelen, All Souls' Day
ſeelenvoll (full), feeling
beſeelen, animate; ent—, kill

638. das Segel, *sail*

der Segler, sailing vessel, sailor
das Wett(bet)ſegeln, sailing race
ſegeln, sail; um—, circumnavigate

639. ſehen (ſah, geſehen), *see*

angeſehen, (looked at) respected, prominent
das Anſehen, reputation
das Ausſehen, appearance; Ver—, mistake
anſehnlich, worth looking at, considerable
unverſehens, unforeseen
zuſehends, as you look at it, visibly
abſehbar, within sight, conceivable
der Seher, seer
die Sicht, sight
ſichtbar, visible
erſichtlich, evident; die Erſichtlichkeit
das Geſicht, An—, face; angeſichts, in view of
die Abſicht, (view at) intention, plan; An—, opinion; Auf—, supervision; Aus—, outlook; Ein—, insight; Hin—, respect; Nach—, (looking closely) indulgence; Rück(back)—, regard; Über—, summary; Um—, circumspection; Vor—, foresight,

caution; **Voraus**—, forethought; **Zuver**—, confidence, trust

absichtlich, intentional; **hin**—, regarding; **voraus**—, presumably; **zuver**—, confident

ansichtig, perceiving; **durch**—, transparent; **ein**—, intelligent; **nach**— indulgent; **um**—, circumspect; **vor**—, cautious

die Durchsichtigkeit

beabsichtigen, intend; **beauf**—, superintend; **berück**—, consider; **be**—, inspect

die Beaufsichtigung

aussichtslos, hopeless

rücksichtsvoll, considerate; **—los**, inconsiderate

die Rücksichtslosigkeit, recklessness

unnachsichtig, unrelenting

sichten, sift, winnow; **die Sichtung**

640. sehnen (sich), *long for*

ersehnen, desire eagerly

sehnlich, eagerly, passionately

die Sehnsucht (siech, sick), intense longing

sehnsuchtsvoll, **sehnsüchtig**, passionate

641. die Seide, (*satin*) *silk*

seiden, silken

642. die Seite, *side*

seitlich, lateral

einseitig, one-sided; **viel**(many)—, versatile

die Einseitigkeit, **Viel**—

abseits, apart; **dies**—, on this side; **jen**—, on the other side of

gegen(against, opposite)**seitig**, mutual, reciprocal

die Gegenseitigkeit, reciprocity

das Jenseits, the beyond

seitens, on the part of

beseitigen, remove; **die Beseitigung**

643. selber, selbst, *self*

selbstlos (less), unselfish

die Selbstlosigkeit

Selbstsucht, selfishness

Selbstmord, suicide

644. selten, *seldom, rare*

die Seltenheit, rarity, curiosity

seltsam, (of rare occurrence) strange, odd (silly)

645. senden (sandte, gesandt), *send*

die Sendung, consignment

das Eingesandt, letter to the editor

der Sender, Ab—, remitter

der Versand, shipment; **das —geschäft**, mail order business

der Sendling, missionary

der Gesandte, envoy, ambassador

die Gesandtschaft, embassy

der Abgesandte, emissary

646. sicher, *secure, sure, safe*

sicherlich, surely, certainly

sichern, secure, ensure; **ver**—, assure, insure; **zu**—, promise

die **Sicherheit**, safety
die **Sicherung**, security; **Ver—,
Zu—**

647. ſickern, *ooze, leak*

verſiegen, be drained, dry up
unverſiegbar, inexhaustible

648. Sie, *you*

ſich ſiezen, call each other **Sie**

649. ſiech, *sick*

ſiechen, be sick; **dahin—**, die slowly
das Siechtum, lingering illness
die **Seuche**, contagious disease
verſeuchen, infect
die **Sucht**, (*in compounds only; in
cases not referring to ailments it
may be construed as mania, but
not as a derivation of* **ſuchen**,
seek) disease, mania
die **Bleich**(bleach, pale)**ſucht**, ane-
mia; **Fall—**, epilepsy; **Fett**(fat)**—**, obesity; **Gelb**(yellow)**—**,
jaundice; **Schwind**(vanish)**—**,
consumption; **Waſſer—**, dropsy
bleichſüchtig, anemic; etc.
die **Hab**(have)**ſucht**, greed; **Herrſch**(master)**—**, imperiousness; **Ge**-
fall(please)**—**, coquetry; **Sehn**-
(longing)**—**, passionate desire;
Selbſt(self)**—**, selfishness
habſüchtig, greedy; etc.

650. ſiedeln, *settle*

anſiedeln, settle down
der **Anſiedler**, die **Anſiedelung**

der **Ein**(one)**ſiedler**, hermit; die
Einſiedelei

651. der Sieg, *victory*

der **Sieger**, victor
ſiegreich (rich), victorious
ſiegen, be victorious; **be—**, vanquish

652. das Siegel, *seal*

der **Siegellack** (lacquer, wax), **—**-
ring
ſiegeln, seal; **be—**, set one's seal
to; **ver—**, close by sealing
die **Beſiegelung**

653. das Silber, *silver*

das Queckſilber
ſilbern, made of silver
verſilbern, silver, plate; sell

654. ſingen (ſang, ge-
ſungen), *sing*

der **Sänger**, die **—in**, singer
der **Geſang**, song, singing
geſanglich, vocal

655. ſinken (ſank, ge-
ſunken), *sink*

ſenken, cause to sink, lower
die **Verſenkung**, drop (stage)
ſenkrecht (directed), perpendicular,
vertical
das Senkblei (lead), plummet; die
—rechte, perpendicular
das Geſenke, valley

656. der Sinn, *sense, meaning, mind*

das Sinnbild (picture), symbol

versinnbildlichen, symbolize

der Leicht(light)sinn, levity; Scharf=(sharp)—, sagacity; Un—, nonsense; Wahn(vain)—, insanity

leichtsinnig, scharf—, un—sinnig, thoughtful; die Sinnigkeit

sinnlich, sensual; die Sinnlichkeit

übersinnlich, transcendental

sinnlos, senseless; die Sinnlosigkeit

sinnreich (rich), ingenious

sinnen (sann, gesonnen), meditate, reflect

sich besinnen, sich ent—, recollect; er—, devise, contrive

das Ansinnen, expectation, imputation

die Besinnung, consciousness

besinnungslos (less), unconscious

die Besinnungslosigkeit

besonnen, cautious; die Besonnenheit

gesinnt, disposed; die Gesinntheit

die Gesinnung, intention, mind

657. die Sitte, *custom, fashion, morals*

die Unsitte, bad habit, abuse

sittlich, moral; die Sittlichkeit

sittsam, modest; die Sittsamkeit

658. sitzen (saß, gesessen), *sit*

der Sitz, seat; die Sitzung, session

der Vor(front)sitz, chairmanship

der Vorsitzende, chairman

der Beisitzer, associate, deputy

der Besitz, possession

der Besitzer, die —in; das —tum property

besessen, possessed, mad; die Besessenheit

angesessen, ansässig, eingesessen, seßhaft, settled, domiciled, established

versessen auf, bent upon

die Ansässigkeit, Seßhaftigkeit; Versessenheit, obsession

der Insasse, inhabitant

setzen, cause to sit, set

absetzen, sell, depose, disqualify; an—, start; auf—, set up, compose, put on; aus—, expose; auseinander—, analyze, explain; be—, occupy, trim; durch—, enforce; ein—, set in a game, risk; ent—, unset, frighten; er—, offset, replace; fort—, continue; hintan(behind on)—, set aside; hinzu—, add; über—, translate; ver—, transfer, pawn; vor—, propose, offer; wider(against)—, oppose; zer—, decompose; zu—, add; zurück—, set back, slight

die Absetzung, removal; Auseinander—, explanation, falling out; Be—, occupation; Ein—, installation; Fort—, continuation; Über—, translation; Zurück—, setback

das Entsetzen, horror

entsetzlich, horrible, dreadful

der **Vorgesetzte**, superior

die **Widersetzlichkeit**, obstinacy

das **Gesetz**, (that which is set down) law (that which is lain down)

der **Gesetzgeber**, legislator; die —gebung

gesetzt, dignified; die **Gesetztheit**

der **Setzer**, type-setter; die —ei, printing-office

der **Satz**, set of words, sentence, proposition

der **Absatz**, paragraph, landing (stairs), heel (shoe); **An**—, start; **Auf**—, composition; **Be**—, trimmings; **Ein**—, stake (game); **Ent**—, relief, succor; **Er**—, restitution; **Vor**—, proposition; **Zu**—, addition

der **Boden**(bottom)**satz**, sediment

der **Grund**(ground)**satz**, principle

grundsätzlich, on general principles

die **Satzung**, statute; **Be**—, garrison

659. die Skizze, *sketch*

skizzieren, sketch

660. der Sklave, *slave*

die **Sklavin, Sklaverei,** sklavisch

661. die Sohle, *sole*

besohlen, ver—, sole

die **Besohlung, Ver**—

die **Sole**, salt water, brine

662. der Sold, (*solid money*) *pay*

besolden, give salary; die **Besoldung**

der **Söldner, Söldling,** hireling, mercenary

der **Soldat**, soldier; soldatisch

663. der Sommer, *summer*

sommerlich

der **Altweiber**(old women's)**sommer**, Indian summer

664. sonder, (*sundry, asunder, different, apart*) *particular, especial*

sonderbar, odd; die **Sonderbarkeit**

sonderlich, particular; die **Sonderlichkeit**

der **Sonderling**, singular person, crank

der **Sonderzug**, special train

absondern, separate; die **Absonderung**

absonderlich, odd; die **Absonderlichkeit**

besonder, special; —s, especially

die **Besonderheit**, peculiarity

sondern, but, on the contrary

samt und sonders, jointly and severally

665. die Sonne, *sun*

der **Sonnenaufgang** (rise), —untergang; die —finsternis (darkness), eclipse; der —stich, (stechen, prick), sunstroke

der **Sonnabend,** (Sunday eve), Saturday; —tag

sonnig, sunny

sonnenklar (clear), evident

fich fonnen, bask in the sun

666. die Sorge, *sorrow, care*

die Fürsorge, Vor—, precaution

forglos, careless; **—fam,** careful

die Sorglosigkeit, —famkeit

forglich, anxious, careful

forgenfrei (free), **—voll** (full)

die Sorgfalt, carefulness, attention

forgfältig, careful, painstaking

beforgt, anxious; **die Beforgtheit**

forgen, be anxious, care for, provide for

beforgen, care for, attend to, procure

verforgen, provide with, maintain

die Beforgung, Ver—

667. fpähen, *spy, explore*

der Späher, spy, scout

der Spion, spy; **die Spionage, die Spioniererei**

fpionieren, spy; **aus—,** spy out

668. fpalten, *split, cleave*

der Spalt, split, cleft, rent

der Zwie(two)fpalt, dissension

die Spalte, (split page) column

die Spaltung, dissension, disunion, schism

669. fpannen, *span, stretch, strain*

abfpannen, aus—, unharness; **an—,** harness

abgefpannt, enervated; **die Abgefpanntheit,** exhaustion

abfpenftig machen, alienate; **wider-** (against)**—,** obstinate; **die Widerfpenftigkeit**

angefpannt, harnessed, strenuous

die Angefpanntheit

die Spannung, tension, strain, expectation

die Abfpannung, fatigue; **An—,** strenuousness; **Aus—,** recreation; **Be—,** team of horses

fpannend, fpannungsvoll (full), exciting, fascinating

das Gefpann, team of horses, oxen

der Vorfpann, additional horse(s)

der Einfpänner, one-horse carriage

670. fparen, *spare, save*

auffparen, er—, put off, spare

fparfam, thrifty; **die Sparfamkeit**

fpärlich, sparing, scanty; **die Spärlichkeit**

die Erfparnis, savings

die Sparkaffe (cash), savings bank

671. der Sparren
spar, raft

fperren, shut, block up, embargo

abfperren, block up, close; **auf—,** open wide; **ein—,** imprison; **ver—, zu—,** close, obstruct

die Abfperrung, Ein—

die Sperre, closing, embargo

die Bahn(railroad)fperre, space reserved for passengers; **Hafen-** (haven, harbor)**—,** embargo; **Mund(mouth)—,** lockjaw

der Sperrſitz (seat), orchestra seat

672. der Spaß, *jest, joke*
ſpaßhaft, —ig, laughable, jocose
ſpaßen, joke, jest

673. ſpät, *late*
ſpäterhin, at a later time
ſpäteſtens, no later than
ſich verſpäten, be late
zehn Minuten Verſpätung, ten minutes late

674. ſpeien (ſpie, geſpieen), *spew, spit*
der feuer(fire)**ſpeiende Berg,** volcano
der Speichel, saliva, spittle
ſpucken, spit; **die Spucke**

675. die Speiſe, *food*
die Speiſekarte, bill of fare; **der —wagen,** dining car
ſpeiſen, feed, dine; **auf—, ver—,** eat up
die Speiſung, feeding

676. die Spende, (*spend*) *distribution, alms*
ſpenden, ver—, spend, deal out
der Spender, dispenser
der Spund (*from Lat. punctus*), bung
verſpunden, bung up

677. der Spiegel, (Lat. speculum) *mirror, reflector, lookingglass*
der Meeres(sea)**ſpiegel,** sea level

ſpiegeln, be reflected from a mirror
vorſpiegeln, show in a mirror, deceive
die Spiegelung, reflection, mirage; **Vor—**

678. das Spiel, *play, game*
der Spieler, player, gambler
das Schauſpiel, play; **der —er,** actor; **die —in,** actress
der Geſpiele, die Geſpielin, playmate
das Beiſpiel (spell, story), byword, explanation, example
zum Beiſpiel, for instance
beiſpielsweiſe, by way of illustration
koſt(cost)**ſpielig** (spill, waste), expensive
ſpielen, play, gamble; **ab—,** play at sight; **ſich ab—,** be enacted; **an— auf,** allude to; **ver—,** lose by gambling; **ſich ver—,** strike the wrong key; **vor—,** play for others
verſpielt, fond of playing
die Verſpieltheit

679. der Spieß, (*spit, a pointed prong*) *spear, lance, pike*
der Spießgeſelle (companion), accomplice
Spießruten (rod) **laufen,** run the gauntlet
ſpießen, spear; **auf—,** impale
ſpitz, ſpitzig, pointed, sharp, poignant
die Spitze, point, peak, lace

spitzfindig, subtle, crafty; die Spitz=
    findigkeit
spitzen, an—, zu—, sharpen to a
    point

680. spinnen (spann, gesponnen), spin

der Spinner; die —ei, spinning
    mill
die Spinnwebe (weave), cobweb
das Gespinst, spun yarn; Hirn=
    (brain)—, fancy
anspinnen, plot, contrive; aus—,
    spin out
die Spinne, spider; —feind, hating
    mortally

681. spleißen (spliß, gesplissen), split

der Splitter, splinter
splittern, zer—, splinter, dissipate

682. der Sporn (Sporen), spur

spornen, an—, spur, stimulate
spornstreichs, with spurs struck,
    poste-haste

683. der Spott, mockery, irony

spotten, ver—, deride, scoff at
der Spötter, scoffer
die Spötterei, das Gespött, derision
spöttisch, satirical
bespötteln, rally, ridicule

684. sprechen (sp=r=echen) (sprach, gesprochen), speak

ansprechen, address, please; aus—,
    pronounce; be—, discuss; ent—,
    answer; frei(free)—, acquit;
    ver—, foretell, predict, promise;
    sich ver—, make a mistake in
    speaking; vor—, call on; wi=
    der(against)—, contradict
die Besprechung, Frei—
das Versprechen, die Versprechungen
unaussprechlich, unspeakable, un-
    pronounceable
die Sprache, speech, language
die Ansprache, address; Aus—,
    pronunciation; Für—, interven-
    tion; Rück—, (back, talking to
    and fro) consultation; Umgangs=
    (umgehen, go about, associate)—
    —, colloquial language
die Ein(into)sprache, protest; Zwie=
    (two)sprach, dialogue
der Sprecher; Für—, advocate;
    Fern(far)—, telephone
sprachlich, linguistic
das Gespräch, conversation; —=
    buch (book)
das Selbstgespräch, soliloquy, mon-
    ologue; Zwie—, dialogue
gesprächig, affable; die Gesprächig=
    keit
das Sprichwort, proverb; sprich=
    wörtlich
der Spruch, saying, sentence, de-
    cree

der **Anspruch**, appeal, claim; **Aus=**
—, utterance; **Ein**—, protest;
Wahr(true)—, verdict; **Wider=**
(against)—, contradiction; **Zu=**
—, consolation, run of cus-
tomers

spruchreif (ripe), fit for judgment

anspruchsvoll, hard to please;
—**los**, unassuming

die **Anspruchslosigkeit**, frugality

beanspruchen, demand, claim; die
Beanspruchung

widerspruchsvoll, contradictory

685. spreiten, *spread, extend*

spreizen, aus—, spread open, open

spreizbeinig (bone, leg), straddle-
legged

die **Gespreiztheit**, putting on airs

686. sprießen (sproß, ge=
sprossen), (*sprit*), *sprout*

entsprießen, sprout forth

ersprießlich, useful, beneficial

der **Sproß**, sprout, shoot, germ

der **Sprößling**, shoot, scion

sprossen, sprout, shoot, germinate

die **Sprosse**, step, rung (ladder)

spritzen, spout, squirt

ausspritzen, syringe; **be**—, splash;
ein—, inject; **ver**—, squirt away,
shed

die **Ausspritzung**, **Ein**—

die **Spritze**, syringe, fire engine

687. springen (sprang,
gesprungen), *spring, jump*

aufspringen, spring up, chap; **ent=**
—, escape; **über**—, skip; **vor**—,
project; **zer**—, crack

der **Springbrunnen**, fountain; die
—**kraft** (power), elasticity

der **Sprung**, leap, bound, chink,
flaw

der **Ursprung**, (offspring) origin;
ursprünglich, original; die **Ur=**
sprünglichkeit

der **Vorsprung**, projection, advantage over

sprengen, cause to jump, (a rock)
blast, (a horse) gallop, (water)
sprinkle

aussprengen, divulge; **be**—, sprinkle; **ver**—, disperse; **zer**—, blow
up

der **Sprengwagen**, sprinkler

die **Sprengung**, blasting; der
Sprengstoff (stuff), explosive

der **Sprengel**, scattered parishes,
diocese

sprenkeln, speckle

688. spröde, *brittle*

spröde, (prude) forbidding, prudish

die **Sprödigkeit**, brittleness, pru-
dishness

689. sprühen, *sprinkle in*
small drops, emit sparks

der **Sprudel**, boiling well

sprudeln, bubble

690. spülen, *rinse, wash*

ausspülen, fort—, **weg**(away)—

der **Spülstein**, sink; das —**wasser**
Spülicht, dish water

691. die Spur, (*spur, trail of a wild animal*) *track, trace, vestige*

die Spurweite (width), gauge (railroad)

breitspurig, standard gauge; schmal= (narrow)—

spurlos, traceless, trackless

spüren, trace, feel; auf(up)—; ver= —, be aware of, perceive

verspürbar, perceivable

der Spürhund, bloodhound; der —sinn (sense), scent

692. der Staat, *state*

staatlich, federal, national

verstaatlichen, turn into state property

die Verstaatlichung

der Staat, state attire, pomp, finery

693. der Stab, *stave, staff, rod*

der Buchstab(e), letter, character

buchstabieren, spell

694. die Stadt, (*stead*) *town, city*

das Städtchen, Städtlein

die Haupt(head)stadt, capital

die Vorstadt, suburb; vorstädtisch

städtisch, municipal

der Städter, die —in, resident of a town

die Statt, Stätte, stead, place

der Statthalter (holder), lieutenant-governor, governor-general

die Werkstatt, workshop

stattfinden, take place

anstatt, instead of

stattlich, portly; die Stattlichkeit

statthaft, having a place (existence), permissible

abstatten (Besuch, visit) (Dank, thanks); aus—, fit out; be—, put down, bury; er—, put in place, draw up; ge—, make room, permit

die Ausstattung, outfit, endowment, trousseau; das —stück (piece), extravaganza

die Bestattung

wiedererstatten, zurück—, (put again, back in its place) restore, return

die Wiedererstattung, Zurück—

695. der Stahl, *steel*

der Stahlstich (stechen, stick, prick), engraving

stählen, steel, harden, brace

stählern, made of steel

696. der Stamm, *stem, trunk, tribe, race*

der Stammbaum (tree), pedigree; das —buch, autograph album

Stamm, *referring to clubs or restaurants, indicates regular patronage:*

der Stammgast (guest); —tisch, reserved table

stämmig, stout, strong; die Stämmigkeit

stammen, ab—, ent—, her—, proceed from, originate, descend

angestammt, inherited, hereditary

ſtemmen, stem, dam up; ſich —, resist; ſich an—, press against

697. ſt a m m e l n, *stammer, stutter*

die Stammelei, das Geſtammel
ſtumm, dumb, mute; die Stumm=heit
taubſtumm, deaf and dumb
die Taubſtummenanſtalt (institute)

698. d i e S t a n g e, *(sting) pole, stick*

der Stengel, stalk

699. ſt a r k, *(stark) strong, robust*

die Stärke, strength, vigor
ſtärken, strengthen; be—, confirm; ver—, reinforce
die Stärkung, Be—, Ver—
die Stärke, starch; ſtärken, ein—, starch

700. ſt a r r, *(stare) benumbed, rigid*

ſtarren, be stiff, benumbed
ſtieren, stare; an—, stare at

701. ſt a u n e n, *(a-stound) be astonished*

anſtaunen, gaze at with astonish-ment; er—, be amazed
ſtaunenswert (worth), erſtaunlich, astonishing, amazing
das Staunen, Er—

702. ſt e ch e n (ſt a ch, g e ſt o = ch e n), *stick, stab, sting, prick*

ein Boot (boat) abſtechen, push from shore
beſtechen, break the law, corrupt, bribe
abſtechen von, remove from, con-trast with
der Abſtecher, side excursion
die Beſtechung, bribe; beſtechlich, die Beſtechlichkeit
der Stich, stitch, stab, engraving
der Durch(through)ſtich, cut (rail-road); Holz—, wood-engrav-ing; Kupfer(copper)—, Stahl=(steel)—
ſtichhaltig, (stabproof) valid, sound
die Stichhaltigkeit
ſticheln, taunt, chaff; die Stichelei
der Stachel, sting, prickle, thorn
ſtachelig, prickly, thorny
ſtacheln, prick; auf—, goad
die Aufſtachelung
ſtecken, (cause to stick) fix, set
abſtecken, mark off by poles; an—, stick on, infect; be—, plant with, stick with; ein—, arrest, imprison, pocket; ver—, hide; zu—, convey secretly
die Stecknadel (needle), pin
der Steckbrief (letter), warrant of arrest
die Anſteckung, infection, contagion
das Beſteck, knife, fork
ſtecken, stick fast, be stuck
ſticken, stitch, embroider; die Sticke=rei

703. ſtehen (ſtand, ge=
ſtanden), *stand*

beſtehen, stand together, consist of;
bei—, assist; bevor—, approach;
ent—, stand up from, arise;
ge—, stand for, confess; nach—,
be inferior; über—, overcome;
ver—, understand; vor—, pre-
side; wider—, withstand, resist
die Entſtehung, origin
der Stand, stand, state, condition,
rank
der Abſtand, distance, difference;
An—, suitable conduct, de-
cency; Auf—, uprising; Bei—,
assistance; Gegen—, (standing
against, opposite) object; Übel=
(evil)—, drawback; Um—, cir-
cumstance; Ver—, understand-
ing, intellect; Vor—, management, chairman; Wider—, re-
sistance; Zu—, state, condition
der Stand, stand, state, rank
das Standbild (picture), statue;
der —punkt, standpoint, view-
point
das Standesamt (office), bureau of
vital statistics
das Ständchen, serenade
der Schirmſtänder, umbrella stand
ſtandhaft, steadfast; die Standhaf=
tigkeit
ſtandesgemäß (meſſen, measure),
according to one's rank
ſtändiſch, relating to the states of a
country
ſtändig, stationary, fixed; an—,

suitable, decent; be—, steady,
constant; ge—, confessing; ver=
—, judicious, sensible; voll—,
complete; zu—, in perfect condition, competent
die Beſtändigkeit, Ver—, Voll—
das Geſtändnis, confession
ſich verſtändigen, agree; die Ver=
ſtändigung
vervollſtändigen, complete; die Ver=
vollſtändigung
umſtändlich, ceremonious; ver—,
intelligible
die Umſtändlichkeit, Ver—
beanſtanden, stop, object; die Be=
anſtandung
abgeſtanden, (stood off) stale
unausſtehlich, intolerable
die Unausſtehlichkeit
der Stehplatz (place), standing
room

704. ſtehlen (ſtahl, ge=
ſtohlen), *steal*

beſtehlen, steal from
der Stehler, die Stehlerei
verſtohlen, stealthily
der Dieb(thief)ſtahl, theft

705. ſteif, *stiff, inflexible*

ſteifen, stiffen, starch
die Steifheit, stiffness, formality

706. ſteigen (ſtieg, geſtie=
gen), *mount, ascend, rise*

abſteigen, alight; an—, grow in
elevation; aus—, get off a car;

be—, ascend; ein—, board a car;
er—, mount, scale; um—, change
cars; sich ver— zu, go as far as to
der Steigbügel (biegen, bow), stirrup
der Abstieg, descent; An—, Auf—,
ascent
die Stiege, stairs
die Steigung, upgrade (track);
Be—, Er—
steigern, cause to rise, raise; ver—,
raise prices, sell at auction
die Steigerung, Ver—
steil, ascending, steep; die Steilheit

707. der Stein, stone

der Steinbruch (brechen), quarry;
—druck (print)
der Bern(burn)stein, amber; Edel=
—, precious stone; Meilen=
(mile) —
das Gestein, rock
steinern, steinig, stony, rocky
versteinern, petrify; die Versteine=
rung
steinigen, stone to death; die Stei=
nigung
steinreich, very rich

708. stellen, (stall) place, put, set

anstellen, appoint, employ; aus—,
expose, exhibit; be—, put down
on the bill, order; dar(there)—,
represent; sich ein—, (place oneself into a position) turn up;
ent—, deform; fest(fast)—, ascertain; her—, restore; sich her=

aus—, (place itself outside) reveal itself, become known;
ver—, displace; sich ver—, dissemble; vor—, present, intro-
duce
nachstellen, lay snares, lie in wait
for
die Anstellung, Aus—, Be—, Dar=
—; Ein—, (placing inside) suspension; Ent—, Fest—, Her—;
Vor—, introduction, representation, performance
das Stelldich(thee)ein, trysting-
place
die Nachstellung, snare, ambush
der Besteller, customer; Aus—,
exhibitor; Dar—, actor
sich gestellen, enlist; die Gestellung
das Gestell, stand, frame, rack
anstellig, (fit to be placed at a
thing) skilful; die Anstelligkeit
die Stelle, place, situation
stellenlos (less), unemployed
die Stellenlosigkeit, lack of em-
ployment
die Gestalt, shape, form, figure, size
die Anstalt, institute
die Gestaltung, formation
veranstalten, put in shape, arrange
der Veranstalter, die Veranstaltung
die Bestallung, appointment, salary
wohl bestallt, regularly appointed
der Stall, die Stallung, stable

709. sterben (starb, ge= storben), (starve, perish) die

aussterben, die out

sterblich, mortal; die Sterblichkeit
abgestorben, dry, dead
der, die Verstorbene, deceased

710. der Stern, *star*

der Unstern, disaster
die Sternkunde (kennen), astronomy
die Sternwarte (watch), observatory
das Gestirn, constellation
gestirnt, starred, starry

711. stetig, stätig, *steady,*
stable

die Stetigkeit
stets, steadily, continually
bestätigen, corroborate; die Bestätigung
das Gestade, (steady land) shore,
coast

712. steuern, *steer*

das Steuer, rudder, helm
der Steuermann, das —ruder
(helm)
die Steuerung, steering-gear, re-
versing gear (engine)
aussteuern, steer out, give a start,
endow
die Aussteuer, dowry
steuern, steer, govern, tax, assess
steuerbar, taxable; —frei, free of
duty
besteuern, tax; ver—, pay duty
on
die Besteuerung, Ver—
besteuerbar, taxable
beisteuern, contribute

713. stieben (stob, gesto-
ben), *be scattered, fly about*

zerstieben, fly away in dust
stöbern, auf—, scatter; durch—,
rummage
das Schnee(snow)gestöber (drift)
der Staub, dust
staubig, bestaubt, dusty
stäuben, raise dust; ab—, dust;
zer—, atomize, change into
spray
der Zerstäuber, atomizer

714. der Stiefbruder
step-brother

der Stiefvater (father), die —mutter, —schwester
das Stiefmütterchen, pansy
stiefmütterlich, cruel(ly)

715. der Stiefel, *boot*
gestiefelt, booted

716. der Stift, *tag, pin,*
peg, pencil

der Blei(lead)stift, Rot(red)—
das Stift, charitable foundation
die Stiftung, institution; das —s-
fest (festival), founder's day,
anniversary celebration
der Stifter, founder
stiften, establish, found; an—,
contrive, instigate
der Anstifter, die Anstiftung

717. still, *still, quiet, silent*
das Stillleben (life), —schweigen
(silence)

der Stillstand, standstill
stillen, quiet, quench, appease
die Stillung

718. die Stimme, *voice, tune,*
vote, suffrage

der Stimmer, tuner; stimmen, tune
die Stimmung, (from the tuning
of musical instruments) disposition, humor
die Mißstimmung, discord
mißgestimmt, ill-humored; die Miß=
gestimmtheit
verstimmt, out of humor, ill-
humored
die Verstimmtheit, Verstimmung
es stimmt, (it is in tune) it is correct
die Stimme, (acclamation) vote
die Stimmenein(one)heit, unanim-
ity; —gleich(like)heit, tie; —=
mehr(more)heit, majority
das Stimmrecht (right), suffrage
ein(one)stimmig, unanimous
die Einstimmigkeit
stimmen, speak, determine; bei—,
agree; überein—, agree; zu—,
agree to, consent
die Übereinstimmung, Zu—
bestimmen, give a name, determine
die Bestimmung, destiny, destina-
tion
bestimmt, outspoken, determined
die Bestimmtheit, positiveness

719. der Stock, *stick, cane*
der Stockfisch, codfish

der Stock, das —werk (work), floor
der Stecken, stick; das —pferd,
hobby-horse
stockblind, stone blind; —finster,
pitch dark; —taub, deaf as a
post

720. der Stoff, *stuff,*
matter, goods

der Kohlen(coal)stoff, carbon;
Sauer(sour)—, oxygen; Stick=
(choke)—, nitrogen; Wasser—,
hydrogen
kohlenstoffhaltig (holding), car-
bonic; etc.
ausstaffieren, equip; die Ausstaffie=
rung

721. stolz, *(stout) proud*
der Stolz, pride
stolzieren, walk proudly, strut,
flaunt

722. stopfen, *stuff, fill,*
darn, mend
verstopfen, stop, constipate
die Verstopfung, Verstopftheit

723. stören, *(stir) disturb,*
trouble
auf(up)stören; zer—, destroy
die Störung, disturbance; Zer—
der Störenfried (peace), mischief-
maker
ungestört, unmolested
verstört, disturbed; die Verstörtheit

724. ſtoßen (ſtieß, ge=
ſtoßen), *thrust, push*

abſtoßen, push off a boat, repel;
an—, offend, clink glasses;
aus—, cast out, utter; ein—,
smash; um(about)—, over-
throw; ver—, repudiate, transgress; vor—, push forward;
zer—, pound; zu—, happen, befall; zuſammen—, clash together,
collide
die Abſtoßung, Aus—, Um—, Ver—
der Stoß, shock, blow, jolt
der Anſtoß, collision, offense; Ver—,
(wrong blow) blunder; Zuſam=
men—
anſtößig, shocking; die Anſtößigkeit
unumſtößlich, irrefutable
ſtutzen (abſtoßen), curtail, crop
der Stutzer, (*originally,* person
wearing shortened clothes)
beau, dandy, dude
ſtutzerhaft, dandyish
ſtutzen, be startled at
ſtutzig, startled

725. ſtrafen, *punish*

beſtrafen, punish; die Beſtrafung
ſtrafbar, punishable; die Strafbar=
keit
ſtraflos (less), exempt from punishment
die Strafloſigkeit, impunity
ſträflich, punishable; die Sträflich=
keit
der Sträfling, convict

726. ſtraff, *straight,
tight, tense*

die Straffheit
anſtraffen, tighten

727. ſtrahlen, *emit rays,
radiate, beam*

ausſtrahlen, emit rays; be—, beam
upon
die Ausſtrahlung, Be—
der Strahl, beam, ray

728. ſtramm, *tight,
sturdy, burly*

die Strammheit

729. der Strand, *strand,
shore, beach*

ſtranden, be beached, run ashore
die Strandung

730. der Strang, *string, rope*

abſträngen, (string off) unharness;
an(on)—
anſtrengen, strain, exert; ſich über=
(over)—
die Anſtrengung, Über—
ſtreng, ge—, (strong) severe, rigid
die Strenge

731. ſtreben, *strive, endeavor*

anſtreben, strive for; be—, exert,
endeavor; wider(against)—, resist
das Streben, effort, endeavor;
Be—; Wider—, reluctance

der Streber, ambitious person

strebsam, ambitious; die Strebsam=
keit

732. strecken, *stretch, extend*

ausstrecken, sich er—, extend; voll=
(full)—, stretch to the end,
carry out, execute; vor—, advance

der Testamentsvollstrecker, executor

die Strecke, stretch, extent, distance

streckbar, ductile; die Streckbarkeit

stracks, schnur(snare, string)—,
straightways, immediately

der Strick, line, rope; die —leiter,
rope ladder

stricken, knit

bestricken, um—, ver—, entangle,
ensnare

**733. streichen (strich, ge=
strichen), *strike, pass softly
over***

abstreichen, check off; an—, check
off, paint with a brush; aus—,
cancel; be—, spread over; her=
aus—, underscore, praise; um=
her—, roam about; ver—,
elapse, pass away

der Streich, stroke, blow

der Anstreicher, house-painter;
Land—, vagrant

streicheln, caress; die Streichelei

der Strich, stroke, line, dash,
tract

der Anstrich, house painting; Land=
—, tract of land

strichweise, here and there

**734. der Streif, Streifen
*stripe, streak***

streifen, move in narrow lines,
leave a mark, graze

der Streifband (binden), newspaper
wrapper

streifen, strip; ab(off)—, an(on)—,
über(over)—

**735. der Streit, *strife,
dispute, quarrel***

der Wett(bet)streit, contest

der Streiter, warrior, disputant

streitbar, able to fight; —ig, dis-
putable

die Streitbarkeit, Streitigkeit

streiten (stritt, gestritten), quarrel,
fight

abstreiten, deny; be—, contest,
dispute

bestreitbar, contestable

unbestritten, uncontested

736. streuen, *strew*

ausstreuen, scatter; be—, sprinkle;
ver—, disperse; zer—, scatter;
sich zer—, seek diversion

die Zerstreuung

zerstreut, absent-minded; die Zer=
streutheit

das Stroh, straw

die Streu, litter, bed of straw

737. ſtrolchen, *stroll about*
der Strolch, tramp, vagabond

738. der Strom, (*stream*)
river
die Strömung, current
ſtromabwärts (downward), —auf=
wärts
ſtrömen, stream, flow; aus—,
ent—, escape; über—, overflow
die Ausſtrömung, escape, puff
(steam)

739. das Stück, *piece, part,
cannon*
das Bruch(brechen)—, fragment;
Früh(early)—, breakfast, lunch;
Grund(ground)—, lot, property
frühſtücken
ſtückeln, patch up; zer—, dismember
die Zerſtückelung

740. die Stufe, *step,
degree, grade*
ſtufenweiſe, by degrees, gradually
abſtufen, grade; die Abſtufung
die Staffel, step, rundle, round
die Staffelei, easel

741. der Stumpf, *stump,
trunk*
ſtumpf, blunt, obtuse, dull
abſtumpfen, stupefy; die Abſtump=
fung
abgeſtumpft, blunted, dull, obtuse
der Stümper, bungler; die —ei,
bungling

ſtümperhaft, unskilled
der Stummel, stump, remnant, end
verſtümmeln, mutilate; die Ver=
ſtümmelung

742. die Stunde, (*stand, stop,
mark on the dial*) *hour, lesson*
der Stundenplan, schedule of studies
ſtündlich, every hour
ſtunden, allow an extension of time
die Stundung

743. der Sturm, *storm*
der Anſturm, assault by storm
ſtürmiſch, stormy
ſtürmen, storm, assault, roar; be—,
assault, importune; er—, take
by assault
die Beſtürmung, Er—

744. ſtürzen, (*start, startle*)
tumble, overthrow, rush, plunge
einſtürzen, cave in; ſich über—, act
rashly; um—, upset, overturn
der Sturz, rush, fall, tumble
der Einſturz, Um—
der Umſtürzler, revolutionist
die Überſtürzung, rash act
die Stürze, pot-lid
beſtürzt, perplexed; die Beſtürzung

745. ſuchen, (*sough-t*) *seek,
search, look for*
ausſuchen, pick out; be—, seek at
home, visit; er—, seek a favor,
request; heim—, search the
home, afflict; nach—, apply for;

unter—, search, examine; ver—, search for, experiment, try, tempt

der Besuch, visit; das Gesuch, application; der Ver—, experiment, trial

der Besucher; Ver—, tempter

die Heimsuchung, Unter—; Ver—, temptation

die Suche, search, quest; der Sucher

das Ansuchen, application; Er—, request

746. der Sumpf, (s-w-amp)
bog, marsh

sumpfig, boggy, marshy

versumpfen, become marshy, lose one's character

747. die Sünde, sin

der Sünder, sinner; die —in

sündhaft sinful; die Sündhaftigkeit

sündig, sinful; die Sündigkeit

sündigen, sin; sich ver—, sin against, wrong

die Sündflut, Sintflut, world's flood, deluge

748. süß, sweet

süßlich, sweetish; versüßen

749. der Tadel, blame,
fault, censure, reproach

tadelhaft, faulty; —los (less)

tadeln, blame, censure

der Tadler, faultfinder

750. die Tafel, table,
tablet, board, plate

tafeln, enjoy a meal

täfeln, board, wainscot

die Täfelung, das Getäfel

751. der Tag, day

täglich, daily

der Tagesanbruch (brechen, break), dawn

betagt, aged, elderly; die Betagtheit

tagen, dawn, hold a meeting; ver—, adjourn

die Tagung, convention; Ver—

752. tändeln, dandle, trifle

der Tändler, die Tändelei

der Tand, prattle, trifles

753. die Tanne, pine tree

der Tann, pine forest

tannen, made of pine

754. der Tanz, dance

der Tänzer, die —in

tanzen, dance; ver—, wear out by dancing

tänzeln, skip about, prance

das Tänzchen, short dance

755. die Tapete, (tapestry)
wall-paper

der Tapezier(er), paper-hanger

tapezieren, paper

aufs Tapet bringen, (bring on the table) broach

756. tapfer, (*dapper, lively*)
    brave, gallant

die **Tapferkeit,** valor, bravery

757. die Tasche, *pocket,*
    pouch

der **Taschendieb** (thief), pickpocket;
    das **—geld** (money), **—messer**
    (knife); das **—tuch** (cloth), hand-
    kerchief; die **—uhr,** watch

758. tasten, *feel, grope about*

betasten, touch, handle
die **Taste,** key; **Tastatur,** keyboard
    (typewriter)
die **Tatze,** paw

759. der Tau, (*thaw*) *dew*

der **Mehltau,** mildew
tauen, dew, thaw
verdauen, digest
verdaulich, digestible; die **Verdau-
    lichkeit**
die **Verdauung,** digestion
das **Tau,** tow, cable

760. taub, *deaf*

taubstumm, deaf and dumb
die **Taubheit,** deafness
betäuben, deafen, stun; die **Be-
    täubung**

761. tauchen, (*duck*)
    dive, dip

auftauchen, loom up; ein—, dip in;
    unter—, dip, dive
der **Taucher,** diver

762. taufen, (*dip*) *christen,*
    baptize

die **Taufe,** baptism, christening
der **Taufname,** Christian name;
    —pate, god-father; die **—patin;**
    der **—schein,** certificate
der **Täufer,** baptist
der **Täufling,** child to be baptized

763. taugen, (*doughty, deft*)
    be worth, fit, be good for

tauglich, able, fit; die **Tauglichkeit**
der **Taugenichts** (nothing), ne'er-
    do-well, good-for-nothing
tüchtig, (doughty) able, apt, quali-
    fied
die **Tüchtigkeit**
die **Tugend,** virtue
tugendhaft, virtuous

764. taumeln, *reel, stagger*

der **Taumel,** reeling, giddiness
tummeln, put in motion; **sich
    herum—,** bustle about
der **Tummelplatz,** wrestling place
das **Getümmel,** bustle, turmoil

765. tauschen, *exchange, barter*

vertauschen, mistake for
der **Tausch,** exchange, barter
täuschen, exchange, substitute, de-
    ceive
die **Täuschung,** illusion, deception
enttäuschen, disillusion, disappoint
die **Enttäuschung**
der **Roßtäuscher,** horse-dealer

766. tausend, *thousand*

der Tausend, (*stands for the devil*) deuce

Potz(*corruption of* Gottes)tausend, the deuce

767. der Teich, (*dike*) *pond*

der Deich, dike

ein(in)deichen, um(around)—, protect by a dike

768. der Teil, *deal, part, share, portion*

der Anteil, share, share in other persons' misfortune, sympathy; Hinter(hind)—, stern; Border= (further, front)—, prow

der Vor(fore, first)teil, first, best part, profit, advantage; Nach—, disadvantage

vorteilhaft, advantageous

übervorteilen, defraud; die Über= vorteilung

nachteilig, disadvantageous, injurious

benachteiligen, prejudice, injure, hurt

die Benachteiligung

das Teilchen, particle

teilbar, divisible; die Teilbarkeit

teilhaben, have a share in, participate

der Teilhaber, partner; die —schaft

teilnehmen, share in, sympathize

die Teilnahme, sympathy

teilhaftig, partaking

teils, partly; teilweise, in part

teilen, divide

abteilen, partition off; aus—, deal out; ein—, arrange; er—, issue; mit—, share with others, impart; ver—, distribute; zer—, dissect, dismember; zu—, assign

die Teilung, Ab—, Aus—, Ein—, Er—, Mit—, Ver—, Zer—, Zu—

der Abteil, section of a car

tel (teil), *is used in the formation of fractions:* das Siebentel, seventh

sich beteiligen, participate in

die Beteiligung

der Beteiligte, party concerned

769. teuer, *dear, costly, expensive*

die Teuerung, Teuerkeit, dearth

verteuern, raise the price

die Verteuerung

beteuern, (make true) aver, affirm

die Beteuerung

770. der Teufel, *devil*

die Teufelei, deviltry

teuflisch, diabolical

verteufelt, with a vengeance

der Zauber, incantation, spell, enchantment

der Zauberer, sorcerer; die Zau= berin

zauberisch, enchanting

zaubern, practise witchcraft; be—, charm

die Bezauberung

771. der Thron, *throne*

thronen, sit enthroned, reign

772. tief, *deep*

der Tiefgang (gehen), draught of a ship; —sinn (sense), melancholy

die Tiefe, depth; Un—, shallow place

vertiefen, deepen; sich ver— in, be lost, be absorbed in

die Vertiefung, deepening, cavity, recess

die Teufe, depth of a mine

teufen, deepen a mine

773. das Tier, (*deer*)
animal, beast

tierisch, animal, brutal, bestial

die Tierheit, animal nature

vertiert, bestial, savage

774. tilgen, *efface, annul*

austilgen, ver—, exterminate

die Tilgung, liquidation, payment; Aus—, Ver—

tilgbar, redeemable; die Tilgbarkeit

775. der Tisch, (*dish*) *table*

der Tischler, cabinet-maker; die —ei (shop)

auftischen, serve up, dish up

776. toben, *act foolishly, rage*

die Tobsucht (siech, sick), madness, delirium, insanity

tobsüchtig

austoben, sow one's wild oats

777. der Tod, *death*

tödlich, mortal, deadly

tot, dead

der Scheintod, apparent death, coma

töten, kill; ab—, deaden, mortify

die fahrlässige (let go, careless) Tötung, homicide

778. toll, (*dull*) *mad, frantic*

die Tollheit, madness; das —haus, lunatic asylum

sich austollen, sow one's wild oats

779. der Ton, *tone,*
sound, accent

tonangebend, (giving the tone) leading the fashion; —los (less), unaccented

ein(one)tönig, monotonous; die Eintönigkeit

tönen, sound, resound

wohl(well)tönend, melodious

betonen, accentuate, emphasize

die Betonung

780. der Topf, (*tub*) *pot*

der Töpfer, potter

781. der Tor, (*dizzy*) *fool,*
simpleton

die Torheit, folly

töricht, foolish, silly

betören, delude; die Betörung

782. tosen, *roar*

das Tosen, Getöse

783. traben, *trot, run*

der Trab, trot
der Traber, trotter
die Trabrenn(run)bahn (track),
speedway

784. trachten, (Lat. *tractare*)
strive after, endeavor

betrachten, (aim at) view, contemplate, consider
beträchtlich, considerable, important
die Betrachtung
in Anbetracht, in consideration of
die Eintracht, (one aim) harmony
einträchtig, die Einträchtigkeit
die Zwie(two)tracht, discord
zwieträchtig
niederträchtig, base, abject
die Niederträchtigkeit

785. tragen (trug, getragen), (*draw*) *carry, bear, wear*

antragen, carry to, offer, propose;
auf—, put on one's shoulders,
give an order, instruct; be—,
accumulate, amount to; sich
be—, carry oneself, conduct oneself, behave; bei—, add, contribute; ein—, make an entry,
bring profit; er—, bear; über—,
transmit, transfer; ver—, bear,
endure; sich ver—, bear each
other, agree; vor—, carry before an audience, lecture, recite;

sich zu—, carry itself (move)
toward, turn up, take place
die Eintragung, Er—, Über—
das Betragen, conduct
der Antrag, offer, proposal; Auf—,
order; Be—, amount; Bei—,
contribution; Er—, produce,
profit, output; Ver—, agreement; Vor—, lecture
beantragen, make a motion
beauftragen, commission, order
einträglich, (bringing in) profitable
erträglich, tolerable
nachträglich, (brought afterward)
subsequent; ver—, peaceable;
zu—, carrying to, adding, beneficial
die Unverträglichkeit, incompatibility of temper
tragbar, portable; über—, transferable
die Übertragbarkeit
die Trage, litter
der Träger, carrier, beam
der Brief(letter)träger; Hosen(hosiery)—, suspenders
die Tracht, load, fashion, costume

786. die Träne, *tear*

tränenleer (empty), tearless
tränen, run with tears

787. die Traube, *grape*
die Weintraube, bunch of grapes

788. die Trauer, (*drear-y*)
mourning, sorrow, affliction

der Trauermarsch, funeral march;

das —spiel, tragedy; die —weide, weeping willow

traurig, (dreary) sad, sorrowful

die Traurigkeit

trauern, mourn; be—, bemoan

789. der Traum, *dream*

das Traumbild (picture); —gesicht (sight), vision

der Träumer, dreamer

träumerisch, fanciful, visionary

träumen, dream; ver—, dream away

790. treffen (traf, getroffen), *(drub) hit, catch, meet*

anbetreffen, regard; an—, meet at home; be—, hit, point at, regard; ein(in)—, hit into, reach, arrive; über—, (overhit) surpass, excel; zu—, hit at, prove right; zusammen—, meet, collide

treffend, striking

trefflich, making a hit, excellent; unüber—, unsurpassable; vor—, (outstriking) excellent

die Trefflichkeit, Unüber—, Vor—

betreffend, betreffs, in Betreff, regarding, in regard to

der Treffer, hit, prize (lottery)

das Treffen, collision, battle, fight; Hinter(be-hind)—, rear-guard; Vorder(forward, front)—, vanguard; Zusammen(together)—, coincidence

triftig, striking, weighty, cogent

die Triftigkeit

791. treiben (trieb, getrieben), *drive*

abtreiben, drive away, drift off (boat); an—, drive on, incite; aus—, expel; be—, carry on, operate; ein—, drive in(to), collect (money, *originally* cattle); hinter—, drive behind, remove, frustrate; über—, drive too far, exaggerate; ver—, drive away, pass (time), sell (goods); zurück(back)—

die Austreibung, Ein—, Hinter—, Über—, Ver—

das Treiben, carrying on, act, doings; Be—, instance, instigation

der Treiber, driver, beater (hunt)

das Treibeis, floating ice; —haus, hothouse; die —jagd (hunt); die —kraft, impulsive power

der Trieb, impulse, bent, propensity

der Antrieb, impulse; Be—, operation, instigation; Ver—, carting away, sale

betriebsam, industrious; die Betriebsamkeit

das Getriebe, machinery

die Triebfeder (feather, spring), elastic spring; die —kraft, propelling power; das —rad, spring wheel; der —sand, quicksand; das —werk, machinery, mechanism

die Trift, drift, pasturage

792. t r e n n e n, *(tear)*
separate, sever

die Trennung, separation
trennbar, separable; die Trennbar=
keit
abtrünnig, rebellious, faithless·
die Abtrünnigkeit

793. die Treppe, *step, stairs*
die Wendeltreppe, winding stairs

**794. t r e t e n (t r a t, g e =
t r e t e n),** *tread, step (trade)*

abtreten, step away, cede; an—,
step near, fall in line, take the
first step; auf—, step upon (the
stage), appear; aus—, step out,
resign; be—, step upon, enter;
bei—, step by, near, join a club;
über—, transgress, trespass,
change party, religion; ver—,
step into a person's place, substitute; den Weg (way) ver—,
step across, obstruct; zer—,
tread under foot; zurück(back)=
—, withdraw, resign
die Abtretung, cessation; Über—,
misdemeanor; Ver—
der Übertreter, transgressor; Ver=
—, representative, agent
betreten, disconcerted, confused;
die Betretenheit
der Tritt, pace, step, kick
der Antritt, beginning; Auf—, appearance of an actor, scene,
falling out; Aus—, resignation;
Bei—, admission to a club;

Ein—, entrance; Rück—, withdrawal; Über—, conversion;
Vor,— precedence
das Trittbrett, foot board

795. t r e u, *true, loyal, faithful*

untreu, faithless, perfidious
veruntreuen, embezzle; die Verun=
treuung
treulos faithless; die Treulosigkeit
die Treue, fidelity, loyalty
der Treubruch (brechen), breach of
faith
treubrüchig, faithless
treulich, truly, trustily
getreu, —lich, faithful, trusty, loyal
trauen, trust, confide
sich trauen, sich ge—, venture, dare
trauen, (troth) marry
sich trauen lassen (let), get married
der Trauring; die —ung, wedding
ceremony
antrauen, unite in marriage
traulich, genial, familiar; ver—, confidential; zu—, confiding, trustful
die Traulichkeit, Ver—, Zu—
das Vertrauen, Zu—, confidence,
trust
vertraut mit, (entrusted with)
familiar with
die Vertrautheit
der Trost, (trust in God) consolation, comfort
trostlos, inconsolable; —reich
(rich), consolatory
die Trostlosigkeit

tröftlidj, comfortable
getroft, confident, courageous
tröften, comfort, console; ver—,
give fair hopes
die Tröftung, Ber—, der Tröfter

796. triefen (troff, ge= troffen), *drip*

das Triefauge, running eye; trief=
äugig
die Traufe, eaves
träufeln, drip, drop; ein—, infuse
by drops
der Tropfen, drop; der Tropf, dunce
tropfenweife, by drops
der Tropffftein (stone), stalactite
tropfen, drop, drip; tröpfeln, trickle

797. trinfen (tranf, ge= trunfen), *drink*

fidj betrinfen, become intoxicated,
get drunk
ertrinfen, (drench) drown
der Trinfbedjer (beaker), drinking
cup; das —geld (money), tip;
die —halle, soda fountain; der
—fprudj (fpredjen, speak), toast;
das —waffer (water)
der Trinfer, drinker, drunkard
der Trunf, draught, drinking, drunkenness
trunfen, drunk, drunken, elated
der Trunfenbold, drunkard; die
—heit, drunkenness, intoxication
der Tranf, das Getränf, drink,
beverage
trinfbar, drinkable; die Trinfbarfeit

tränfen, (cause to drink) drench,
water, soak, saturate; durdj=
(through)—, saturate
ertränfen, (cause to be drowned)
drown
die Tränfe, watering-place

798. trocfen, *dry, arid, barren*

die Trocfenheit, dryness
abtrocfnen, wipe, dry; aus(out)—,
dry up, parch; ein—, dry in,
shrink; ver—, dry up, wither

799. die Trommel, *drum, barrel*

das Trommelfell (pelt, skin), tym-
panum
der Trommler, trommeln

800. die Trompete, *trumpet*
der Trompeter, trompeten

801. der Trofj, *baggage of an army*

der Trofjbube (boy), —fnedjt (servant), das —pferd (horse), der
—wagen (wagon)

802. der Trott, *trot*
trotten, trottieren, trot, drudge
das Trottoir, sidewalk

803. der Trofj, *scorn, spite*
der Trofjfopf (head), pig-headed
fellow
trofjig, defiant, sulky

tro𝔷en, defy, be obstinate; ab—,
er—, obtain by defiance
tro𝔷, (*prep. with gen.*) in spite of
das Tru𝔷bündnis (binden), offensive
alliance

804. trübe, *gloomy, cloudy,
dull*

die Trübfal, affliction, misery
trübfelig, woeful; die Trübfelig=
keit
der Trübfinn (sense), sadness, de-
jection
trübfinnig, die Trübfinnigkeit
die Trübheit, cloudiness, dulness
trüben, trouble, sadden; be—,
afflict, grieve
die Betrübtheit, affliction, grief,
distress

805. trügen (trog, getro=
gen), *deceive*

betrügen, deceive, cheat, defraud
der Trug, deceit, fraud
Lug (lügen, lie) und Trug, fraud
and falsehood
das Trugbild (picture), phantom;
der —fchluß (fchließen, close,
conclude), fallacy
trügerifch, fallacious, deceitful
trüglich, fallacious, illusory
die Trüglichkeit
der Betrug, fraud; der Betrüger,
impostor; die Betrügerei, fraudu-
lence
betrügerifch, fraudulent, deceitful

806. der Trümmer, (*thrum*)
fragments, ruins, wreck

trümmerhaft, ruinous
zertrümmern, demolish; die Zer=
trümmerung

807. der Truthahn, *turkey*

die Truthenne (hen), die Truthühner
(chickens)

808. das Tuch, (*duck, light
canvas*) *cloth;* plur. Tuche
(*goods*), Tücher (*cut cloth*)

das Hals(throat)tuch, neckerchief;
Schnupf(snuff)—, handkerchief;
Tafchen(pocket)—, handkerchief; Tifch(table)—; Wifch=
(wash)—, rag
das Tüchelchen, Tüchlein, little shawl
tuchen, made of cloth

809. die Tücke, *malice*

tückifch, malicious, trickish
die Heimtücke, malice, malignity
heimtückifch

810. tun (tat, getan), *do*

abtun, (do off, doff) do away with,
settle; an—, (do on, don) put
on; auf—, put on, pour on,
open; genug(enough)—, satisfy;
groß(great)—, boast; fich hervor=
(forward)—, distinguish oneself;
mit(with others)—, join; wohl=
(well)—, benefit, befriend; zu—,
(put towards, add) help

tunlich, feasible, practicable
die Tunlichkeit
der Großtuer, braggart; die —ei
die Genugtuung, satisfaction
der Untertan, (underdone, underling) subject
untertänig, humble, obsequious
die Untertänigkeit
die Tat, deed, act, action
die Groß(great)tat, achievement, exploit; Wohl(well)—, good action, benefit; Un—, misdeed; Zu—, addition, ingredient
der Tatbestand (standing, state), facts of a case; die —kraft (power), energy; die —sache, matter of fact
tatkräftig, energetic; —sächlich, actual, based on facts
tatenlos, deedless, inactive; —reich (rich), fruitful in achievements
die Tatenlosigkeit
der Täter, doer
der Übel(evil)täter, perpetrator; Wohl—, benefactor
tätig, active; mild(mild)—, benevolent; wohl—, charitable
die Tätigkeit, Mild—, Wohl—
sich betätigen, take an active part in
die Betätigung

811. die Tünche, (tinge)
whitewash

der Tüncher
tünchen, über—, whitewash, gloss over

812. der Turm, tower, steeple

das Türmchen, turret
der Aussichts(outlook, view)turm, observatory; Kirch(church)—, steeple; Leucht(light)—, lighthouse
der Türmer, warden of a tower, jailer
türmen, auf—, pile up; sich auf—, rise high

813. turnen, practise
gymnastics

das Schau(show)turnen, gymnastic contest
der Turner, gymnast; Vor—, leader
die Turnerschaft, athletic association
das Turnen, gymnastic exercises
die Turnanstalt (institute), gymnasium; —fahrt (fare, ride), excursion of gymnasts; das —gerät (apparatus); die —halle, der —saal (saloon), gymnasium; der —lehrer (teacher); der —platz (place), drill ground; der —verein (one, union), athletic club

814. das Turnier
tournament

der Turnierplatz (place), tilt-yard

815. tuschen, (re-touch) draw
with Indian ink

die Tusche, Indian ink

der Tuſchkaſten (chest), color box
vertuſchen, obliterate, hush up
die Vertuſchung

816. der Tyrann, *tyrant*

die Tyrannei, tyranniſch, tyranni=
ſieren

817. übel, *evil, ill, bad*

übelnehmen, take amiss; übelneh=
miſch), cross-grained, touchy
verübeln, take amiss; die Verübe=
lung
das Übel, evil, injury, hurt
die Übelkeit, nausea; der —ſtand
(standing, state), defect, drawback; die —tat, misdeed, crime;
der —täter, evil-doer, criminal;
das —wollen (will, will), hostile
disposition
übelwollend, malevolent

818. üben, *operate, exercise;*
practise

ausüben, execute, exercise; ein=
(in)—, study, train; ver—, commit, perpetrate
die Übung, exercise
das Übungsbuch (book); der —ſtoff
(stuff), material
ungeübt, untrained, inexperienced
üblich, usual, customary
die Ausübung, Ein—, Ver—
die Fingerübung, Leſe(reading)—,
Schieß(shoot, target)—; Vor-
(fore)—, preliminary exercise

819. über, *over*

überdies (this), besides, moreover
übrig, left over; die —en, the others
übrigens, for the rest, besides
erübrigen, (keep over) save, spare

820. das Ufer, *bank*

uferlos, shoreless

821. die Uhr, (*hour*) *watch,*
clock

die Uhrfeder (feather, spring); das
—gehäuſe (house), case; die
—kette (chain), der —macher
(maker), das —werk (work)
die Normal(normal, standard)-
uhr; Sonnen—, sun dial; Ta=
ſchen(pocket)—, Turm(tower)—,
Weck(wake, alarm)—
zwei Uhren, two clocks
zwei Uhr, two o'clock

822. der Unflat, *filth, dirt*

unflätig, filthy, nasty; die Unflätig=
keit

823. ungeheuer, *monstrous,*
prodigious, immense

geheuer, unhaunted
das Ungeheuer, monster, prodigy

824. ungestüm, *uncheckable,*
impetuous

das Ungestüm

825. das Urteil (*ordeal,* ancient
form of trial by fire or water,

divine decision) judgment, sentence, *opinion, verdict*

urteilsfähig, capable of judgment
die Urteilsfähigkeit
urteilslos, brainless; die Urteils=
losigkeit
das Todes(death)urteil; Vor—,
prejudice
urteilen, judge, decide
aburteilen, decide finally; be—,
judge, decide; ver—, condemn
die Aburteilung, Be—, Ver—
der Beurteiler, judge, critic

826. der Vater, *father*

das Vaterland, native country; die
—stadt, native town; —stelle,
father's place; das —unser,
Lord's Prayer
der Vaterlandsfreund, patriot; die
—liebe, patriotism
der Vatersname, surname
vaterlandslos (less)
der Groß(great, grand)vater, Ur=
groß(great grand)—; Raben=
(raven)—, unnatural father;
Schwieger—,   father-in-law;
Waisen—, superintendent of an
orphan asylum
väterlich, paternal; —erseits (die
Seite, side)
der Gevatter, (co-father) god-father; die —in, god-mother; die
—schaft, godfather(mother)ship
der Vetter, cousin; die — schaft, relationship

827. verblüffen (*bluff*), *dumbfound, startle*

die Verblüfftheit

828. verdrießen (verdroß, verdrossen), *vex, annoy, cause disgust*

verdrießlich, vexatious, peevish
die Verdrießlichkeit
verdrossen, displeased, unwilling
die Verdrossenheit
unverdrossen, indefatigable
die Unverdrossenheit
der Verdruß, vexation, annoyance
der Überdruß, disgust, satiety
überdrüssig, weary of, tired of

829. vergessen (vergaß, vergessen), *forget*

die Vergessenheit, oblivion
vergeßlich, forgetful; die Vergeß=
lichkeit
das Vergißmeinnicht, forget-me-not

830. vergeuden, *waste, lavish, squander*

die Vergeudung

831. verletzen, (*let* in the sense of hinder) *injure, hurt*

verletzbar, —lich, violable, vulnerable
die Unverletzlichkeit, inviolability
die Verletzung, violation, hurt,
offense

832. **verlieren (verlor, verloren)**, *lose*

der Verlierer, die —in, loser
der Verlust, loss; die —liste, list of casualties
verlustig gehen (go), be lost

833. **der Vers**, *verse, stanza*

der Versbau (building), versification; das —maß (messen, measure), meter
der Bibel(bible)vers, scriptural quotation

834. **versehren**, (*sore*) *injure, hurt*
unversehrt

835. **das Vieh**, (*fee*, originally cattle used in trading) *beast, brute, cattle*

das Viehfutter, fodder, forage; der —handel (trade), der —händler (dealer), der —hof (hoof, yard), der —markt (market); die —seuche (siech, sick), cattle plague; der —stall; der —stand (standing, state), stock; der —treiber (driver), drover; die —trift (drift), pasture; die —weide (wade), pasture; die —zucht (ziehen draw, produce), cattle breeding; der —züchter, stockraiser
das Hornvieh, Rind—, black cattle; Zucht—, cattle for breeding
viehisch, beastly, brutal

836. **viel**, *much, many*

vieldeutig (deuten, mean), ambiguous; —ecfig (die Ecke, edge, corner), polygonal; —erlei, of many kinds, various; —fach, fältig, manifold; —jährig, of many years; —köpfig, many-headed; —mal, many times; —malig, often done, repeated; —mehr (more), rather; —sagend (saying), significant; —seitig (die Seite, side), versatile; —silbig, polysyllabic; —stimmig, many-voiced; —wissend, knowing much
die Vieldeutigkeit, —fältigkeit, —seitigkeit
der Vielwisser, smatterer
die Vielgötterei (Gott, God), polytheism; die —weiberei (Weib, wife), polygamy
das Vielliebchen, fillipeen
vielleicht, (very lightly) perhaps
der wievielte (*imitation of ordinal numbers;* the how-many-eth?), which of a certain number?
vervielfältigen, manifold
die Vervielfältigung

837. **vier**, *four*

das Viereck (die Ecke, edge, corner), square, quadrangle; der —füßler (foot), quadruped; das —tel, fourth, quarter
viereckig; —fältig, quadruple; —füßig, —jährig; —räderig (das Rad, wheel); —seitig (die Seite, side), quadrilateral; —silbig,

quadrisyllabic; —ſiţig, with four seats; —ſpännig, drawn by four horses; —tägig, of four days
viertens, fourthly
das Geviert, square

838. der Vogel, (fowl)
bird; plur. Vögel

das Vogelbauer (building), cage; der —fänger (fangen, catch), fowler; das —haus, aviary; das —neſt; die —perſpektive, bird's-eye view; die —ſcheuche (shy), scarecrow; der —ſteller, fowler.
der Vogler, fowler
vogelfrei (free), outlawed, proscribed
der Raub(rob)vogel, bird of prey; Sing(song)—; Waſſer—, water fowl; Zug(ziehen, pull, travel)—, migratory bird

839. das Volk, (folk) people,
nation; plur. Völker

das Volksfeſt, public festival; der —haufe (heap), mob, crowd; die —herrſchaft (mastery), democracy; die —hymne, national anthem; das —lied (lay), folk-song, folk-lore; die —menge (many), crowd; die —ſchule, public school; der—ſtamm (stem), tribe; die —zählung (telling, counting), census
die Völkerkunde (kennen, know), ethnology; das —recht (right), international law; die —ſchaft

(ship), tribe, people; die —wanderung (wandering), migration of nations
völkerrechtlich, relating to international law
volkstümlich, popular; die Volkstümlichkeit
bevölkern, populate; ent—, depopulate
die Bevölkerung, population; Ent—

840. voll, *full*

das Vollbad, plunge bath; das —blut(blood)pferd, thoroughbred horse; die —macht (might), power of attorney; der —mond (moon)
vollblütig (blood), plethoric; — giltig (gelten, be worth), unexceptionable; —jährig (year), of age; —kommen, perfect, complete; —ſtändig, complete; — wichtig, of full weight; —zählig (tell, count), complete
die Vollblütigkeit; —jährigkeit, full age, majority; —kommenheit, —ſtändigkeit
vervollkommnen, perfect; die Vervollkommnung
vervollſtändigen, complete; die Vervollſtändigung
bevollmächtigen, authorize; die Bevollmächtigung
vollbringen, (bring to an end) accomplish, perform, execute
vollenden, (end fully) finish, accomplish

vollführen, (lead to the end) execute

vollstrecken (stretch), execute, carry out

vollziehen (draw), execute, fulfil

die Vollendung, —führung, —streckung, —ziehung

vollends, fully, altogether, wholly

völlig, fully, entirely

die Völlerei, gluttony

voller, full of

841. vor (be-fore), before, in front of

voran, before, in front, ahead; —auf, in front; —aus (out), beforehand; —bei, past, over, finished; —her, a short time before; —hin, a little while ago; —über (over), by, past, finished; —wärts, forward; —weg (way), from before

vordem (this), formerly, of old

vorder, anterior, fore

der vorderste, foremost

842. der Vulkan, volcano

vulkanisch

843. wach, (wake) awake

wachsam (some), watchful

die Wachsamkeit

wachen, wake, be awake, watch over

aufwachen, er—, awake; be—, über—, guard

die Wache, guard, watch; Nacht=(night)—

wachthabend (having), on guard, acting

das Wachthaus, guardhouse; der —meister (master), sergeant, major; die —parade, review of the soldiers on guard; der —posten, sentinel; das —schiff, guard-ship

der Wächter, watchman; Nacht=(night)—

wacker, awake, lively, gallant, brave

wecken, (cause to be awake) wake, awake, rouse, call; auf(up)—, rouse from sleep; er—, resuscitate (the dead)

die Erweckung der Toten (dead)

der Wecker, die Weckuhr (hour, clock), alarm clock

844. das Wachs, wax

die Wachsfigur (figure), das —enkabinett (cabinet, museum); die —leinwand (linen), oilcloth

wächsern, waxen

wichsen, wax, polish; die Wichse, blacking

845. wachsen (wuchs, gewachsen), (wax) grow

anwachsen, grow on, increase; aus—, grow out, shoot out; be—, overgrow; ent—, outgrow; er—, grow up, accrue from; über—, overgrow das **Wachstum** (dom), growth, increase

der **Erwachsene**, adult

verwachsen, ill-grown

der **Zuwachs**, increase

der **Wuchs**, growth

der **Anwuchs**, increase; **Aus—**, outgrowth, excrescence; **Nach—**, aftergrowth

halbwüchsig, half-grown; **ur**(old, first)**—**, original, strong

die **Urwüchsigkeit**

das **Gewächs**, plant, vegetable, excrescence; das **—haus**, hothouse

846. die Waffe, *weapon, arm*

der **Waffenstillstand**, armistice

die **Feuer**(fire)**waffe**, **Hand—**, **Schutz**(protective, defensive)**—**

waffnen, **be—**, arm; **ent—**, disarm

die **Bewaffnung**, armament; **Ent—**

das **Wappen**, escutcheon, coat of arms

wappnen, arm

847. wagen, *dare, venture*

waghalsig (der **Hals**, neck), audacious

die **Waghalsigkeit**

das **Wagnis**, risk, hazard; das **—stück** (piece), hazardous enterprise

verwegen, daring, audacious, bold

die **Verwegenheit**

848. der Wagen, (*wain*) *wagon, carriage, car*

die **Wagenburg** (borough), barricade of wagons; das **—gestell** (stellen, place), body; die **—ladung** (load); die **—remise** (remit, put back), shed; das **—rennen** (run), chariot race; der **—schuppen** (shop), shed

der **Kinderwagen**, baby carriage; **Last**(laden, load)**—**, truck; **Pack**(pack, baggage)**—**, **Post**(mail)**-—**, **Schlaf**(sleep)**—**; **Speise—** (food)**—**, dining car

849. die Wahl, (*will, wish*) *choice, election, option*

die **Auswahl**, choice; **Neu**(new)**—**, re-election; **Stich**(stechen, stick, cut)**—**, second ballot (*when no candidate has received a majority on the first ballot*), supplementary ballot

der **Wahlbezirk** (circle, district); **—könig**, elective king; die **—liste** (list), register of electors; der **—mann**, elector, constituent; der **—spruch** (sprechen, speak), device, motto; die **—stimme** (voice, acclamation), vote; der **—tag** (day); die **—urne** (urn), ballot-box; die **—versammlung** (assembly); die **—verwandtschaft**, elective affinity; der **—zettel** (schedule), ticket, vote

wählen, elect, select
wählbar, eligible; **die Wählbarkeit**
wahlberechtigt (right), entitled to
vote
wahlfähig (fit), eligible
die Wahlfähigkeit
der Wähler, elector, voter

850. **der Wahn,** (*ween*) *erroneous opinion, illusion, delusion*

der Wahnsinn (sense), madness,
frenzy; **der —witz** (wit), insanity, madness
wahnsinnig, —witzig, die —witzigkeit
der Größen(greatness)**wahn,** exaltation, megalomania
wähnen, fancy, presume
arg(bad)**wöhnen,** (ill fancy) suspect
der Argwohn, suspicion, mistrust
argwöhnisch

851. **wahr,** *true, real, genuine*

wahrhaft, truthful, veracious; **—ig,**
positively, really
die Wahrhaftigkeit, veracity, truth
wahrlich, truly, in truth
die Wahrheit, truth; **die —sliebe**
(love), veracity
wahrheitsgetreu (true to), in keeping with the truth
wahrsagen (say), tell fortunes
der Wahrsager, die —in, fortune-teller; **die —sagung,** prediction

wahrscheinlich (shine, appear),
probable, likely
die Wahrscheinlichkeit
der Wahrspruch (sprechen, speak),
verdict; **das —zeichen (Wortzeichen,** word token), emblem
bewahrheiten sich, come true
sich bewähren, prove true, stand
the test

852. **wahren,** (*a-ware, be-ware, wary*) *guard, watch over*

bewahren, aufbe—, ver—, (beware) take care of, keep, preserve
die Bewahrung, Aufbe—, Ver—
sich gegen (against) **etwas verwahren** (protect)
verwahrlosen (guardless), neglect,
slight
wahrnehmen (nahm wahr, wahrgenommen), take notice of, observe
die Wahrnehmung, perception
gewahr, aware

853. **die Waise,** (*wid-ow*) *orphan*

das Waisenhaus (house, asylum)
verwaist, fatherless and motherless

854. **der Wal, Walfisch**
(*fish*) *whale*

der Walfischfang (finger, catch);
—fänger, whaler; **der —tran,**
train-oil

855. der Wald, (wold) woods, forest

das Wäldchen, grove

der Waldbrand (brand, fire); das —horn, French horn; der —meister, woodruff

der Eich(oak)wald, Laub(leaf)—; Nadel(needle)—, pines and firs; Schwarz(Black)—, Tannen(pine)—

die Waldung, Wäldereien (plur.), woodland

der Vierwaldstättersee, lake of the four forest towns

waldreich (rich), bewaldet, woody

der Waldreichtum (riches), abundance of forests

856. der Wall, (wall) rampart

der Festungs(fast, fortress)wall

die Wallpromenade, rampart turned into a promenade

umwallen, surround with ramparts

die Umwallung

857. wallen, go on a pilgrimage

der Wallfahrer (fare, ride), pilgrim; die —fahrt, pilgrimage

wallfahrten, go on a pilgrimage

wallen, (billow) wave, undulate; see Welle

858. walten, (wield) rule, handle, manage, control

ob(above)walten, exist, prevail; ver—, manage, administrate

der Verwalter, die —in, die —ung

das walte Gott, God grant it

schalten und walten, rule absolutely

der Anwalt, (manager of legal affairs) attorney; Rechts(right, law)—, attorney at law; Staats(state)—, district attorney

die Anwaltschaft, attorneyship; Staats—, district attorney's office

der Sach(case before court)walter, attorney

die Gewalt, power, force, violence

der Gewalthaber (have), person in authority; die —herrschaft (mastery), despotism; der —streich (stroke), illegal measure; die —tat (deed), violence

gewalthaberisch, despotic

gewalttätig (die Tat), violent, outrageous

gewaltsam, forcible, violent; die Gewaltsamkeit

die All(all)gewalt, omnipotence; Amts—, official power; Straf—, power of punishment

allgewaltig, omnipotent

vergewaltigen, treat brutally

die Vergewaltigung

bewältigen, über—, overcome, overpower, subdue

die Bewältigung, Über—

859. die Wand, wall, partition

die spanische Wand, folding screen

die Wanze (Wandlaus, wall-louse), bedbug

860. die Wanne, (*van*)
bath tub

die Bade(bath)wanne, das Wannen=
bad

861. die Ware, *ware,*
merchandise

das Warenhaus (house), department store; das —lager (layer),
warehouse

die Eisen(iron)waren, hardware;
Eß(eat)—, eatables; Glas—,
Korb(wicker)—; Kurz(short)—,
notions; Rauch(rauh, rough)—,
furs; Schnitt(cut)—, haberdash-
ery

862. warm, *warm*

lau(luke)warm
die Wärme, warmth
der Wärmegrad (degree); —leiter
(leader), conductor of heat; —=
messer (measure), thermometer;
—stoff (stuff, matter), caloric
die Wärmflasche (flask), warming
bottle; die —pfanne (pan)
wärmen, warm, heat; auf—, warm
up; er—, warm
die Erwärmung

863. warnen, *warn*

verwarnen, admonish
die Warnung, Ver—

864. der Wart, *ward-en,*
keeper, guardian

der Hauswart, janitor; Schrift=
(script)—, secretary

die Warte, watch-tower, lookout;
Stern(star)—, observatory
warten, guard, attend to, wait
for
abwarten, await the end of; auf—,
wait on; er—, wait for, expect
die Erwartung, unerwartet; Auf—,
attendance; seine — machen, pay
one's respects
der Wärter, attendant, waiter;
An—, person waiting for an
appointment, candidate
die Anwartschaft, expectancy, candidacy
die Wartefrau, female attendant;
das —geld (money), charges for
nursing; der —raum (room),
—saal (saloon), das —zimmer,
waiting-room
der Aufwärter, waiter; Bahn=
(track)—, switchman; Kranken=
(sick)—, nurse; die —in; der
Schank(tap)—, bartender
der Wirt, (warden, person in charge
of) landlord, host, innkeeper
die Wirtin, landlady
der Hauswirt, landlord; Land(land,
country)—, farmer
wirtlich, economical, thrifty, hospitable
die Wirtlichkeit
das Wirtshaus, inn, tavern; die
—leute (people), landlord and
landlady
die Wirtschaft, (wardenship) house-
keeping, inn; der —er, housekeeper, manager; die —erin

die Volfs(folks, people)wirtschaft, political economy

bewirten, entertain, treat; die Bewirtung

bewirtschaften, manage an estate

die Bewirtschaftung

verwirtschaften, darauf los (loose) wirtschaften, mismanage

865. wärts, ward

abwärts, downward; auf(up)—, aus(out)—, ein(in)—, rück=(back)—, vor(for)—

auswärtig, outward, foreign; gegen=(against)—, directed against, opposite, near, present; wider=(with, against)—, adverse, repulsive

das Auswärtige Amt, Foreign Office

die Gegenwart, presence, present time

sich vergegenwärtigen, (direct toward oneself) imagine, realize

die Widerwärtigkeit

866. waschen (wusch, ge=waschen), wash

ab(off)waschen, aus(out)—; ver—, obliterate; zer—, destroy by washing

waschbar, washable; —echt (genuine), having fast colors

die Waschanstalt (institute), laundry; das —becken (basin); die —frau (woman), laundress; die —leine (line), die —maschine; das —maul (mouth), gossip; der —tisch (desk, table), das —was=ser; der —zettel (schedule), laundry bill

die Wäsche, linen; das —geschäft (shop, store)

der Wäscher, die —in

das Gewäsch, stuff and nonsense, twaddle

867. das Wasser, water

der Wasserfall (fall), cataract; die —heil(heal)anstalt (institute), hydropathic establishment; die —hose (spout); der —kopf (head), hydrocephalus; die — =leitung (leading), aqueduct; die —nixe (nymph); die —scheu (shy), hydrophobia; der — =spiegel (mirror), water level; der —stand (standing), height of the water; der —stoff (stuff, matter), hydrogen; die —straße (street), waterway; die —sucht (siech, sick), dropsy; die —wage (wiegen, weigh), water balance; das —zeichen (token), water mark

die Wassersnot (need), inundation, flood

das Ab(off)wasser, sewerage; Fahr=(fare, ride)—, channel; Regen=(rain)—, Salz(salt)—, See=(sea)—; Spül—, dishwater; Süß(sweet)—, fresh water; Wasch(wash)—

wasserdicht (tight), waterproof; —scheu (shy), hydrophobic; —süchtig, dropsical

das Gewässer, body of water
wässerig, watery, insipid
wässern, be—, irrigate; ent—, drain; ver—, overwater, dilute
die Bewässerung, Ent—, Ver—

868. waten, *wade*

das Watt, shallow, ford

869. die Watte, *wadding, wad, cotton*

wattieren, wad; die Wattierung

870. weben (wob, ge= woben), *weave*

anweben, weave to; ein(in)—, ver—, interweave
der Weber, die —in; die —ei, spinning-mill
der Webstuhl (stool), loom
das Gewebe, texture, tissue, weft
die Honigwabe, honeycomb

871. der Wechsel, *change, bill of exchange*

wechseln, transform, change
abwechseln, change, alternate; aus=(out)—, exchange; ein(in)—, change, realize (bank notes); um(about)—, change places, alternate; ver—, mistake for
die Abwechselung, variety; Aus—, Ein—, Um—, Ver—
der Wechsel, change, bill of exchange
die Wechselbank (bank), das —fie=ber, intermittent fever; der —gesang, alternate song; das

—geschäft, banking business; der —kurs (course), rate of exchange
der Wechsler, Geld—, money-changer, banker
der Brief(letter)wechsel, correspondence; der Jahres—, New Year; Prima—, first of exchange; Sekunda—, second of exchange; Wort—, quarrel
wechselseitig (Seite, side), mutual, reciprocal; —weise, reciprocally
abwechselnd, alternately

872. der Weg, *way*

das Wegegeld (money), turnpike toll; der —lagerer, waylayer; das —recht, right of way; der Wegweiser (show), sign-post
der Ab(off)weg, wrong way, vice; Aus(out)—, issue, expedient; Fahr(fare)—, carriage road; Fuß(foot)—, Heim(home)—; Hohl(hollow)—, notch; Reit=(ride)—, bridle path; Um=(around)—, roundabout way
unentwegt, unswerving
unwegsam, impassable
weg (*short vowel*), away; durch(all the way through)—, without exception; hin(hence)—, away, off

873. weh, (*woe*) *painful, sore*
weh tun (do), cause pain, hurt
das Weh, (woe) grief, pang; die —mut (mood), sadness
wehmütig

das Halsweh, sore throat; Heim—, homesickness; Kopf—, headache; Leib(stomach)—, Zahn= (tooth)—

die Nachwehen (*plur.*), after-pains

874. das Wehr, *weir*

die Wehr, (war) defense, weapon of defense

die Ab(off)wehr, defense; Feuer—, fire department; Land—, the oldest class of reserves, veterans; Not(need, emergency)—, self-defense

der Feuerwehrmann, fireman; Land= —, veteran

das Gewehr, weapon, gun; Sei= ten(side)—, sword

das Gewehrfeuer, rifle fire; der —lauf (laufen, leap, run), barrel

das Wehrgehänge (hang), shoulder belt; der —stand (stand, state), military classes

wehrhaft, (able to fight) able-bodied; —los, defenseless, unarmed

die Wehrhaftigkeit, —losigkeit

wehren, restrain, hinder, forbid

abwehren, keep off, avert; ver—, forbid

875. das Weib, (*wife*) woman

as opposed to man, *wife, married woman*

das Weibchen, female of animals

der Weiberhaß, hatred of women; der —hasser; die —herrschaft

(mastery), petticoat government; der —narr (narrow mind, fool), ladies' man

das Weibsbild (picture, likeness); das Weibsen, female

die Weibsleute (people), women folks; die —person, female; das —volk (folks), womankind

weiberhaft, womanlike; —scheu (shy), afraid of women

weibisch, effeminate; —lich, female, feminine

die Weiblichkeit, womanhood

die Viel(many)weiberei, polygamy

sich beweiben, take a wife, marry

876. weich, (*weak*) tender, soft

die Weichheit, softness; der —ling, tenderfoot

weichherzig, soft-hearted; —lich, effeminate; unerweichlich, unrelenting

die Weichherzigkeit, —lichkeit

verweichlichen, emasculate

die Verweichlichung

weichen, steep, soften, soak

aufweichen, moisten, soak; ein= (in)—, soak; er—, soften, move, touch

die Erweichung

die Weichen, soft parts of the body, side, flank

877. weigern, refuse, decline

sich weigern, deny, be unwilling; ver—, deny, decline, refuse

unweigerlich, without a refusal

die Weigerung, Ver—
das Geweih, (fighters) antlers

878. weihen, *consecrate, dedicate*

ein(in)weihen, consecrate, initiate, inaugurate; ent—, desecrate
die Einweihung, consecration, dedication, inauguration; Ent—
eingeweiht, initiated, familiar with
die Eingeweihtheit, thorough familiarity
die Weihe, consecration, ordination
der Weihkessel (kettle), holy water fount; die —nacht (night), Christmas; der —rauch (smoke), incense; das —wasser (water), der —wedel (waft, sprinkler)
der Weihnachtsabend (eve); der —feiertag, Christmas-day; das —fest (festival), das —geschenk (present), das —lied (lay, carol), der —tag (day), die —zeit (time)
zu (at) Weihnachten
weihevoll, sacred, inspiring

879. die Weile, *while*

die Kurz(short)weile, (shortening time) pastime, sport, jest; Lange—, (time appearing long) tediousness, weariness, boredom
kurzweilig, lang—
langweilen, tire, bore; sich —, find time hanging heavy on one's hands
die Langweiligkeit, tediousness
bis(by)weilen, at times; einst—,

for a while, for the present; zu—, at times, once in a while
mittler(middle)weile, in the meantime
zeit(time)weilig, (lasting some time) temporary
weilen, ver—, tarry, stay

880. der Wein, *wine*

der Weinbau (build), wine culture; der —bauer (grower); der —berg (mountain), vineyard; der —geist (ghost, spirit), spirit of wine; die —lese (pick), vintage; die —ranke (ring, vine branch, tendril), die —rebe (grape, vine); die —säure (acid), vinegar; der —stein (stone), tartar; der —stock (stick), vine; die —traube, bunch of grapes
der Apfel(apple)wein, cider; Brannt(burnt)—, brandy; Firne-(old)—; Rhein(Rhine)—; Rot-(red)— claret; Schaum(foam)—, champagne; Tisch(table, dinner)--, Ungar(Hungarian)—, Weiß-(white)—
weinartig (die Art, variety), vinous; —reich (rich), abounding in wines
der Winzer, vintner; die —ei, vintner's house

881. weinen, *weep, cry, lament*

beweinen, weep for; —swert

(worth), deplorable; **ſich aus—,**
cry one's eyes out
weinerlich, inclined to weep
winſeln, whine, wail
das Gewinſel, die Winſelei, wailing
verweinte Augen, eyes red with
weeping

882. weiſe, *wise, prudent*

der Weiſe, sage, philosopher; **der
Stein der Weiſen,** philosophers'
stone
die Weisheit, wisdom, prudence;
der —szahn (tooth), grinder
weislich, wisely, prudently; **naſe-**
(nose)**weis,** pert, forward, saucy
weisſagen (say), prophesy, foretell
der Weisſager, die —in, soothsayer
die Weisſagung prophesy, divina-
tion
einem etwas weis machen, make a
person believe a thing

883. die Weiſe, (*wise*)
mode, manner

die Denkweiſe, way of thinking;
Lehr—, method of teaching
dutzendweiſe, by the dozen; **grup-
pen**(groups)**—, haufen**(heap)**—,
länder**(lands, countries)**—, leih-**
(loan)**—, paar**(pairs)**—**

**884. weiſen (wies, gewie-
ſen),** (*make wise, enlighten*)
demonstrate, point out, show,

abweiſen, (point off) refuse, reject;
an—, point at, assign, order;

aus—, turn out, eject; **ſich —,**
(point oneself out) prove one's
identity; **be—,** demonstrate,
prove; **er—,** prove; **hin**(hence)**=
—,** point at, refer to; **nach**(toward)**—,** show, demonstrate;
ver—, banish, reprimand; **zurück**(back)**—,** reject
die Abweiſung; An—, assignment;
Poſtan—, money order; **Aus—,**
expulsion; **Zurück—**
der Ausweis, identification; **Be-
—,** proof; **Hin—,** reference;
Nach—, proof; **Ver—,** reprimand
der Weg(way)**weiſer,** sign-board

885. weiß, *white*

das Weiß, whiteness; **das Weiße,**
glair (egg), white (eye)
weißglühend (glowing), at a white
heat; **—lich,** whitish
die Weißglühhitze, incandescence
der Weißkohl (cauli-flower), white
cabbage; **die —waren** (wares),
linen, drapery
ſchneeweiß (white); **Schneewittchen,**
little Snowwhite

886. weit, *wide far, distant*
weitaus (out), by far
weitblickend (der Blick, look), far-
sighted; **—läufig** (laufen, leap,
run), extensive, ample, detailed,
elaborate; **—ſchweifig** (sweep,
swerve), prolix, circumstantial;
—ſichtig, far-sighted; **—ſpurig**

(spur, trail), wide-tracked; — =
tragend (carrying), of large
range, portentous

die Weitläufigkeit, diffuseness; —en,
(*plur.*) formalities, difficulties;
—schweifigkeit, —sichtigkeit

die Weite, width

das Weite ergreifen, (grasp the distance) run away

der Handschuhweiter, glove widener

weiter, farther, further; —hin,
furthermore

des weiteren, further; ohne —es,
without further proceedings

die Weiterreise, continuation of a
journey

die Weiterungen, (*plur.*) complica-
tions, difficulties

aus(out)weiten, widen, enlarge;
die Ausweitung

erweitern, widen, extend, expand

die Erweiterung, die Herz(heart)—,
dilatation

**387. die Welle, *wave,
billow***

wellig, wellenförmig, waving, un-
dulating

wallen, auf—, wave, undulate,
bubble

die Wallung, Auf—, ebullition,
agitation, excitement

die Walze, roller, cylinder

das Walzwerk (work), rolling-mill

walzenförmig (form), cylindrical

walzen, roll

wälzen, (cause to roll) turn about

sich wälzen, wallow, welter; um—,
revolve

die Umwälzung, revolution

888. die Welt, *world, universe*

die Mitwelt, (world with us) present generation; Nach(after)—,
posterity; Vor(before)—, primitive world, former ages

die feine (refined) Welt, society

die Außen(outside)welt, Ober(upper)—; Pflanzen(plant)—, vegetable kingdom; Tier(animal)—,
Unter(under, lower)—

das Weltall (all), universe; —alter
(old), age of the world; die —an-
schauung (look at), view of the
world, philosophy; die —aus-
stellung (put out, expose),
world's fair; der —bürger (citizen), cosmopolite; die —gegend
(region), cardinal point; die
—geschichte, universal history;
die —kenntnis (kennen, know),
worldly wisdom; die —kugel
(ball), terrestrial globe; das — =
meer (sea), ocean; der —post-
verein, universal postal union;
der —schmerz (smart, pain),
melancholy, pessimism; der — =
teil (part); der —umsegler (sail
around), circumnavigator of
the globe; der —weise (wise),
philosopher; die —weisheit, das
—wunder (wonder)

weltberühmt, far-famed; —flug,
wordly wise, prudent; —lich,

worldly, temporal, secular; — = müde (tired), world-worn

verweltlichen, secularize; die Verweltlichung

889. werden (ward, wurde, geworden), (*weird* in the sense of fate. Cf. weird sisters, the Fates) *become, turn into, grow*

der Werdegang (gehen, go), development

890. werfen (warf, geworfen), (*warp*) *cast, throw, fling*

ab(off)werfen, throw off (a rider), yield a profit; be—, throw at; ein(in)—, throw in (a word), protest; ent—, make a rough cast, design; um—, throw about (the shoulders), overthrow; unter(under)—, subdue; ver—, reject; vor—, throw before (a gauntlet), challenge, reproach; zu—, throw at, slam (a door)

die Unterwerfung, Ver—

der Wurf, thrust, throw, cast

der Auswurf, refuse, expectoration, dregs; Ein—, protest, objection; Vor—, challenge, reproach

verwerflich, objectionable; die Verwerflichkeit

verworfen, abject; die Verworfenheit

unterwürfig, submissive; die Unterwürfigkeit

vorwurfsvoll, reproachful

der Schein(shine, light)werfer, searchlight

das Wurfgeschoß (schießen, shoot), projectile; die —maschine, catapult; der —spieß (spit), javelin

das Zerwürfnis, (throwing apart) dissension

der Würfel, die, cube; der —becher, dice-box; das —spiel (game)

würfelförmig, cubiform, cubical

würfelig, cubical, checkered

würfeln, play at dice

891. das Werk, *work, action, deed, workmanship*

das Bollwerk, bulwark; Feuer (fire)—; Hand—, handicraft; Mach(make)—, worthless compilation; Pracht(pretty)—, parlor edition, edition de luxe

der Feuerwerker, artilleryman

der Werkeltag, workday

der Werkführer (leader), foreman; die —statt (stead), workshop; das —zeug (instrument), tool

das Gewerk, die —schaft, guild, corporation, union

bewerkstelligen, (put into the workshop) effect, perform

die Bewerkstelligung

wirken, operate, have effect, act, weave

bewirken, ein—, influence, weave in; er—, aus(out)—, procure, obtain from; ver—, forfeit

die Wirkung, effect; Be—, Ein—, Er—, Ver—

wirklich, actual, real, true, genuine
die Wirklichkeit
verwirklichen, realize; die Verwirk=
lichung
wirksam, effective, efficient; die
Wirksamkeit

892. wert, *worth, worthy, dear, valuable*

entwerten, depreciate; ver—, utilize
die Entwertung, Ver—
verwertbar, available; die Verwert=
barkeit
der Wert, worth, value
die Wertangabe (geben, give, state),
valuation; die —papiere (pa-
pers), stocks; die —sachen
(things), valuables
wertvoll (full), valuable
wertlos, worthless; die Wertlosigkeit
gleich(like) wertig, equivalent; min=
der(minus)—, of inferior quality; voll(full)—, of full value
die Gleichwertigkeit, Minder—,
Voll—
ein(one)wertig, univalent; zwei=
(two)—, bivalent; viel(many)-
—, polyvalent
die Einwertigkeit, Zwei—, Viel—

893. wetten, (*wed*, originally to pledge) bet

verwetten, lose by betting
der Wetteifer (zeal), emulation,
contention; wetteifern
die Wette, bet, wager
der Wettbewerb, (application) competition; die —fahrt (fare, ride),
boatrace; das —fieber (fever),
racing mania; der —kampf,
pugilistic combat; der —lauf
(laufen, leap, run), running
match; das —rennen, running
match; das —rudern (rudder,
oar), rowing contest; das — =
schwimmen, swimming contest
der Wettkämpfer, —läufer

894. das Wetter, *weather*

das Unwetter, stormy weather
die Wetterfahne (vane); das — =
leuchten (light), sheet lightning;
der —prophet, die —prophezeiung
wetterfest (fast), weather-proof;
—wendisch (wind), changeable,
irritable
anwettern (einen), rush at a person
like a cyclone, burst out
das Gewitter, electrical storm
wittern, scent, smell; die Witterung
verwittern, be weather-beaten, become disintegrated
die Verwitterung

895. wetzen, *whet, sharpen*

der Wetzstein (stone)

896. der Wickel, (*wick*) roll, roller, filler (*cigars*)

das Wickelband, swathing band;
das —kind, child in swaddling
clothes
wickeln, roll, wrap
abwickeln, wind off, wind up,

liquidate; au§(out)—, unwind, extricate, disentangle; ein(in)—, wrap up, envelop, implicate; ent—, unfold, develop; ver—, entangle, complicate

die Abwicfelung, Ent—, Ver—

897. w i d e r , (*with-stand, resist*) *against, contrary to*

wieder, again. *Compare* again *and* against

widerlid, disgusting, disagreeable, repulsive; —wärtig (ward), adverse, repulsive; —willig (will), reluctant, cross-grained

widrig, contrary, repulsive

die Widerwärtigfeit, der Widerwillen

anwidern, excite loathing, disgust; er—, (speak against) retort, reply, answer

die Erwiderung

898. w i d m e n , *dedicate, inscribe a book*

die Widmung

899. w i e g e n (w o g , g e w o = g e n), *weigh, ascertain the weight*

abwiegen, ver—, weigh; auf—, counterbalance; nach(after)—, verify the weight; über(over)—, outweigh, prevail over

vorwiegend, prevailing, predominating

wiegen, (*reg.*) weigh, balance, rock

ein(in)wiegen, (balance into sleep) lull

die Wiege, cradle

da§ Wiegenfeft (feast), birthday; —lied (lay, song), lullaby

da§ Wiegemeffer (balancing), chopping knife

da§ Gewidt, weight, importance, consequence

gewidtig, weighty, ponderous, important

vollwidtig, of full weight

widtig, weighty, important; die Widtigfeit

da§ Gleich(like)gewidt, equilibrium; Über—, overweight, preponderance

einem gewogen fein, balance toward, be kindly disposed

die Gewogenheit

die Wudt, weight, stress

die Wage, balance, pair of scales

wagerecht, (directed like scales) horizontal, level

wägen, weigh; er—, weigh, consider

die Erwägung

wägbar, ponderable; die Wägbarfeit

bewegen, (*reg.*) move

bewegen (bewog, bewogen), move, touch

bewegbar, —lid, movable

die Bewegbarfeit, —lidfeit

bewegt, touched, deeply affected

die Bewegtheit

der Beweggrund (ground), motive

die Bewegung, motion, emotion, movement

bewegungslos, motionless

aufwiegeln, (move up, stir up) inveigle, incite to rebellion

die Aufwiegelung

abwiegeln, (cease balancing) pacify, settle (business)

die Abwiegelung

900. wild, *wild, savage*

der Wilde, savage

das Wild, wild animals, venison, game; das —bret, —pret (braten, fry), roast game; der —dieb (thief), poacher; die —dieberei, poaching; der —fang (catch), lively child, romp; die —heit, wildness, savageness; das —leder (leather), deerskin; die —nis, wilderness, desert; das —schwein (swine), wild boar

wildern, poach; der Wilderer

wildfremd, quite strange

901. der Wille, *will, wish, mind, purpose*

willig, willing, ready; die Willigkeit

bereit(ready) willig, ready, willing; bös(malicious)—, malevolent; eigen(own)—, self-willed, wilful; frei(free)—, voluntary; gut-(good)—, friendly, easy; mut-(mood, humor)—, mischievous, wanton; un(bad)—, indignant; wider(against)—, reluctant

die Bereitwilligkeit, Bös—, Eigen—, Frei—, Gut—, Mut—

der Eigenwille, Mut—, Un—, Wider—

die Willkür (choice), arbitrariness, discretion; der —kommen, welcome

willkürlich; un—, involuntary

bewillkommnen, welcome; die Bewillkommnung

willfahren (fare, ride), go according to one's wish, comply with, gratify one's wishes

willfährig, die Willfährigkeit, die Willfahrung

willenlos (less), weak; die Willenlosigkeit

die Willenskraft, strength of will

willentlich, intentionally

gewillt, willing

ich will (wollen, gewollt), I will, wish

bewilligen, (be willing to grant) allow, appropriate; ein(in)—, consent, assent, agree

die Bewilligung, Ein—

übel(evil) wollend, malevolent; wohl(well)—, benevolent

das Wohlwollen

902. der Wind, *wind, breeze*

der Windbeutel, puff, paste (pastry), windy fellow; die —büchse (shooting-box), air-gun; der —hund, greyhound; die —mühle (mill); die —rose (rose), compass card

die Windsbraut (bride), gust of wind

windig, windy, empty, doubtful

windschief (shifting), warped, bent; —**still** (still), calm; —**wärts** (ward)

der Ost(east)**wind, West**—, **Nord**—, **Süd**(south)—

der Passat(trade)**wind, Sturm**=(storm)—, **Wirbel**(whirl)—

903. winden (wand, ge= wunden), *wind*

entwinden, wrest from; **über**=(over)—, overcome, conquer; **ver**—, get over, get the better of

die Windung, winding, convolution

die Entwindung, Über—, **Ver**—

unüberwindlich, invincible

die Unüberwindlichkeit

unumwunden, (nothing being wound around) in plain terms

die Winde, windlass; **das Ge**—, thread (screw)

das Blumen(bloom, flower)**gewinde,** garland

die Windel, swaddling cloth

wenden (wandte, gewandt), (cause to wind, wend) turn

ab(off)**wenden,** avert; **an**—, turn to, apply; **auf**(up)—, turn upon, spend upon; **ein**(in)—, turn in, object, protest; **ent**—, turn away, steal; **ver**—, apply, employ; **vor**—, turn before oneself, protect oneself, pretend; **zu**—, direct to, devote to

sein Bewenden haben, have its turn, change the subject

die Wendung

die Abwendung, An—, **Auf**—, appropriation; **Ein**—, **Ent**—, **Ver**—, **Zu**—

der Aufwand, ostentatiousness; **Ein**—, protest, objection; **Vor**=—, pretence, pretext

notwendig, (turning to the needful) necessary; **die Notwendigkeit**

abwendig machen, (make to turn away) alienate; **aus**—, (turning to the outside) by heart, from memory; **in**—, inward, internal

auswendig lernen (learn), commit to memory; — **wissen** (know)

abwendbar, preventable; **an**—, applicable; **ver**—, ready for use

die Abwendbarkeit, Ver—

gewandt, (quickly winding) dexterous, clever

die Gewandtheit

verwandt, (turning to each other) related

der, die Verwandte, relative

die Verwandtschaft, relationship

wandeln, (cause to wind, turn) change, transform

anwandeln, come over one; **um**=(around)—; **ver**—, change, transform

die Anwandlung, paroxysm, fit; **Um**—, **Ver**—, transformation

unwandelbar, immutable, unchangeable

die Unwandelbarkeit

der Nachtwandler, night-walker, somnambulist

wandern, wander

der Wanderer, Wandersmann; die Wanderung, die —schaft, migration

auswandern, emigrate; ein—, immigrate

der Auswanderer, Ein—, die Auswanderung, Ein—

904. der Winkel, *angle, corner*

der rechte (right) Winkel; spitze (spit, pointed) —, acute angle; stumpfe (stump, blunt) —, obtuse angle

winkelig, angular

rechtwinkelig, rectangular; spitz—, stumpf—

der Winkeladvokat, pettifogger; das —maß (measure), protractor

905. winken, *wink, make a sign, nod*

abwinken, call off by a nod

der Wink, sign, nod

906. der Winter, *winter*

winterlich, wintry

über(over)wintern, winter

die Überwinterung

907. der Wirbel, *whirlpool*

die Wirbelsäule, vertebral column, spine; der —sturm (storm), der —wind

der Trommelwirbel, roll of a drum

werben (warb, geworben), (whirl about, try hard to obtain) apply for, woo, court, recruit

anwerben, enlist, enroll; sich be—, apply for, woo; er—, acquire

die Anwerbung, Be—, Er—

der Werber, recruiting officer; Be—, candidate, suitor

der Wett(bet)bewerb, competition; Er—, profit, wages, salary

das Gewerbe, business, industry, profession

die Gewerbeausstellung (put out, exhibit), industrial exhibition; der —schein (shine, evidence), license; die —schule (school); gewerblich, gewerbtätig (tun, do); —treibend (driving, pushing), manufacturing

die Gewerbtätigkeit

908. wirren, *perplex, puzzle, entangle*

verwirren, perplex, puzzle, entangle; ent—, disentangle, extricate

die Verwirrung, Ent—

der Wirrwarr, jumble, hurly-burly

das Gewirr, confusion

verworren, confused, crazy; die Verworrenheit

909. wissen (ich weiß, wußte, gewußt), (*wit, wise*) *know, have information*

das Wissen, knowledge, science; Ge—, (co-science) conscience

wissend, knowing; all—, omniscient; un—, ignorant

die Allwissenheit, Un—

gewiſſenhaft (having), conscientious, scrupulous; —los (less), unscrupulous

die Gewiſſenhaftigkeit, —loſigkeit

der Gewiſſensbiß (bite), remorse; die —freiheit (freedom, liberty); die —pflicht (pledge), duty in conscience

die Wiſſenſchaft, science

die Naturwiſſenſchaft, natural science; der —ler, scientist

wiſſenſchaftlich, scientific

gewiß, (that which I know, am sure of) sure, certain; —lich, surely, truly

die Gewißheit

vergewiſſern, make certain, ascertain; die Vergewiſſerung

gewiſſermaßen . (meſſen, measure), (in a certain measure), to a certain extent, so to speak

wißbegierig (greedy), curious; die Wißbegierde

wiſſenswert (worth)

wiſſentlich, knowingly, purposely

bewußt, conscious of, aware; —los, senseless, unconscious

die Bewußtloſigkeit

das Bewußtſein, (be,having knowledge) consciousness

der, die Bewußte, (person one knows of) person referred to

910. die Witwe, widow

der Witwer, widower

der Witwenstand (standing, state), widowhood

das Wittum (dom), dower, dowry

der Stroh(straw)witwer, grass-widower; die —witwe

verwitwet, widowed; die Königin Witwe, Queen Dowager

911. der Witz, wit, *brains, joke*

das Witzblatt (blade, sheet), humorous paper; der —bold, wit; der —ling, witling; das —wort (word), sally, witticism

der Aber(aber = false, wrong *as in* Aberglaube)witz, false wit, craziness; Für(fore)—, pertness; Mutter(mother)—, common-sense

witzig, witty, ingenious; die Witzig=keit

aberwitzig, für—

witzigen, teach wit, make wiser

witzeln, affect wit, poke fun at

die Witzelei, witticism

912. die Woche, *week*

das Wochenblatt (blade, sheet), weekly publication; der —tag (day)

die Wochen, childbirth

die Wöchnerin, young mother

die Kar(care, passion)woche, Oster=(Easter)—

der Mitt(mid)woch, Wednesday; Aſcher(ash)—

wöchentlich, weekly

wochenweiſe, by the week, weekly

913. die Woge, *billow, wave*
wogen, wave, fluctuate
wogig, wavy

914. das Wohl, (*weal*)
welfare, health

das Wohlbefinden (ich befinde mich,
find myself, am), good health;
das —behagen, pleasure, gratification; das —ergehen (go, fare),
welfare; die —fahrt (fare), welfare, prosperity; das —gefallen
(delight); der —geruch (riechen,
smell), fragrance, perfume; der
—geschmack (smack), pleasant
flavor; der —klang (sound),
euphony; das —sein (being),
good health; der —stand (standing, state), prosperity; die —
tat (deed), good action, charity;
das —wollen (will), benevo-
lence
der Wohltäter, benefactor
wohltätig, charitable; die Wohl-
tätigkeit
wohlauf (well up), healthy, cheer
up; —behalten (held, kept), in
good condition; —feil (for sale),
cheap; —gemut (mood), merry;
—habend (having), wealthy;
—riechend (smelling), sweet-
scented, fragrant; —wollend
(willing), benevolent
Ew. (Euer) Wohlgeboren, Your
Honor
die Wohlgemutheit, —habenheit
wohltun, do good, benefit

das Lebe(live)wohl, farewell
unwohl, indisposed; das Unwohlsein

915. wohnen, (*wont, habit*) *in-
habit, dwell, live, reside*

bewohnen, occupy; bei(nearby)—
assist, attend; inne(within)—
bewohnbar, habitable, comfortable
der Bewohner, occupant, tenant;
Ein—, inhabitant
die Einwohnerschaft, population
wohnbar, habitable; —haft (having), residing; —lich, cozy
die Wohnbarkeit, —lichkeit
das Wohnhaus, residence; der
—ort, —platz (place), residence;
der —sitz (seat), domicile; die
—stätte (stead), abode; das
—zimmer (room), sitting-room
die Wohnung, dwelling, habitation,
residence, flat, apartment
die Wohnungssuche (seek), flat
hunting
gewöhnen (won-t), accustom
angewöhnen, acquire a habit; ab—,
break a habit
entwöhnen, disuse, disaccustom;
ver(wrongly)—, spoil
verwöhnt, fastidious; die Verwöhnt-
heit
gewöhnt, (wonted) accustomed,
used
die Gewohnheit, An—, custom,
habit
der Gewohnheitsmensch, slave of
custom; das —recht (right),

common law; der —trinker,
habitual drunkard

die Gewöhnung, acquiring a habit

gewöhnlich, customary, usual

916. wölben, *vault, arch*

die Wölbung, vault, vaulting

das Gewölbe, vault; das feuer=
(fire)feste (fast, proof) —, safe
deposit vault

917. die Wolke, *cloud*

der Wolkenbruch (brechen, break),
cloudburst

wolkenlos, cloudless, serene

sich bewölken, become cloudy, over-
cast

die Bewölktheit

918. die Wolle, *wool*

der Wollenstoff (stuff), goods; der
—weber (weaver)

die Wollarbeit, work in wool; der
—handel (trade), der —markt
(market), die —spinnerei (mill)

wollen, wollig, woolly

die Baum(tree)wolle, cotton;
Schieß(shoot)baum—, gun cotton

919. die Wonne, (*win-some*)
delight, bliss, rapture

der Wonnemonat (month), May

wonnig, delightful, blissful

920. das Wort, *word;* plur.
Wörter, *disconnected words,*

vocabulary; **Worte,** *connected
words, text*

die Worterklärung (clear), defini-
tion; der —führer (leader),
spokesman; die —fülle (fill),
wordiness; der —klauber
(cleave), hair-splitter; der — =
laut (loud, sound), wording,
text; der —schwall (swell),
bombast; das —spiel (play),
pun; der —wechsel (exchange),
dispute

das Für(for, instead)wort, pro-
noun; Haupt(head, principal)—,
noun; Ja(yes)—, acceptance;
Macht(might)—, absolute command; Vor(fore, front)—, prep-
osition, preface; Zeit(time)—,
verb

das Wörterbuch (book), dictionary

wortarm, poor in words; —brüchig
(brechen, break), faithless; — =
karg, of few words, laconic;
—los (less); —reich (rich),
wordy, verbose

die Wortarmut, —kargheit, — =
brüchigkeit

wörtlich, verbal, literal

befürworten, (speak a word for)
advocate

die Befürwortung

die Antwort, answer, reply

antworten auf, reply to; be—,
answer (a letter)

die Beantwortung

verantworten, answer for, assume
the responsibility

verantwortlich, responsible; die
Verantwortlichkeit
die Verantwortung, justification,
defense

921. wühlen, *root up, dig up,
agitate, incite*

auf(up)wühlen, durch(through)—,
unter(under)—, zer—, root up
der Wühler, agitator, demagogue;
die Wühlerei
das Gewühl, crowd, bustle

922. wund, *(wound) sore*

die Wunde, wound, hurt
der Wundarzt (physician), sur-
geon; —fieber (fever)
die Brand(brennen, burn)wunde,
burn; Schnitt(cut)—,
wundärztlich, surgical
verwunden, wound, injure, hurt;
die Verwundung
verwundbar, vulnerable; die Ver-
wundbarkeit

923. das Wunder, *wonder,
marvel, miracle*

wunderbar, wonderful, miraculous;
—hübsch, exceedingly handsome; —lich, strange, odd; —
sam, wonderful; —schön, wondrous fair; —tätig (tun, do),
miraculous, —voll, wonderful,
miraculous
wundern, wonder, amaze; be—,
admire; ver—, surprise
sich wundern, amaze

die Bewunderung, Ver—
bewundernswert (worth), admi-
rable
bewunderungswürdig (worthy), ad-
mirable
der Bewunderer admirer

924. wünschen, *wish, desire,
long for*

erwünschen, wish for, desire; ver-
(ill)—, curse, bewitch
wünschenswert (worth), desirable
die Verwünschung, curse, maledic-
tion
verwunschen, enchanted
der Wunsch, wish, desire
der Wunschzettel (schedule), list of
presents wished
die Wünschelrute (rod), magic wand
der Geburtstags(birthday)wunsch,
congratulation; Glück(luck)—,
congratulation; Herzens—,
heart's desire
beglückwünschen, congratulate
die Beglückwünschung

925. die Würde, *(worthy)
dignity, honor*

der Würdenträger (carrier), dig-
nitary
würdig, worthy, deserving
die Würdigkeit, worthiness, merit
anbetungs(anbeten, pray to, adore)-
würdig, adorable; ehr(honor)—,
reverend, venerable; glaub(belief)—, credible, authentic; lie-
bens(love)—, amiable, lovable;

nid)ts(nothing)—,   worthless,
contemptible;   fel)ens(see)—,
worth seeing
die Glaubwürdigkeit, Liebens—,
Nichts—,   Sehens—,   Ehr(hon-
or)—; Hoch(high)—, right reverend
würdevoll (full), dignified
würdigen, (consider worthy) appreciate
die Würdigung

**926. würgen, (worry) choke,
strangle**

erwürgen, strangle, throttle
der Würgeengel (angel)

**927. der Wurm, worm
(die Würmer)**

der Band(binden, bind; ribbon)=
wurm, tapeworm; Bücher(book)=
—; Lind—, dragon; Regen=
(rain)—, earthworm
das Glühwürmchen, glowworm,
firefly
wurmen, (curb like a worm) fret,
vex
wurmförmig, vermiform; —ftid)ig
(ftechen, stick, prick), worm-
eaten
das Gewürm, vermin, reptiles

928. die Wurzel, (wort) root

die Quadratwurzel, square root;
Kubik—
wurzeln, root, be rooted; ent—,
unroot

eingewurzelt, deeply rooted
das Gewürz, spices, groceries
das Gewürznägelchen (nail), clove
gewürzreich (rich), spicy, aromatic
die Würze, seasoning, spice

**929. wüft, waste, deserted,
confused**

der Wuft, confused mass, rubbish,
trash
die Wüste, Wüftenei, desert, wilderness
der Wüftling, reprobate
verwüften, lay waste, devastate,
ravage
die Verwüftung
unverwüftbar, —lich, indestructible
die Unverwüftbarkeit, —lichkeit

930. die Zacke, (tack) prong

der Drei(three)zack, trident
zackig, pronged, indented
aus(out)zacken, ein(in)—, notch,
indent

**931. die Zahl, (tale, tell; all
told = all counted) number,
figure**

die Anzahl, number, amount;
Bruch(brechen, break)—, fraction; Ein(one)—, singular;
Grund(ground)—, cardinal number; Jahres(year)—, historical
date; Mehr(more)—, plural, majority; Minder(minus)—, minority; Ordnungs(order)—, ordinal
number; Über(over)—, greater

force; **Un**—, indescribable number, no end of

überzählig, supernumerary; **un**—, innumerable; **voll**(full)—, complete

zahllos (less), innumerable; **—reich** (rich), numerous

zahlen, (enumerate coins) pay

ab(off)**zahlen**, **abbe**—, (pay off, reduce the amount) make a partial payment; **an**(on, onward)—, **anbe**—, make the first payment, give a deposit; **aus**(out)—, **ausbe**—, pay down, in full; **be**—, pay, honor; **nach**(after)—, **nachbe**—, make an additional payment

die Abzahlung, Abbe—, **An**—, **Aus**—, **Ausbe**—, **Be**—, **Nach**—, **Nachbe**—

auf Abzahlung, on the instalment plan

zahlbar, payable; **unbe**—, invaluable

der Zahlkellner, head-waiter; **der —tag**, pay-day; **das —wort**, numeral

zahlungsfähig (fit), solvent

die Zahlungsfähigkeit

die Zahlungseinstellung (put inside, suspend), suspension of payments; **das —mittel** (middle, means), legal tender; **das —vermögen** (might), solvency

zählen, count, number

ab(off)**zählen**, count over; **auf**(up)—, enumerate, pay down;

er—, account, narrate, tell, relate; **hinzu**(hence to)—, add; **nach**(after)—; **über**(over)—, count over; **sich ver**—, make a mistake in figuring; **zusammen**(together)—, add

die Abzählung, Auf—, **Er**—, **Zusammen**—

die Volks(folks, people)**zählung**, census

der Erzähler, **die —in**, narrator

der Zähler, numerator

932. z a h m , *tame, domestic*

die Zahmheit, tameness

zähmen, tame, curb, break; **sich be**—, restrain oneself

die Zähmung, taming, domestication

zähmbar, **be**—, tamable, manageable

933. d e r Z a h n , (*dent-ist*)
**   *tooth, cog***

der Zahnarzt (physician), dentist; **die —bürste** (bristle, brush); **die —fäule** (foul), caries; **das —fleisch** (flesh), gum; **das —geschwür** (**schwären**, ulcerate), ulcer; **das —pulver** (pulverize), powder; **die —schmerzen** (smart, pain), toothache; **der —stocher** (stick), toothpick; **das —weh** (woe), toothache

das Zahnrad, cog-wheel; **die —bahn** (track), cog railroad

der Backen(back, cheek)**zahn**, molar; **Milch**(milk)—, **Vorder**

(forward, front)—, Weisheits (wisdom)—

zahnförmig (form), tooth-shaped; —los (less)

das Zähneklappern (chattering)

zahnen, cut one's teeth, tooth, indent

934. zapfen, *tap, draw*

ab(off)zapfen, draw (blood); an—, tap (barrel); ver—, sell liquor

der Zapfen, tap, peg; am Zapf, on draught

der Eiszapfen, icicle; Tannen—, pine cone

der Zapfenstreich (stroke), tap, tattoo

935. zart, *tender, delicate*

zartfühlend, tender of feeling, delicate

unzart, rude; die Unzartheit

die Zartheit, das —gefühl

zärtlich, tender, soft, amorous, fond; die Zärtlichkeit

verzärteln, spoil by too much tenderness

die Verzärtelung

936. zaudern, *linger,*
hesitate

der Zauderer, die Zauderei

zauderhaft, lingering, tarrying

die Zauderhaftigkeit, dilatoriness

937. der Zaun, *(town, enclosed settlement;* **Zaun** *is the enclosing structure itself) fence*

der Zaunkönig (king), wren

der Bretter(board, plank)zaun, Garten(garden)—; Stachel(stechen, stick, prick)draht (thread, wire)—, barbed wire fence

ein(in)zäunen, um(around)—, fence in

die Einzäunung, Um—

938. zechen, *take (food and drink), consume, drink, tipple*

sich bezechen, become intoxicated

die Zeche, sum total of food and drink orders, bill, check

der Zechgenoß (genießen, enjoy), —kumpan (companion); das —gelage, drinking bout

der Zecher, drinker, toper

die Kohlen(coal)zeche, coal mine

939. die Zehe, *toe*

die Zehenspitze (spit, spear), tiptoe

940. zehren, *(tear) waste,*
consume

ab(off)zehren, aus(out)—, waste, emaciate; ver—, (tear up with the teeth) eat, feed

das Zehrfieber, hectic fever; das —geld (money), der —pfennig (penny), viaticum, provisions for a journey

die Abzehrung, Aus—, emaciation, consumption

zerren, tear, pull, tug, drag

verzerren, (pull out of shape) distort, wrest

das Zerrbild (distorted picture), caricature

zergen, tease, annoy

zergeln, (make many short pulls) annoy, harass

941. das Zeichen, *token, sign, mark, symptom*

die Zeichensprache, language of signs

das Ab(off)zeichen, distinctive mark; An(on)—, indication, symptom; Kenn(know)—, characteristic mark; Kreuzes(cross)—, sign of the cross; Lebens(life)—; Schrift(script)—, written character; Vor(fore, advance)—, omen, musical annotation; Wahr(Wort)—, emblem

das Ausrufungs(call out)zeichen, exclamation mark; Frage(pray, question)—

zeichnen, sign, mark, draw (lines)

abzeichnen, draw from, copy; aus—, mark out, distinguish; be—, supply with a mark, denote, denominate; unter(under)—, subscribe, sign (a letter); ver—, note down, record

die Zeichnung, drawing, subscription, signature; Aus—, Be—

das Verzeichnis, list, record; Inhalts(held inside, contents)—, table of contents, index; Namens(name)—

ausgezeichnet, distinguished, excellent

bezeichnend, kenn—, characteristic

die Feder(feather, pen)zeichnung,

Kreide(crayon)—, Kohlen(charcoal, crayon)—

der Zeichenlehrer (teacher), das —material, die —stunde (hour, lesson)

der Zeichner, draftsman, designer

942. die Zeit, (*betide, happen*) *time*

der Zeitabschnitt (cut off, section), epoch, period; das —alter (old), age; die —angabe (give, state), date; der —geist (ghost, spirit); der —genoß (companion), contemporary; der —raum (room), space of time; die —rechnung (reckoning), chronology; die —schrift (script), periodical; der —verlust (loss); der —vertreib (drive off), pastime; das —wort (word), verb

zeitgenössisch, contemporary

die Bedenk(think over)zeit, respite, delay; Essens(eat)—, dinner time; Jahres(year)—, season; Neu(new)—, modern times; Un—, unseasonable time; Ur(original)—, prehistoric period; Vor(before, previous)—, remote antiquity

unzeitig, unseasonable; vor—, premature

zeitig, timely, early, mature; früh(early)—, premature; recht(right)—

zeitgemäß (messen, measure by), seasonable, opportune; —lich, temporal, earthly; —weilig (while, last), temporary; — = weife (wise, manner), from time to time

zeitlebens, as long as one lives, for life

zeitigen, ripen, mature; die Zeitigung

bei seinen Lebzeiten, in his lifetime

die Zeitung, (tidings, news) newspaper

943. der Zettel, (*schedule*) *slip of paper, bill, poster*

der Theaterzettel, play bill, program; Wasch—, laundry bill

anzetteln, (post a proclamation) plot, contrive, lay a plot; ver—, scatter, disperse, squander

die Anzettelung, Ver—

944. der Ziegel, *tile, brick*

der Ziegelbrenner (burner), tiler; die —ei, brick-kiln; der —decker (coverer), bricklayer; die —erde (earth), clay; der —ofen (oven, kiln); der —stein (stone), brick

die Ziegelei, brick-kiln

der Ziegler, tiler

945. ziehen (zog, gezogen), (*tug*) *pull, draw, cultivate* (active transitive)

abziehen, pull off, subtract; an—, (pull on clothing) dress, pull near, attract; aus(out)—, undress; be—, (pull near) procure,

purchase; ent—, withdraw; er—, (pull out) bring up, educate; über(over)—, cover with; ver—, educate wrongly, spoil; voll= (full)—, draw out fully, accomplish; vor—, draw forth, pick out, prefer

sich anziehen, dress; sich aus—, undress; sich um—, (re-dress) change clothes

einen aufziehen, pull up like a puppet, tease, mock at

die Anziehung, attraction; Be—, (drawing near, establishing a connection), reference; Ent—, withdrawal; Er—, education; Voll—, execution, performance

der Erzieher, educator; die —in, governess

erzieherisch, educational

der Vollzieher, executor; die —in, executrix

der Überzieher, overcoat

der Zug (tug, pull), train, draught (air), outline, feature (drawing), trait (pen picture)

der Charakterzug, trait, feature; Eisenbahn(railroad)—, (pulled cars) train; der Luft—, draught of air; Namens(name)—, monogram

der Abzug, deduction; An—, suit of clothes; Aus—, extract, abstract, digest; Be—, purchase, relation, reference; Über—, cover; Ver—, (drawing along) delay; Vor—, preference abzüglich, deducting; an—, (drawing in a person's character) allusive, offensive, personal; be—, relating to; unver—, without delay; vor—, preferable, excellent; zu—, (drawing to) adding

die Anzüglichkeit, Vor—

die Abzugs(draw off, drain)röhre, (pipe)

der Güter(goods)zug, freight train; Personen(person)—, accommodation train; Post(mail)—; Schnell(fast)—, express train

der Zugführer (leader), conductor

die Zugbrücke, drawbridge; die —kraft, tractive power, attractiveness; die —luft, draught of air; das —pflaster (plaster), blister; das —vieh, draught cattle

zugig, windy, draughty

der Zügel, (tugger, puller) rein, bridle

zügellos (less), unbridled, dissolute

die Zügellosigkeit

zügeln, bridle, curb

eingezogen, (drawn in) retired, solitary, modest; un—, (untrained) naughty; zurück—, retired, modest

die Eingezogenheit, Un—, Zurück—

der Zögling, pupil, scholar

ziehen, (*active intransitive*) move, march, remove

ab(off)ziehen, depart; auf(up)—, march in procession; aus(out)=

—, remove from; ein(in)—, move into; nach(after)—, follow; um(about, around)—, remove to another house; ver—, remove (*not mentioning the place*)

der Abzug, Aus—, Ein—, Um—

der Feld(field)zug, campaign, war; Kreuz(cross)—, crusade

der Nach(after)zügler, straggler

zeugen, (draw from the soil) produce, grow; er—, produce, generate

das Erzeugnis, product; Boden=(bottom, soil)—, product of the soil

das Zeug, artificial product, goods, material, contrivance, instrument

das Zeughaus, arsenal

das Fahr(fare, ride)zeug, vessel, craft; Spiel(play)—, toy; Werk=(work)—, tool

die Zucht, training, discipline, brood

das Zuchthaus, house of correction, State's prison; der —meister, severe master; das —vieh, cattle for breeding

die Manns(man)zucht, discipline; Vieh—, cattle breeding

züchten, breed (animals), cultivate, grow (flowers, plants)

der Blumen(bloom, flower)züchter, Vieh—

die Züchtung

zuchtlos (less), undisciplined

die Zuchtlosigkeit, want of discipline

züchtig, (well-trained) modest, chaste
die Züchtigkeit
züchtigen, chastise; die Züchtigung
der Züchtling, Zuchthäusler

946. das Ziel, (*tiller,* lever used to determine the course of a vessel) *objective point, aim, end*
das End(end)ziel, objective point
der Zielpunkt, objective point; die —scheibe, target
ziellos, aimless; —bewußt (know), sure of success
zielen, ab— auf—, aim at, drive at, allude to

947. ziemen, *be suitable, becoming*
geziemen, befit, be decent
ziemlich, seemly, suitable, proper
ziemlich gut, apparently well, fairly well
die Unziemlichkeit, unseemliness, uncomeliness

948. die Zier, *harmonious arrangement, ornament*
die Zierde, ornament; Un—, inelegance
der Zierat, ornament, finery
der Zierbengel, dude; die —puppe (puppet), girl very fond of finery
der Ziergarten, ornamental garden; die —pflanze, ornamental plant

zierlich, elegant, neat; die Zierlichkeit
zieren, ver—, decorate, adorn; sich —, adorn oneself, put on finery, act like a girl, be bashful
die Verzierung, decoration, ornament
verunzieren, disfigure; die Verunzierung

949. die Ziffer, (*cipher*) *figure*
das Zifferblatt (blade, sheet), dial
entziffern, decipher, unravel
die Entzifferung

950. das Zimmer, (*timber*) *room, chamber, apartment*
zimmern construct, build, make
die Zimmerarbeit, carpenter's work; der —herr (master), room tenant; das —holz (wood), timber; der —mann, timberman, carpenter
das Bade(bath)zimmer, Eß(eat)—, Schlaf(sleep)—; Speise(food)—, dining-room; Sprech(speak)—, consultation room; Studier(study)—, Warte(wait)—
das Hinter(hind, rear)zimmer, Mittel(middle)—, Vorder(fore, front)—
das Frauenzimmer, (*originally* separate room for women) female

951. zingeln, um—, *surround, encompass, enclose*
die Umzingelung

952. der Zins, plur. die Zinsen, (Lat. census, censere) *interest*

die Zinsenberechnung (reckoning), interest account; der —fuß (foot), rate of interest; der —herr (master), lord of the manor; die —rechnung (reckoning), percentage; die —tabelle (table)

die Zinseszinsen, compound interest

zinsbar (bearing), tributary; —frei, free of rent; —pflichtig (pledged), tributary, subject to rent

verzinsen, pay interest; die Verzinsung

verzinslich, bearing interest

953. der Zirkel, *circle, compass*

zirkelförmig (form), circular

abzirkeln, measure by means of compasses

der Bezirk, district

der Regierungs(regency, government)bezirk, largest subdivision of a province, *abbreviated* Rgbz.; Stadt(town)—, ward

954. zittern, *shiver, tremble*

erzittern, tremble, shake, shiver

der Zitteraal, electric eel

955. der Zoll, *inch*

der Zollstock (stick), inch ruler

der Zoll, (toll) custom, duty

das Zollamt (office), customhouse; der —aufseher (overseer), surveyor of the customs; der —beamte (officer); die —deklaration, bill of entry, manifest; der —einnehmer (take in), collector; die —freiheit (freedom), exemption from duty; die —gebühr (bearing), duty; die —revision, examination of baggage; der —speicher (storage), bonded warehouse; die —spesen (expenses), charges; der —tarif, der —verband (binden, bind), —verein (one, union), customs union

unter Zollverschluß (schließen, close), in bond

der Einfuhr(fahren, fare, ride, bring in)zoll, entrance duty; Schutz(protection)—, protective duty, high tariff

der Schutzzöllner, protectionist

der Zöllner, publican (Bible)

zollen, pay, give; ver—, pay duty on

die Verzollung, custom-house examination

zollbar, ver—, dutiable; —frei (free); —pflichtig (pledged), dutiable

956. der Zopf, (*tuft of hair*) *braid, tail, pigtail, cue*

die Zopfzeit (time), grandfather's time

zopfig, old-fashioned

zupfen, pull, pluck, pick

957. der Zorn, *wrath,*
anger

zornig, wrathful, angry

zürnen, be angry; er—, make
angry

958. der Zucker, *sugar*

der Zuckerbäcker (baker), confec-
tioner; die —ei; der —hut (hat),
loaf; die —dose, bowl; der —guß
(gießen, pour, cast), crust of
sugar; der —kandis (candy); das
—mäulchen (mouth), sweet
tooth; die —pflanzung (planta-
tion), die —raffinerie (refinery);
das —rohr (pipe), sugar-cane;
die —rübe (rape), beet sugar;
das —werk (work), confection-
ery; die —zange (tongs)

der Stücken(piece)zucker, lump sugar

zuckerhaltig (holding), sacchariferous;
 —ig, sugary; —füß, as
sweet as sugar

das zuckersaure (sour) Salz (salt),
saccharate

verzuckern, sugar over

959. der Zunder, *tinder*

zünden, catch fire; an—, ignite,
light; ent—, inflame

die Entzündung, inflammation;
Selbst(self)—, spontaneous combustion

die Bauch(belly)fell(skin)entzün-
dung, peritonitis; Blind(blind)-
darm(bowel)—, appendicitis;
Hals(throat)—; Gehirn—, brain

fever; Kehl(throat)kopf(head)-
—, laryngitis; Lungen(lung)—,
pneumonia; Mandel—, tonsil-
itis; Rippen(rib)fell(skin)—,
pleuritis

zündbar, inflammable; die Zünd-
barkeit

entzündbar, inflammable, combustible

die Entzündbarkeit

der Zünder, fuse, match; der La-
ternenanzünder, lamplighter

das Zündhölzchen (wood), match;
das —hütchen (hat), cap; das
—loch (leak), touch-hole; das
—nadelgewehr, needle gun; der
—stoff (stuff, matter), explosive

960. die Zunge, *tongue*

das Züngelchen, hand (scales)

die Landzunge, neck of land

doppel(double)züngig, deceitful

die Doppelzüngigkeit, duplicity

züngeln, shoot out in tongues
(flames)

das Gezüngel

961. zwacken, *pinch, torture*

abzwacken, pinch off, extort

zwicken, pinch, twitch, nip

der Zwicker, eye-glasses

die Zwickmühle (mill), merils

962. der Zweck, (*wooden nail
in the center of the target*) *aim,
purpose, design*

das Zweckessen (eating), public
dinner

zweckdienlich (serving), expedient; —entsprechend (answering), practical; —los, useless; —mäßig (messen, measured on to), suitable, proper; —widrig (against, contrary to), inexpedient

die Zweckdienlichkeit, —losigkeit, —mäßigkeit, —widrigkeit

bezwecken, aim at, have in view

die Zwecke, (wedge) tack

bezwecken, fasten with tacks

963. z w e i , *two*

zweierlei, of two different sorts; —deutig (meaning), ambiguous; —fach, twofold

entzwei, in two, asunder, broken

entzweien, disunite, set at variance

die Entzweiung, disunion

die Zweideutigkeit, ambiguity; das —gespann (span); der —kampf (fight), duel, single combat; das —rad (wheel), bicycle

der Zwieback, (two-cake) biscuit; der —spalt (split), dissension, disunion; die —sprache (sprechen, speak), dialogue, conversation; die —tracht (two objects in view), discord, dissension

zwieträchtig, discordant

964. z w e i f e l n , (*waver between two views*) *doubt, question*

bezweifeln, doubt, question; ver— (be harassed by doubts), despair

die Verzweiflung, despair, desperation

der Zweifel, doubt, question

der Zweifler, skeptic

zweifelhaft, doubtful; —los, doubtless

965. d e r Z w e i g , *twig, branch, bough*

die Zweigbahn (railroad), branch line; das —geschäft (shop), branch store; der —verein (one, union), branch of an association

abzweigen, branch off; sich ver—, ramify

die Abzweigung, Ver—

966. z w e r ch , *across, awry, askance*

verzwerch, athwart, across

das Zwerchfell (pelt, skin), diaphragm

967. d e r Z w e r g , *dwarf*

die Zwergin

968. d i e Z w i e b e l , *onion*

das Zwiebelbeet (bed); das —gewächs (wachsen, wax, grow), bulbous plant

zwiebeln, rub with onions, cause to shed tears, treat cruelly

969. d e r Z w i l l i n g (*twin-ling*) *twin*

der Zwillingsbruder (brother), die —schwester (sister)

970. zwingen (zwang, ge=
zwungen), (*twinge*) *constrain,
compel*

bezwingen, subdue, vanquish, conquer; er—, enforce, extort

die Bezwingung, Er—
-gezwungen, constrained, forced;
die Gezwungenheit

die Zwinge, ferule

der Zwinger, (constrainer) bear-
pit, prison, dungeon

der Zwingherr (master), despot;
die —schaft, despotism

der Zwang, constraint, coercion,
compulsion

die Zwangsanleihe, compulsory
loan; die —arbeit, hard labor;
die —jacke, straight-jacket

zwanglos (less), unconstrained, in-
formal; —weise, by force

die Zwanglosigkeit

zwängen, (cause to be pressed between two objects) press, force
into

einzwängen, squeeze in

971. der Zwirn, *twine,
linen thread*

der Zwirnsfaden (fathom, thread)

zwirnen, of linen thread

zwirnen, twist, twine

972. zwischen, (*be-twixt*)
between

der Zwischenakt, (between the
acts) intermission; das —deck
(deck), steerage; der —fall (fall,
case), incident; der —handel,
carrying trade; der —raum
(room), interval, intermediate
space; die —station, intermediate station; die —zeit (time),
interval, interim

zwischendurch (through), between
the two, midway between

973. der Zwist, (*splitting into
two*) *dissension, dispute*

zwistig, at variance, discordant

die Zwistigkeit, discord, quarrel,
dispute

V. SUPPLEMENTARY VOCABULARY, SHOWING THE LO-CATION OF THOSE WORDS WHICH, OWING TO THEIR RELATIONS TO OTHER WORDS, COULD NOT BE AR-RANGED IN THE PRECEDING GROUPS IN STRICTLY ALPHABETICAL ORDER

Aas, 63
abfinden, 79
abgemattet, 340
Abgeordnete, 406
abgeschieden, 561
abhängig, 163
abhärmen, sich, 164
abkarten, 218
abknipsen, 249
Abkömmling, 256
abkühlen, 273
Abschied, 561
abspenstig, 669
abstufen, 740
abtrünnig, 792
abwechselnd, 871
abwesend, 19
abzirkeln, 953
ähnlich, 55
Anbetracht, 784
Andacht, 39
angenehm, 390
Ankömmling, 256
anlangen, 285
anläßlich, 286
anrüchig, 518
ansässig, 658
ansehnlich, 639
Anstalt, 708

anstatt, 694
anstößig, 724
anstrengen, 730
antworten, 920
Anwalt, 858
anwesend, 19
Anwuchs, 845
anzetteln, 943
argwöhnen, 850
Ärmel, 3
Armut, 3
aufmerksam, 349
Aufruhr, 521
ausgezeichnet, 92
ausklügeln, 243
ausrotten, 509
äußern, 5
ausstaffieren, 720
austollen, 778
ausweiten, 886

Ballen, 9
Band, 20
bändigen, 20
barmherzig, 3
Baumwolle, 918
beanspruchen, 684
bedacht, 39
bedächtig, 39

Geſchworene, 636
Geſchwulſt, 630
Geſchwür, 620
Geſenke, 655
Geſetz, 658
Geſicht, 639
geſinnt, 656
Geſinnung, 656
Geſpann, 669
Geſpiele, 678
Geſpinſt, 680
Geſpött, 683
Geſpräch, 684
Geſtade, 711
Geſtalt, 708
Geſtändnis, 703
Geſtein, 707
Geſtell, 708
Geſtirn, 710
Getäfel, 750
Getöſe, 782
Getränk, 797
getreu, 795
Getriebe, 791
getroſt, 795
Getümmel, 764
Gevatter, 826
Geviert, 837
Gewächs, 845
gewahr, 852
Gewalt, 858
gewandt, 903
Gewäſch, 866
Gewäſſer, 867
Gewebe, 870
Gewehr, 874
Geweih, 877

Gewerbe, 907
Gewerk, 891
Gewicht, 899
gewillt, 901
Gewirr, 908
gewiß, 909
Gewiſſen, 909
Gewitter, 894
Gewogenheit, 899
gewöhnen, 915
Gewohnheit, 915
gewöhnlich, 915
Gewühl, 921
Gewürm, 927
Gewürz, 928
geziemen, 947
—gezogen, 945
gezwungen, 970
giltig, 124
Gipfel, 258
Gitter, 114
gläubig, 135
Glut, 139
Gnade, 398
gnädig, 398
gönnen, 149
Göttin, 141
Götz(e), 141
Grab, 142
Graben, 142
grämen, ſich, 143
Griff, 144
Grimm, 143
Größe, 146
Grübchen, 142
Grube, 142
grübeln, 142

Oberſt, 403
Obrigkeit, 403
obwalten, 859
öffentlich, 404
öffnen, 404
ölen, 405
ölig, 405
Ölung, 405
ordentlich, 406
Ordnung, 406
Organiſt, 407
örtlich, 409

päbſtlich, 410
Pächter, 411
Pack, 412
packen, 412
Papſt, 410
päpſtlich, 410
Paſſatwind, 902
peinlich, 415
perſönlich, 417
pfänden, 420
Pfänderſpiel, 420
pfiffig, 422
placken, 429
plätten, 431
platzen, 432
Plunder, 434
Poliziſt, 438
poſſierlich, 441
poſtaliſch, 442
Pottztauſend, 766
Pracht, 443
predigen, 446
Predigt, 446
preiſen, 447

probieren, 450
prophezeien, 452
Prunk, 443
pünktlich, 457
Putz, 458

quälen, 459
Quecke, 460
quellen, 461
Quere, 462
Quittung, 464

rächen, 466
radebrechen, 467
radeln, 467
—räderig, 467
rädern, 467
Ranke, 507
Ränke, 496
ranken, 507
Rappe, 465
Rat, 475
—rat, 475
Rätſel, 475
Raub, 476
Räuber, 476
rauchen, 502
räuchern, 502
Rauchwaren, 477
räumen, 478
räumlich, 478
Rechnung, 479
Reck, 488
recken, 488
Rede, 481
redlich, 481
Redner, 481

Schäfer, 545
Schaffner, 546
schälen, 548
Schalter, 550
Schaltjahr, 550
schämen, 551
Schande, 551
schändlich, 551
Schärfe, 552
schartig, 554
schattieren, 555
schattig, 555
schätzen, 556
Schau, 558
schaudern, 557
schäumen, 559
scheiden, 561
Schein, 562
Scheit, 561
Scheitel, 561
scheitern, 561
Schenke, 564
Schere, 565
scheuchen, 566
Scheusal, 566
scheußlich, 566
schicklich, 130
Schicksal, 130
Schiedsrichter, 561
Schirm, 571
Schlacht, 573
schlachten, 573
Schlächter, 573
Schlaf, 572
Schläfe, 572
schlaff, 572
schläfrig, 572

Schlag, 573
Schlägel, 573
schlängeln, 575
schlapp, 572
Schlappe, 572
Schläue, 576
Schleim, 574
schleppen, 580
Schleuder, 581
Schlich, 578
schlicht, 577
schlichten, 577
Schliff, 580
Schloß, 582
Schlucht, 585
schlüpf(e)rig, 585
Schlupfwinkel, 585
Schluß, 582
Schlüssel, 582
schlüssig, 582
schmachten, 588
schmächtig, 588
schmälern, 586
Schmalz, 591
schmatzen, 588
Schmelz, 591
Schmiß, 590
schmücken, 594
schmutzig, 595
schnäbeln, 596
Schnalle, 601
schnalzen, 601
schnaufen, 598
Schneide, 600
Schneider, 600
schneien, 599
Schnitt, 600

Sole, 661
sonnen, 665
spärlich, 670
Speichel, 674
sperren, 671
Spinne, 680
Spion, 667
spitz, 679
Splitter, 681
Spötter, 683
Sprache, 684
spreizen, 685
Sprengel, 687
sprengen, 687
sprenkeln, 687
Sprichwort, 684
spritzen, 686
Sproß, 686
Sprosse, 686
Sprößling, 686
Spruch, 684
Sprudel, 689
Sprung, 687
spucken, 674
Spülicht, 690
Spund, 676
spüren, 691
Stachel, 702
Städtchen, 694
Städter, 694
städtisch, 694
Staffel, 740
stählen, 695
stählern, 695
Stall, 708
stämmig, 696
Stand, 703

Ständchen, 703
Ständer, 703
ständig, 703
ständisch, 703
stärken, 699
Statt, 694
Stätte, 694
Staub, 713
stäuben, 713
stecken, 702
Stecken, 719
steigern, 706
steil, 706
steinern, 707
Stelle, 708
stemmen, 696
Stengel, 698
Stetigkeit, 711
stets, 711
Steuer, 712
Stich, 702
sticheln, 702
sticken, 702
—stieg, 706
Stiege, 706
stieren, 700
Stimme, 718
stöbern, 713
stolzieren, 721
Stoß, 724
stracks, 732
sträflich, 725
Sträfling, 725
Strahl, 727
Strecke, 732
Streich, 733
streicheln, 733

träufeln, 796
traulich, 795
Träumer, 789
traurig, 788
Treffen, 790
trefflich, 790
Treue, 795
Trieb, 791
Trift, 791
triftig, 790
Tritt, 794
trocknen, 798
Tropfen, 796
tröpfeln, 796
Trost, 795
tröstlich, 795
Trottoir, 802
Trug, 805
Trunk, 797
Trutz, 803
Tüchelchen, 808
tüchtig, 763
tückisch, 809
Tugend, 763
tummeln, 764
tunlich, 810
Türmchen, 812
türmen, 812
Turner, 813
Tusche, 815

Übel, 817
Überdruß, 828
überraschen, 472
überwintern, 906
üblich, 818
übrig, 819

Übung, 818
unbeholfen, 181
unbescholten, 563
unersättlich, 536
unerschrocken, 607
unflätig, 822
Ungemach, 325
ungeschlacht, 573
ungeschliffen, 580
Unkosten, 260
unleugbar, 322
unmittelbar, 356
unpäßlich, 413
Unterricht, 480
Unterschied, 561
Untertan, 810
unterwürfig, 890
unumstößlich, 724
unversehrt, 834
Urkunde, 226
Urlaub, 62
Ursache, 525
urwüchsig, 845

väterlich, 826
veranstalten, 708
verantwortlich, 920
verbissen, 14
Verbot, 17
Verbrechen, 26
Verdacht, 39
verdauen, 759
verdrossen, 828
Verdruß, 828
Verein, 55
vergegenwärtigen, 865
vergeßlich, 829